Cracking the
SAT Spanish
Subject Test

Cracking the SAT Spanish Subject Test

By George Roberto Pace
Revised by David Stewart

2005–2006 Edition

Random House, Inc.
New York

www.PrincetonReview.com

The Independent Education Consultants Association recognizes The Princeton Review as a valuable resource for high school and college students applying to college and graduate school.

Princeton Review Publishing, L.L.C.
2315 Broadway
New York, NY 10024
E-mail: booksupport@review.com

ISBN 0-375-76453-4
ISSN 1076-6200

SAT is a registered trademark of The College Board.

Edited by: Omar Amador
Production Editor: Patricia Dublin
Production Coordinator: Marc Williams

Manufactured in the United States of America.

10 9 8 7 6 5 4 3 2

2005–2006 Edition

ACKNOWLEDGMENTS

Para Roberto, Carmina y Enrique, sin quienes no estuviese donde estoy.

To Ernie and Bert, for helping me learn to speak English.

G.R.P.

For Eric Holt, the one who inspired me to continue studying Spanish in college and who provided invaluable assistance during the revision process of this book.

For my mom, my first Spanish teacher and one of the best bilingual teachers the Los Angeles Unified School District has ever had.

For my wife, Lisa, who inspires me in so many ways.

D.S.

Special thanks to Adam Robinson, who conceived of and perfected the Joe Bloggs approach to standardized tests and many of the other successful techniques used by The Princeton Review.

CONTENTS

PART I

Orientation

Introduction

YOU'RE ON YOUR WAY

Congratulations! By purchasing this book, you've taken the first step toward raising your score on the SAT Spanish Subject Tests. Now you just have to read the book, practice the strategies, and take the practice tests. We know that taking a standardized test is about as exciting as watching paint dry, but we've done everything possible to make working through this book as painless and fun as possible.

To get the most out of this book, you should tackle it in bite-sized pieces. You'll drive yourself crazy and lose interest if you try to read through the entire book in one sitting or one weekend. We recommend that you figure out how much time you have left before you take the actual test and then come up with a game plan that makes sense. Just be sure to set aside a solid hour to take each one of the practice tests. You won't do yourself any good or get an accurate assessment of your performance if you take the practice tests in pieces or if you give yourself extra time to finish them.

WHO WE ARE

The Princeton Review is a test-preparation company based in New York City. We have branches across the U.S. and abroad. We've developed the techniques you'll find in our books, courses, and online resources by analyzing actual exams and testing their effectiveness with our students. What makes our techniques unique is that we base our principles on the same ones used by the people who write the tests. We don't want you to waste your time with superfluous information; we'll give you just the information you'll need to get great score improvements. You'll learn to recognize and comprehend the relatively small amount of information that's actually tested. You'll also learn to avoid common traps, to think like the test writers, to find answers to questions you're unsure of, and to budget your time effectively.

You need to do only two things: trust the techniques, and practice, practice, practice.

WHY OUR BOOK

Welcome

Remember — this test shows little of your Spanish abilities, only how well you do on this particular test.

The Princeton Review is on your side. We didn't create the tests and we don't force anyone to take them. We simply help students do better on them. In this book, you'll find a thorough review of the content that will be covered on the test, test-taking strategies that will help you apply your existing knowledge, and enough practice tests for you to determine your own personal strengths and weaknesses.

WHAT ARE THE SPANISH SUBJECT TESTS?

There are two different Spanish Subject Tests, the traditional Spanish Subject Test and a newer called Spanish with Listening Subject Test. Most of you will take the traditional Spanish Subject Test, and the majority of this book will be dedicated to that exam. However, for those of you who are planning to take the Spanish with Listening Subject Test, we will provide you with some strategies to help you do your best.

Both SAT Spanish Subject Tests are hour-long, multiple-choice exams that are supposed to measure your knowledge of Spanish. In fact, the College Board claims that the subject tests ". . . provide a reliable measure of your academic achievement" and "can help in assessing how well prepared you are for different programs of college study." Do the SAT Spanish Subject Tests really accomplish this? Absolutely not. If you want to know how well you speak Spanish, you should try reading a Spanish newspaper, watching a Spanish television show, or speaking Spanish with a native speaker. Each of these activities will give you a better idea of how well you speak the language than will the results of the SAT Spanish Subject Tests.

WHY SHOULD YOU TAKE A SPANISH SUBJECT TEST?

Other than wanting to get a higher score than one of your friends got, there are only two good reasons to take an SAT Spanish Subject Test. The first of these reasons is that one of the colleges to which you are applying either requires or strongly recommends that you take several different SAT Subject Tests. If this is the case, you will want to make sure that you pick the three subjects that will best demonstrate your academic achievement. Evaluate your own strengths and weaknesses, and contact colleges to see which tests they suggest or require. The second reason you might take the SAT Spanish Subject Test is that one of the colleges to which you're applying plans to use the Spanish Subject Test as a placement exam.

WHEN SHOULD YOU TAKE IT?

The first thing you need to decide is whether to take one of the Spanish Subject Tests. These tests are appropriate for students who have completed a minimum of two years of high school Spanish or the equivalent, but are more often taken by students who have completed or are in the middle of their third year of high school Spanish.

The second thing you need to decide is whether to take the Spanish Subject Test or the Spanish with Listening Subject Test. If you have a lot of experience speaking Spanish, you might want to take the Spanish with Listening Subject Test. If you learned most of your Spanish from reading a book, you should probably take the Spanish Test that does not contain a listening section.

The Spanish Subject Test is given five times each year: October, December, January, May, and June. The Spanish with Listening Subject Test is given only once each year, in November. There is really no advantage to taking the test in a particular month, though there are plenty of rumors going around that certain administrations are easier than others. Don't pay any attention to those rumors — just take the test when you feel most ready to do so. Of course, if you decide to take the Spanish with Listening Subject Test, you don't really have much choice in the matter.

HOW DO I REGISTER FOR THE TESTS?

The easiest way to register is through the College Board's website at **www.collegeboard.com**. Here you will also find up-to-date information on testing sites, dates, and fees. You may also register by mail by picking up a registration form and student bulletin at your guidance office. If you have questions, you can talk to a College Board representative by calling 609-771-7600.

You may have your scores sent to you, to your school, and to four colleges of your choice. Additional reports will be sent to additional colleges for, you guessed it, additional money. The scores take about six weeks to arrive.

STRUCTURE OF THE TEST

Both the Spanish and the Spanish with Listening Subject Tests contain 85 multiple-choice questions. You'll have one hour to complete each of the tests, but you do not necessarily need to finish either test to get a good score.
The structure of each test is as follows:

SPANISH SUBJECT TEST: SPANISH

The Spanish Subject Test contains three sections that measure different skills. Each section is weighted equally and contains approximately the same number of questions (between 27 and 29). The three sections are:

- Part A: Vocabulary and Structure
- Part B: Paragraph Completion
- Part C: Reading Comprehension

SPANISH SUBJECT TEST: SPANISH WITH LISTENING

The Spanish with Listening Subject Test consists of two sections: the Listening section and the Reading section. The Listening section contains about 35 questions and must be completed in about 20 minutes. The Reading section contains about 50 questions and must be completed in 40 minutes. Each of these two sections contains questions that measure different skills. The specific format is as follows:

LISTENING SECTION

- Part A: Pictures—You will be presented with a picture and asked to select the sentence that best reflects what someone in the picture might say or what is portrayed in the picture.

- Part B: Rejoinders—You will listen to a short conversation and then select the answer choice that represents the most likely continuation of the conversation.

- Part C: Selections—You will be asked to listen to extensive selections and then choose the best possible answer.

READING SECTION

- Part A: Vocabulary and Structure

- Part B: Paragraph Completion

- Part C: Reading Comprehension

SCORING

Your overall score on either the Spanish Subject Test or the Spanish with Listening Subject Test is based on the number of questions you answer correctly minus $\frac{1}{3}$ of the questions you answer incorrectly. You get no credit and lose no points for questions you leave blank. On the Spanish Subject Test, the result of this simple calculation (# correct $-\frac{1}{3}$ of number incorrect) represents your raw score. Raw scores can range from –28 to 85. On the Spanish with Listening Subject Test, you receive several different scores: a raw score for each section, a scaled score for each section (20–80), and an overall scaled score (200–800).

Both Spanish Subject Tests are scored on a 200–800 scale. Just like with the SAT, the lowest possible score is a 200 (even if you answer every question incorrectly) and the highest possible score is an 800 (which you can get even if you miss a question or two). The only tricky thing about the scoring is on the Spanish with Listening Subject Test. On this test, the two sections are weighted differently. Since the Reading section represents about $\frac{2}{3}$ of the overall test, your raw score in that section is multiplied by 1.12. The Listening section represents about $\frac{1}{3}$ of the overall test, so your raw score in that section is multiplied by .881. The products of each of these two calculations are added together to determine your overall raw score. This new raw score is then converted to a scaled score between 200 and 800.

You shouldn't get too worked up over the scoring. Just do your best, and follow the techniques you learn in this book.

IS THERE ANY OTHER MATERIAL AVAILABLE FOR PRACTICE?

When preparing for this or any other SAT Subject Test, stay away from the plethora of other test-prep books available. The questions in the majority of books on the market bear little, if any, resemblance to actual SAT Subject Test questions. The College Board publishes a book called *Real SAT II: Subject Tests*, which contains full-length tests in almost all the SAT subjects offered. You can also go to the College Board's website, **www.collegeboard.com**, for more information and practice questions.

> **For book updates, links to more information, and last-minute test changes, visit this book's Online Companion at www.PrincetonReview.com/cracking.**

FINAL THOUGHTS

Preparation is the key to success—not just on this test, but in everything you do. If you want to succeed on the Spanish Subject Test or any other test, make sure you understand the content, practice the strategies, and develop an overall plan to attain your target score. In addition to working through this book, you may want to read a Spanish newspaper (looking up the words you don't know in a dictionary), listen to Spanish-language radio stations or television programs, or engage in conversations in Spanish with your classmates, friends, or family members.

Finally, RELAX. Once you've finished preparing, there's no need to stress about the tests. Just make sure you get plenty of sleep the night before the test, eat a balanced breakfast, walk into the test center with a feeling of confidence, and do your best. In the end, your score is just a number. These tests will never be able to measure the most important aspect of your academic potential: your determination.

How to Take the Test: Overall Strategies

In Chapters 3 through 6 you'll review the Spanish you need to know (as well as some strategies) for the different question types. Right now, let's talk about how to take a standardized test.

Pace Yourself

There is no need to do the whole test, especially since it's designed so that you can't! Use the pacing chart. Not doing all the questions gives you more time to get the ones you *are* doing right. If you walk into the test without a pacing strategy, you're basically unprepared.

PACING

Since your earliest days in school, you were probably taught that when you take a test, finishing is important. Standardized tests, however, are a completely different ball game. The folks who write these tests are interested in how fast you can work, and they design the tests so that it's nearly impossible to finish on time. Because you're so accustomed to the idea that finishing is crucial, you may pressure yourself to answer every question. Have you ever stopped to consider how much sense this makes? It's not as if you get a special prize for finishing! In fact, in order to finish, you usually have to rush through questions, and as a result you make careless errors that could be avoided. Doesn't it make more sense to slow down a bit, answer the questions you're sure of, and leave a few blanks? Well, let's see how pacing yourself on the Spanish Subject Tests relates to actual scores:

PACING CHART

To Get a Score of	Answer About	Leave This Many Blank
400	13	72
450	26	59
500	38	47
550	48	37
600	58	27
650	68	17
700	78	7
750 & up	85	0

Understand that the pacing chart assumes that you'll make fewer than six mistakes, and it doesn't take guesses into account. If you take your time, pick your questions carefully, and learn to guess effectively, making fewer than six errors really isn't as tough as it might sound.

Structure

60 minutes, 85 questions

You should walk into your test with a target score in mind and a pacing strategy that reflects the score you're shooting for. Remember, this is your test, and that means you can answer the questions you want, when you want, how you want, and still get an excellent score. If you want to leave most (or all) of the reading comprehension blank and concentrate on the other questions, go ahead. If you're good at the reading comprehension, but not so good on the grammar, then do more of the reading comprehension and less of the grammar sentence completions. If all the other students at your test site want to race frantically to the end of the test and make careless mistakes along the way, that's their problem. You're going to be sitting there, cool and relaxed, just taking your time and getting a great score.

WHEN SHOULD YOU GUESS?

A lot of people talk about the "guessing penalty" on the SAT and the SAT Subject Tests. What they really mean is that there's no advantage to random guessing. The truth is, there really isn't a penalty either.

Each question on the Spanish Subject Test and the Spanish with Listening Subject Test has four answer choices. If you answer a question correctly, you will receive 1 raw-score point. If you get a question wrong, you will lose $\frac{1}{3}$ of a raw-score point. If you were to randomly guess on four questions with four answer choices each, odds are you would get one question right and three questions wrong. How would this affect your raw score?

1 question correct = +1 point

3 questions incorrect = $-(\frac{1}{3}) \times 3 = -1$ point

Total impact on overall score = 0

So should you guess? Sometimes. If you can eliminate one or more incorrect answer choices, the odds become more favorable. Imagine if you were able to eliminate two answer choices and then randomly guess on the remaining two answer choices for four different problems. In this case, you would likely get two questions right and two questions wrong. How would this affect your raw score?

Guessing

If you can eliminate even one answer choice, guessing is to your advantage.

2 questions correct = +2 points

2 questions incorrect = $-(\frac{1}{3}) \times 2 = -\frac{2}{3}$ point

Total impact on overall score = $+1\frac{1}{3}$ points

The moral of this story is this: If you can eliminate even one answer choice, you should guess. If you can't eliminate any answer choices, there's no reason to guess. You'll just be wasting valuable time.

THREE-PASS SYSTEM

Because the test is written for students with varying levels of expertise in Spanish, the questions vary in difficulty. Unfortunately, they aren't arranged in any particular order of difficulty. There are questions that are much easier than others, but it's up to you to find them if you want to take advantage of them.

Scoring

Raw score = # right $- \frac{1}{3}$ of # wrong, converted to an 800 point scale

THE THREE-PASS SYSTEM SAYS THE FOLLOWING:

- **1st Pass**—Go through an entire section of the test from beginning to end, but only answer the easiest questions, that is, those on which you thoroughly understand all the vocabulary, etc. Skip anything that looks as if it's going to give you grief.

- **2nd Pass**—Go back to the beginning of the same section and take a shot at those questions where you knew some, but not all, of the vocabulary.

- **3rd Pass**—Use the Process of Elimination (which you'll learn about in a moment) on the remaining questions in that section to eliminate some answers. Then take a guess. If you can't eliminate anything, leave the question blank.

Taking a section of the test this way will keep you from getting stuck on a tough question early in the section and spending too much time on it. Your time should be spent both answering questions you're sure of and guessing intelligently, not banging your head against the wall in an attempt to crack a tough question.

Note: The Three-Pass System will not work on the Listening section of the Spanish with Listening Subject Test. During that section, you will be listening to an audiocassette and you must answer the questions in the order in which they appear (or leave them blank).

POE—PROCESS OF ELIMINATION

The usefulness of the Process of Elimination is one of the gifts of a multiple-choice exam. The idea is simple: There are three wrong answers and only one right one; so it is easier to find answers to eliminate. If you can eliminate answers that you know are wrong, you will eventually stumble upon the right answer because it'll be the only one left. Approaching questions in this way will also ensure that you avoid the traps that ETS (Educational Testing Service) sets for students. You'll learn how this applies to each question type later on. POE is going to vary a bit for the different question types, but the general idea is always the same.

The Spanish with Listening Subject Test

OVERVIEW

If you're reading this chapter you must be thinking about taking the Spanish with Listening Subject Test. Good for you! This probably means that you're fairly comfortable listening to spoken Spanish or that you speak it regularly. If not, you may be better off taking the basic Spanish Subject Test.

THE ESSENTIALS

If you plan to take this Spanish with Listening Subject Test, the most important thing you need to remember is to bring a cassette player with you to the test center. That's right, our good friends at ETS are perfectly willing to hand out cassette tapes on the day of the test, but they will NOT provide you with a cassette player in which to play them. In order for your cassette player to be "acceptable," it must have earphones, be small enough to fit in your hand, operate on batteries (bring your own—the test administrator will not have extras), and be able to play a standard audiocassette. Under no circumstances will you be allowed to share your cassette player with another student.

The other thing to keep in mind if you're considering taking the Spanish with Listening Subject Test is that it's only offered once each year—in November. If you're planning to take the test, be sure to register in time for the November exam.

STRATEGIES

The good news is that the strategies that apply to the Spanish Subject Test are also appropriate for the Reading section of the Spanish with Listening Subject Test. Chapters 4–7 contain a thorough review of the vocabulary and grammar you'll need for both tests, as well as a review of the reading and test-taking strategies you'll need for the Spanish Subject Test and the Reading section of the Spanish with Listening Subject Test. However, you'll need to prepare for the Listening section of the Spanish with Listening Subject Test on your own. There are a few ways you can do this:

- Practice speaking Spanish with your friends, classmates, or family members—by speaking Spanish with others, you will get more comfortable with understanding and responding to spoken Spanish.

- Listen to a Spanish-language radio station and practice interpreting the commercials and the conversations.

- Watch a Spanish-language television program and practice interpreting the commercials and the shows.

PART ◆ II

Subject Review

Sentence Completion: Vocabulary

The first section of the Spanish Subject Test and the first part of the Reading section of the Spanish with Listening Subject Test consist of vocabulary and grammar questions tested in a format we call *sentence completion*. Each sentence is missing one or more words, and your job is to select the answer choice that best completes the sentence in terms of meaning. In other words, fill in the blank with the answer that makes the most sense. Like all the questions on the test, each of the questions in this section has four answer choices. Before you go any further, memorize the directions to this question type so that you're so familiar with them you will never have to read them again.

Part A

Directions: This part consists of a number of incomplete statements, each having four suggested completions. Select the most appropriate completion and fill in the corresponding oval on the answer sheet.

HOW TO CRACK THIS SECTION

One of the keys to the sentence completions is understanding the vocabulary. If you know every word that appears in the section, understanding the sentences and choosing the right answers is a breeze. So, one of the things you're going to work on is improving your vocabulary. Later in this chapter you'll find a list of words that are most likely to appear on your test, along with easy ways to remember them. If you think your vocabulary needs help, then start working on that list *today*. We'll see more about vocabulary later. What else can be done to attack this question type?

In order to master this section, you need to combine your vocabulary review with some common sense. You've already read about pacing, POE, and the three-pass system. Now you're going to learn how those ideas, as well as some additional techniques, apply to this section in particular.

First Pass: When You Understand the Entire Sentence

It's pretty obvious that the easiest questions for you to deal with are the ones that don't contain unknown vocabulary words. You should do these questions first. Remember, the questions are not in any particular order of difficulty, so it's up to you to hunt down the easiest ones. Your approach should be to read the sentence, and if it's easy, to answer that question. If you're a bit uncomfortable with some of the vocabulary, move on and come back to that question later, during your second pass.

Be careful. Just because a question is a "first-pass question" doesn't mean you should blow through it as fast as possible and risk making a careless error. Once you've decided to answer a question on the first pass, take the steps listed on the next page.

Think of Your Own Word

The first step after reading the sentence is to fill in the blank with your own word without peeking at the answers. Your word doesn't have to be long or difficult; in fact, short and simple is best. Also, your word doesn't even have to be in Spanish. If it's easier for you to think in English, then write the word in English. The important thing is to choose a word that fits in terms of meaning. After you have a word, write it down next to your sentence (or in the actual blank, if there's room). Try this on the following example:

Hoy hace mucho frío. Por eso voy a ponerme un . . .

What would make sense in this blank? Well, pretty much any article of clothing that would be appropriate in cold weather, like a pair of gloves (**par de guantes**) or a sweater (**suéter**). You shouldn't feel that there's only one possible answer, because there are usually several words that would make sense in the blank. Don't worry about picking the *right* word, just worry about picking a word that makes sense. Once you've done this, move on to the next step.

Eliminate Answers That Are Out of the Ballpark

Now you're going to look at the answers and cross out any answer that does not fall into the same category as your word. You're not looking for the right answer, you're looking to eliminate wrong answers.

Let's say that you filled in the word **suéter** in the example above. Which of the following answer choices would you eliminate?

(A) vestido
(B) abrigo
(C) zapato
(D) lápiz

Does a dress (**vestido**), shoe (**zapato**), or pencil (**lápiz**) have anything at all to do with cold or a sweater? No, and so the correct choice is (B). If you don't know all of the words in the answers, then eliminate whichever ones you can and take a guess at the remaining choices.

Avoid Trap Answers

Once you've filled in your own word, it's crucial that you don't just pick the first answer you see that reminds you of the word you came up with. The folks who write this test are very clever about creating answer choices that are tempting but incorrect. Knowing what types of traps they typically lay out for you will help you to avoid them. In this section, there are a couple of tricks that show up frequently.

Answers That Sound Alike

One way the test writers try to confuse you is by having all four answers sound alike, even though their meanings are different. You can easily avoid this trap by reading carefully and not using your ear. Remember that you're picking the best answer based on its meaning, not on how it sounds.

Try the following example:

> La madre de Pedro no le dejó salir porque todavía
> no había . . . su cuarto.
>
> (A) llamado
> (B) limpiado
> (C) llevado
> (D) llenado

Why wouldn't a mom allow her son to go out? Probably because he hadn't cleaned his room. The word for clean is **limpiar** and, since we're in the pluperfect, **limpiado** would be the correct form (if that doesn't make sense, don't fret—the grammar review is in the next chapter, and you don't need to be an expert on Spanish grammar to do well on this test). Notice how all the other answers sound very similar to **limpiado**. This is why it's important to take your time and concentrate on meaning.

Categories

Another favorite trick of the test writers is to give you four choices that all come from the same category, as in the following example:

> Ricardo quiere lavarse las manos, y por eso
> necesita . . .
>
> (A) un cepillo
> (B) una navaja
> (C) pasta de dientes
> (D) jabón

Each of the answer choices is something you'd find in a bathroom (**jabón** = soap, **navaja** = razor, **pasta de dientes** = toothpaste, **cepillo** = hairbrush). Although these words have very different meanings, seeing them all together like this may be confusing, especially if you're thinking in general terms (bathroom stuff) and not in terms of the specific word you chose for the blank. For this reason it's very important that you fill the blank with a specific word, and not a general category.

SECOND PASS: WHEN YOU DON'T UNDERSTAND THE ENTIRE SENTENCE

Let's say you've answered all of the questions you found to be easy. Now what? The strategy for first-pass questions works just fine when you have a clear understanding of the sentence, but unfortunately, there will probably be some words that you don't know in some of the sentences. Will that keep you from answering the question altogether? Absolutely not, but you *will* leave these questions for the second pass. The approach is different for these questions, but it works just as well as the approach for the first-pass questions. Not knowing some of the vocabulary will hardly be a handicap at all if you are aggressive and use POE, so don't let these questions intimidate you!

One of These Things Is Not Like the Others

One of the nice things about this question type (from your point of view) is that the answer choices are usually very far apart in meaning. In other words, you *rarely* find two answers that are separated by subtle shades of meaning. Instead you find four things that have nothing to do with each other, except perhaps a very general common category, similar to what you saw earlier in the "avoid trap answers" examples. Why is this so helpful? It allows you to eliminate answer choices based on a minimal understanding of the sentence. If you can figure out the general context of the sentence by piecing together one or two words as clues, you can eliminate answers that are unlikely to appear in that context. You'll usually find that there's really only one word that makes any kind of sense in that context. Choose the answer that is *not* like the others.

Eduardo monta en el automóvil y dice que. . .

(A) tiene hambre
(B) hace mucho calor
(C) el perro es grande
(D) necesita gasolina

What if the only word you understand in the above sentence is **automóvil**? Well, your next thought should be, "Which of the answers has a word that has something to do with a car?" Answer (A), which means "he's hungry," doesn't seem likely. Answer (B) talks about the weather, which isn't a car-related topic. Choice (C) probably wins the prize for most ridiculous: "The dog is big." So which answer is not like the others? Choice (D), which means "he needs gas." Notice that if you can make out some of the key words in either the sentence or the answers, you can eliminate some of the answer choices and get the correct answer.

It's important to understand that this technique will *not* always leave you with only one remaining answer, i.e., the right one. Sometimes you will be able to eliminate one or two choices and end up taking an educated guess. However, guessing one out of two is much better than guessing one out of four. Never eliminate an answer simply because you don't understand it. If you're not sure, leave it in and deal with the choices of which you are sure. Also, the technique allows you to get around some of the tough vocabulary, but you still need to know the meanings of some of the words in order to use the technique: If you don't know what the answers mean, you can't determine which one is not like the others. The moral of the story is *don't neglect your vocabulary work!*

Drill

In the following drill, each sentence is missing all but a couple of key words. Eliminate answers that aren't related to the words in the sentence. If you're left with more than one answer, guess the one that is most like the words in the sentence.

1. María *blah blah blah* médico *blah blah* . . .

   (A) enferma
   (B) perfumada
   (C) acostada
   (D) sucia

2. *Blah blah blah* revistas *blah blah blah* . . .

   (A) vacaciones
   (B) obras de teatro
   (C) conciertos
   (D) artículos interesantes

3. No *blah* salir porque *blah* mucha . . .

   (A) comida
   (B) dinero
   (C) nieve
   (D) hambre

4. *Blah* postre me *blah blah* que . . .

   (A) el agua
   (B) las vitaminas
   (C) el helado
   (D) arroz con pollo

5. La película *blah blah blah* miedo porque *blah blah* . . .

   (A) violenta
   (B) graciosa
   (C) corta
   (D) tremenda

6. La casa *blah blah* sucia. *Blah blah* que . . .

   (A) llorar
   (B) limpiar
   (C) llover
   (D) llevar

Answers and Explanations of Drill

1. **A**

   Médico (doctor) would make **enferma** (ill) a very good guess. The other answers (**perfumada** = scented, **acostada** = lying down, **sucia** = dirty) have nothing to do with a doctor.

2. **D**

   Revistas (magazines) would match up with **artículos interesantes** (interesting articles) better than it would with any of the other choices offered (**vacaciones** = vacation, **obras de teatro** = plays, **conciertos** = concerts).

3. **C**

   This is a pretty tough one, but you can still take a good guess. **Salir** (to go out), combined with the **no** that precedes it gives you "no go out." Are any of the answers something that might keep you from going out? Yes, **nieve** (snow). None of the others would really make sense (**comida** = food, **dinero** = money, **hambre** = hunger).

4. **C**

   Postre means dessert, and there is only one answer that is a dessert: **helado** (ice cream). **Arroz con pollo** (chicken with rice), **vitaminas** (vitamins), and **agua** (water) are all edible, but they aren't desserts.

5. **A**

   If you put **película** (movie) and **miedo** (fear) together, what do you get? A scary movie! The closest guess would be **violenta** (violent). **Graciosa** means funny, **corta** means short, and **tremenda** means huge or grand.

6. **B**

   Sucia (which, as you saw earlier, means dirty) is enough to tell you to guess **limpiar** (to clean). **Casa** (house) doesn't really give you any additional helpful information. **Llorar** (to cry), **llover** (to rain), and **llevar** (to carry) all sound similar to the right answer, but their meanings are way off.

THIRD PASS: WHEN YOU HARDLY UNDERSTAND ANY PART OF THE SENTENCE

These questions should be left for last: There's very little you can do if you know only one or two words in the entire sentence. Your goal on the third pass is to go back to those questions that you skipped on the first two passes and see if you can eliminate even one answer choice based on the word or words that you do know in the sentence, using the same approach that you used on the second pass. The only difference is you'll probably have less to base your decision on. If you're unable to cancel anything, no sweat—just move on to the next question.

You don't need to know the hardest words in the sentence in order to knock off some of the answers. Even if you can only determine that the answer is going to be a feminine word based on its article (**la**), that alone could get rid of one or two choices, so be aggressive!

SUMMARY

FIRST PASS: WHEN YOU UNDERSTAND THE ENTIRE SENTENCE

- Fill in your own word (short and simple).

- Eliminate answers that are not in the same category as your word.

- Beware of the little traps: Concentrate on meaning, not sound.

- Out of the remaining choices pick the answer that's closest to your word.

Three Pass

Do all the easy questions first. Do the questions with moderately difficult vocabulary second. For the rest, either use POE to get rid of at least one answer choice and guess, or skip them.

SECOND PASS: WHEN YOU DON'T UNDERSTAND THE ENTIRE SENTENCE

- Determine the meanings of as many individual words as you can.

- Put these words together to try to determine the general context of the sentence.

- Eliminate any choices that don't make sense in that context.

- Pick the one that is most likely to appear in the context out of the remaining choices (it should be the only one left).

THIRD PASS: WHEN YOU HARDLY UNDERSTAND ANY PART OF THE SENTENCE

- Try to locate sentences in which you know at least one or two words.

- See if any of the answers seem impossible based on those words.

- Eliminate those answers and guess.

Never...

- cancel an answer choice because you don't know its meaning—just because you don't know it doesn't mean it's wrong! Use POE on the words you *do* know.

- leave a question blank if you can eliminate even one answer—the odds are with you if you can eliminate one or more of the choices, so guess!

PRACTICE QUESTIONS

Part A

Directions: This part consists of a number of incomplete statements, each having four suggested completions. Select the most appropriate completion and fill in the corresponding oval on the answer sheet.

---

1. El ------- que se pone mi novia huele a rosas.

   (A) calcetín
   (B) esfuerzo
   (C) perfume
   (D) tamaño

2. Buscaba las medicinas para mi abuelo en la -------
   de la esquina.

   (A) librería
   (B) farmacia
   (C) oficina
   (D) panadería

3. Estaba ------- cuando mis empleados llegaron tarde
   por cuarta vez en la misma semana.

   (A) furioso
   (B) encantado
   (C) contentísimo
   (D) abierto

4. Si no comes el ------- por la mañana no tendrás
   energía durante el día.

   (A) café
   (B) almuerzo
   (C) caballo
   (D) desayuno

5. Es un hombre sumamente vanidoso; siempre se
   está mirando en el ------- .

   (A) espejo
   (B) cristal
   (C) gafas
   (D) mismo

6. Los viejos tienen más ------- que los jóvenes porque
   han tenido más experiencias.

   (A) tiempo
   (B) que comer
   (C) sabiduría
   (D) apetito

7. Es bastante evidente que a Alejandro le gusta hacer la tarea; siempre la hace ------- .

(A) de mala gana
(B) con entusiasmo
(C) muy despacio
(D) sin gusto

8. Pedro ------- muy contento cuando nació su hijo.

(A) se cambió
(B) se dio
(C) se hizo
(D) se puso

ANSWERS AND EXPLANATIONS OF PRACTICE QUESTIONS

PART A

Key Words
#1 – huele
#2 – medicinas
#3 – llegaron tarde
#4 – comes ... por la mañana
#5 – vanidoso ... se está mirando en
#6 – más experiencias
#7 – le gusta
#8 – contento

1. The ------- that my girlfriend puts on smells like roses.

(A) sock
(D) effort
(C) perfume
(D) size

The key word in this sentence is **huele**, which is an excellent clue because the only answer that is related to smell is **perfume**.

2. I was looking/looked for medicine for my grandfather in the ------- on the corner.

(A) bookstore
(B) pharmacy
(C) office
(D) bakery

The clue in this question is a cognate (remember those?), **medicinas**, so that even if the rest of the sentence was a blur you could tell that the answer had something to do with medicine. The answer also happens to be a cognate, and is the only choice that relates to medicine.

3. I was ------- when my employees arrived late for the fourth time in the same week.

(A) furious
(B) delighted
(C) very happy
(D) open

Unless you were some sort of lunatic, you'd be pretty peeved if your staff was late all the time. Although three of the answers are emotions, only one of the three is a negative emotion.

4. If you don't eat ------- in the morning you won't
   have energy during the day.

   (A) coffee
   (B) lunch
   (C) horse
   (D) breakfast

Comes and **por la mañana** are the two keys here. What do you eat in the morning? Breakfast, of course. **Café** isn't a bad second choice, but the problem with it is that you drink it, you don't eat it, and the verb that comes before the blank is **comer**. Even though the meaning comes across, you should never use **comer** with **café**.

5. He is an extremely vain man; he's always looking at
   himself in the ------- .

   (A) mirror
   (B) glass
   (C) glasses
   (D) self

Vanidoso is one clue in this one, but that's a pretty tough vocabulary word (add it to your list). You've also got **mirarse** (to look at oneself) later in the sentence to tell you that the best answer is **espejo**. **Cristal** means plain old glass, as in a window or a bottle, or fine glass.

6. Old people have more ------- than young people
   because they've had more experiences.

   (A) time
   (B) to eat
   (C) wisdom
   (D) appetite

Old folks probably have more of lots of things than do young folks, but what might they have more of based on experience? Not time, food, or appetite, which leaves you with only (C). We know this is a hard word, but you could have used POE to get this question right without knowing **sabiduría**.

7. It's evident enough that Alejandro likes doing his
   homework; he always does it ------- .

   (A) reluctantly
   (B) with enthusiasm
   (C) very slowly
   (D) without taste

"Likes" implies a positive answer, such as (B). The others are all negative things, and if you could determine that much you could cancel them without knowing their precise meanings.

8. Pedro ------- very happy when his child was born.

   (A) changed
   (B) gave himself
   (C) made himself
   (D) became

Choices (A) and (B) are really awkward, and although (C) seems like it could work, the verb **ponerse** is generally used to indicate a change of emotions. **Hacerse** is not.

VOCABULARY REVIEW

WHY WORK ON YOUR VOCABULARY?

In case you haven't already noticed, vocabulary is a very important part of this test. You've already seen some ways to get around the tough vocabulary by using certain techniques, but that doesn't mean that you can blow off this section of the book. We know, we know—memorizing vocabulary words is about as much fun as watching grass grow. At the same time, vocabulary work can translate into some easy points on the day of the test: If you know the words, the questions are that much easier. By not working on your vocabulary, you're blowing a golden opportunity to improve your score. We've narrowed down your work so that you only have to deal with the words that are most likely to appear on the test. Now it's up to you to memorize them.

HOW TO USE THIS LIST

The following vocabulary list is broken up into three general categories: beginner, intermediate, and advanced. There are several good reasons for doing this. Perhaps the most obvious is that it supports your Three-Pass pacing strategy. Your review of these lists can help you decide what kind of questions you will attempt to answer right away and which ones you will leave for a second or third pass. Another reason is to address that high-school Spanish classes teach an uneven mix of vocabulary. If you are currently taking an advanced Spanish course, for example, you might have forgotten easier vocabulary words.

If you are taking the SAT Spanish Subject Test, you have probably taken at least two years of Spanish. The following vocabulary lists, like the rest of the review material in this book, are meant to be used in conjunction with your accumulated classroom material. If you feel fuzzy on a concept, by all means return to your textbooks. If there seems to be a concept or a word group that you have never really mastered, then you can set up your third pass or "skip" questions accordingly.

The beginner list is arranged by thematic category, much like a beginner's vocabulary list in any language. At minimum, you should memorize all the words in this section, but you may also want to review other thematic presentations in your textbooks for any categories you need to brush up on. If you are comfortable, move on to the words found in the intermediate list. These are practical words and concepts (such as prepositional phrases and conjunctions) that you'd use if you were comfortable with Spanish. Words like these frequently appear in both the Paragraph Completion and Reading Comprehension portions of the test. We've also provided an advanced vocab list, which contains words that ETS might use to trap you, such as false cognates. Don't forget to add any words you don't know from the practice tests to your study list! See if you can place them into categories, as we do. Then you will have your own, personalized three-part pacing strategy.

BEGINNER LEVEL — THEMATIC VOCABULARY

Don't Forget to Use Your English Cognates

Spanish Word	English Equivalent
profundo	profound
participar	to participate
el automóvil	automobile
el circo	circus
el minuto	minute
el perfume	perfume
el/la dentista	dentist
la farmacia	pharmacy
la música	music
estupendo/a	stupendous
el crítico	critic
criticar	to criticize
la ovación	ovation
el plato	plate
el programa de televisión	television program
el apetito	appetite
las vacaciones	vacation
el teatro	theater
la biología	biology
el empleado, la empleada	employee
el arte	art
el/la artista	artist

Vocabulary
Make sure that vocab review is a routine part of preparing for the exam. Not knowing the vocabulary is the surest way not to do as well as you could otherwise.

la controversia	controversy
la creación	creation
el hotel	hotel
la manifestación	manifestation
furioso/a	furious
cordial	cordial, polite
la residencia	residence, home
practicar	to practice
la operación	operation
el estómago	stomach
falso	false, fake
decidir	to decide
el caso	case (as in "in this case," not suitcase)
la clase	class (as in school, or society)
comparar	to compare
la justicia	justice
defender	to defend
la gloria	glory
misterioso/a	mysterious
la impresión	impression
plantar	to plant
servir	to serve
contemporáneo/a	contemporary
el verso	verse
el acto	act
la gracia	grace

Basic Words and Phrases You Should Know

por eso	that's why
la noticia	news
cada uno	each one
poner	to put
sentado/a	seated
dormido/a	asleep
llamar	to call
muy poco	very little
manejar, conducir	to drive

entrar (en)	to enter
¿Quién eres?	Who are you?
llevar	to take, to carry, to wear
tocar	to touch, to play (an instrument)
tocar a la puerta	to knock at the door
el correo	mail
el buzón	mailbox
sacar	to take out, to remove
dar la vuelta	to turn or flip over
la carrera	race (as in a marathon); career
el negocio	business
sin falta	without fail
terminar	to finish
la calidad	quality
la cantidad	quantity
la revista	magazine
mostrar	to show
el partido	party (as in political, not birthday); game, match
el árbol	tree
devolver	to give back
el almacén	warehouse
el desfile	parade, procession
advertir	to notice, observe; to warn
el estilo	style
tener cuidado	to be careful
envolver	to wrap
ahorrar	to save (as in money, not a life)
algo	something
empezar	to begin

We Are Family

la madre	mother
el padre	father (also sometimes used for priest)
el hijo/la hija	son/daughter
el tío/la tía	uncle/aunt
el sobrino/la sobrina	nephew/niece

el primo/la prima	cousin
el nieto/la nieta	grandson/granddaughter
el niño/la niña	boy/girl (usually used for small children)
el muchacho/la muchacha	boy/girl (usually used for teenagers)
el abuelo/la abuela	grandfather/grandmother
el hermano/la hermana	brother/sister

School Days

¡Despiértate!	Wake up!
¡Levántate!	Get up!
la escuela	school
a tiempo	on time
tarde	late
la tarde	afternoon
el trabajo	work
la tarea	homework
hacer la tarea	to do homework
leer	to read
el cuento	story
saber	to know
escribir	to write
la librería	bookstore
el libro	book
el número	number
tonto/a	boneheaded, silly
estudiar	to study
los estudiantes	students
prestar atención	to pay attention
el idioma	language
preguntar	to ask
la biblioteca	library

Feed Me

el apetito	appetite
tener hambre	to be hungry
comer	to eat
beber, tomar	to drink
la comida	food

el camarero/la camarera	waiter/waitress
la cuenta	the check, the bill
el desayuno	breakfast
el arroz	rice
el pollo	chicken
gordo/a	fat
delgado/a	thin
el vaso	glass
la taza	cup
el helado	ice cream
el olor	smell, odor, aroma
el sabor	flavor
el almuerzo	lunch
la cena	dinner

The Neck Bone's Connected to the

los dientes	teeth
las encías	gums
la muela	molar
el estómago	stomach
las manos	hands
la cintura	waist
la cabeza	head
las piernas	legs
los brazos	arms
los pies	feet
la espalda	back
el pelo/el cabello	hair
los ojos	eyes
la boca	mouth
la nariz	nose
el pecho	chest

Shopping Is My Life

comprar	to buy
ir de compras	to go shopping
la camiseta; la playera	T-shirt

la cartera; la bolsa	purse
la zapatería	shoe store
la corbata	tie
el pañuelo	handkerchief
el calcetín	sock
el vestido	dress
el abrigo	coat
la billetera	wallet
el dinero	money
el zapato	shoe
los pantalones	pants
la camisa	shirt
la blusa	blouse
la falda	skirt
las medias	pantyhose/stockings
los dólares	dollars
de lujo	expensive, luxurious
gastar dinero	to spend money

An Apple a Day

la úlcera	ulcer
diagnosticar	to diagnose
la operación	operation
la extracción	extraction
pálido/a	pale
la herida	injury, wound
enfermo/a	sick
sufrir	to suffer
el dolor	pain
la escayola; el yeso	arm or leg cast
urgencias	emergency room
el médico	doctor
el/la dentista	dentist
la salud	health
sano/sana	healthy

House Stuff

la casa	house
el piso	floor (a level of a building)
el suelo	floor (in a house), ground
los muebles	furniture
la butaca	armchair, easy chair
salir (de)	to leave
volver	to return
el espejo	mirror
el jabón	soap
el sillón	rocking chair; armchair
lavar	to wash
el fregadero	sink
el cesped; la grama	lawn
limpiar	to clean
el cuarto/la sala	room
la cocina	kitchen
el dormitorio	bedroom
el baño	bathroom
las llaves	keys

Comparatively Speaking

antes	before
después	after
demasiado/a	too (as in too much, too late, too funny, etc.)
mayor	older
menor	younger
mejor	better
peor	worse
mediocre	mediocre
bien hecho	well done
(me) da igual	it doesn't matter (to me)

The Meaning of Life

la vida	life
cambiar	to change

con cariño	with affection
los chistes	jokes
reír	to laugh
regalar	to give as a gift
ganar	to win, to earn (money)
saber	to know (facts, how to do things)
la sabiduría	knowledge, wisdom
jugar	to play
aceptar	to accept
ofrecer	to offer
querer	to want; to love (te quiero = I love you)
tranquilo/a	peaceful, tranquil
reposar; descansar	to rest, relax
desear	to want
esperar	to wait
odiar	to loathe, hate
decir	to say
es decir	that is, . . .
tener	to have
buscar	to look for, search for
hacer	to do, to make
sentir(se)	to feel
¿Cómo te sientes?	How do you feel?
la simpatía	sympathy
la pena	sorrow, trouble, pain
escoger	to choose
conocer	to know (people, places—indicates familiarity)
prestar	to lend
empeñarse	to pledge or devote oneself

Too Much Time on My Hands

la última vez	last time
el siglo	century
el centenario	centennial
despacio	slow, slowly
en cuanto	as soon as

inmediatamente	immediately
durante	during
empezar, comenzar	to begin
terminar, acabar	to finish
hace un rato	a little while ago
próximo/a	next
el próximo día	the next day
media hora	half hour
una/la hora	hour; time
¿Qué hora es?	What time is it?
de la noche	P.M. (after sunset)
de la tarde	P.M. (afternoon)
de la mañana	A.M.
apurarse	to hurry oneself
en marcha	on the move, on the go
ahora mismo	right now
la fecha	date (as in calendar)
hoy	today
mañana	tomorrow
la mañana	morning
ayer	yesterday
cada vez	each/every time
el año	year
en seguida	right away
de buena gana	gladly (e.g., I'd be happy to)
a eso de	around (a eso de las ocho = around 8:00)

Places to Go, People to See

ir	to go
la esquina	street corner
la playa	the beach
la obra de teatro	the play
la taquilla	box office
cerca de	near
la calle	street
el viaje	trip

aquí	here
allí	there
el mapa	map
dondequiera	wherever
la ciudad	city
el país	country
la película	movie
el banco	bank; bench
el camino	path, route
el señor	gentleman
la señora	lady
la mujer	woman
el hombre	man
el torero	bullfighter
el cartero/la cartera	mail carrier

How's the Weather?

hacer frío	to be cold out
hacer calor	to be hot out
caliente	hot
caluroso/a	warm, hot
llover/la lluvia	to rain/rain
mojado/a	wet
oscuro/a	dark
nevar/la nieve	to snow/snow
el sol	the sun
el viento	the wind

Music Soothes the Savage Beast

la música	music
la orquesta	orchestra
tocar	to play (an instrument); to touch
practicar	to practice

Life's a Drag

nada más	no more, nothing more
¡De ninguna forma!	No way!
nadie	no one

¡Ya lo creo!	Absolutely! For sure!
ningún/ninguna	none, neither
asco	disgust
falsamente	falsely
romper	to break
tener culpa	to be at fault, guilty
sin querer	unintentionally; against your will
el mendigo/la mendiga	beggar
pedir limosna	to beg
¿Con qué derecho?	How dare you? What gives you the right?
quemar	to burn
rechazar	to push away, repel, reject
olvidar	to forget
sucio/a	dirty
quejarse	to complain
grave	serious
distraído/a	absentminded
poner fin a	to put an end to
de mala gana	reluctantly
de mal humor	in a bad mood
a contrapelo	the wrong way
inconveniente	unsuitable, inappropriate; inconvenient

Life's a Bowl of Cherries

perfumado/a	scented, sweet smelling
cómodo/a	comfortable
lleno/a	full
por favor	please
el premio	prize
premio gordo	grand prize
¡Cómo no!	Of course! I'd be glad to!
empeñarse	to pledge or vow
¡Felicitaciones!	Congratulations!
cortés	courteous
cordial	cordial
estar de acuerdo	to be in agreement

Que Dios lo bendiga.	May God bless you.
el regalo	gift
el regalo de cumpleaños	birthday gift
bastante	enough
gracioso/a	cute, funny

Reflexive Verbs

Low Tech Vocab Review

Make flash cards! Five minutes each day learning and reviewing will make a huge difference.

ponerse	to put on; to become (with verbs of emotion)
hacerse	to make oneself; to become (with nouns: **Me hice abogado.** I became a lawyer)
acostarse	to go to bed
involucrarse	to involve oneself with
lavarse	to wash oneself
peinarse	to comb one's hair
vestirse	to get dressed
sentarse	to sit down
divertirse	to have fun
quitarse	to take off
bañarse	to bathe oneself
ducharse	to shower

INTERMEDIATE LEVEL — PRACTICALITIES

Other Prepositions, Conjunctions, Adverbs, and Phrases to Remember

hacia	toward
enfrente de	in front of
frente a	in front of
dentro de	inside of
fuera de	outside of
a la derecha de	to the right of
a la izquierda de	to the left of
debajo de	underneath
encima de	above, on top of
alrededor de	around, surrounding
en medio de	in the middle of
hasta	until

tras	behind, after
cerca de	close to, near
lejos de	far from
detrás de	behind
delante de	in front of
al lado de	next to
sin	without
contra	against
junto a	next to
respecto a	in regard to
a pesar de	in spite of
en vez de	instead of
en cuanto a	as to, as regards
mientras que	while, meanwhile
aunque	although
sin embargo	nevertheless
a menos que	unless
de antemano	beforehand
ni siquiera	not even
apenas	barely
a no ser que	unless
siempre que	as long as
por más que	no matter how (much)
también	also
de repente	suddenly
en seguida	immediately
por desgracia	unfortunately
al azar	by chance
de todos modos	in any case
tarde o temprano	sooner or later
de nuevo	again
despacio	slowly
acaso	perhaps
tampoco	neither, either
mientras tanto	meanwhile
de una vez	once and for all
en fin	in short

por supuesto	of course
por lo menos	at least

Practical and Useful Nouns

el rincón	corner
el sacapuntas	pencil sharpener
el incendio	fire (as natural disaster)
el seguro	insurance
la herencia	inheritance
la inversión	investment
el salvavidas	lifejacket
el socorrista	lifeguard
la acera	sidewalk
los impuestos	taxes
el guión	script
la red	line, web, network
el recado	message (as in "leave a...")
el despachoa	person's office
el escritorio	desk
el equipaje	luggage
la huelga	worker's strike
la superficie	surface
el silbido	whistle
la moda	fashion
el marco	frame
las joyas	jewelry
la mochila	backpack
la factura	bill (for services rendered)
la fecha	date
el estreno	debut
la empresa	company
el esfuerzo	effort
el/la periodista	journalist
el ordenador (in Spain)	computer
la computadora (in America)	computer
la impresora	printer
el orgullo	pride
la misericordia	mercy

la temporada	season
el descubrimiento	discovery
el peso	weight
la pantalla	screen
los recursos	resources
la propina	tip
la contraseña	password

Verbs: Actions to Take

recuperarse	to recover
respirar	to breathe
dirigir	to direct
encabezar	to lead, head
superar	to overcome
lanzar	to launch
ampliar	to broaden, expand
repasar	to review
encargarse	to take charge of
imprimir	to print
fortalecer	to strengthen
resplandecer	to shine
sostener	to sustain
dar a luz (a)	to give birth (to)
negociar	negotiate
caer en cuenta, dar(se) cuenta	to realize
tener en cuenta	to take into account
hallar	to find
reciclar	to recycle
tranquilizarse	to calm (oneself) down
amueblar	to furnish (a room)
enjuagar	to rinse
rescatar	to rescue
traducir	to translate
viajar	to travel
agradar	to please
madrugar	to get up early
despegar	to take off (said of an airplane)
llevar a cabo	to finish

atreverse	to dare
acertar	to guess correctly

Advanced Level—Traps

Different Genders, Different Meanings

el editorial	editorial
la editorial	publishing house
el mañana	the future
la mañana	morning
el orden	order
la orden	religious order
el coma	coma
la coma	comma
el corte	cut
la corte	court
el frente	front (as in a war)
la frente	forehead
el guía	guide
la guía	phonebook
el policía	police officer
la policía	police force
el capital	capital (as in money)
la capital	capital (of a country)

Feminine Nouns with Masculine Articles

el hambre	hunger
el habla	speech
el ancla	anchor
el aula	classroom
el hacha	ax

el arma	weapon
el alma	soul
el águila	eagle
el alba	dawn
el agua	water

False Cognates and Other Pitfalls

actualmente	at the present moment
sensible	sensitive
embarazada	pregnant
el éxito	success
insólito	uncanny
aterrizar	to land (said of an airplane)
el vidrio	glass (window, bottle)
grabar	to record
el desenlace	climax, denouement, finale
el frenesí	frenzy
el collar	necklace
los parientes	kin
el ámbito	field of activity, environment
cazar	to hunt
la informática	computer science
el temporal	storm
destornudar	to sneeze
la tos	cough
rendirse	to surrender

Sentence Completion:
Grammar

Memorize All Directions

Reading the directions when you take the test is a waste of precious time. Know them beforehand!

Now we're going to take a look at the grammar portion of the sentence completion questions that you'll find in Part A of the Spanish Subject Test and the first part of the Reading section of the Spanish with Listening Subject Test. The good news is that you don't need to review everything about grammar that you ever learned, because only a small portion of Spanish grammar is actually tested, and your review will focus on that portion. The even better news is that the techniques you learned earlier work really well on this section, and, by combining them with a brief review of some grammar, you can do very well. Before you get into strategies or review, memorize the instructions for this question type:

Directions: This part consists of a number of incomplete statements, each having four suggested completions. Select the most appropriate completion and fill in the corresponding oval on the answer sheet.

Each question will be followed by four answer choices. These differ from the vocabulary sentence completion questions because the answer choices will all have the same or very similar meanings, but only one of them will fit the blank and make the sentence grammatically correct. It's not about vocabulary; it's about verbs, pronouns, prepositions, and idioms, but don't let that scare you! After you get through this chapter, you'll know everything you need to know to master this section.

HOW TO CRACK THIS SECTION

The key to success on this section is to focus specifically on those grammatical concepts that are being tested and spend a little time relearning them. Contrary to what the test writers would like you to believe, this section doesn't test everything you learned in Spanish class, but instead sticks to a few grammatical ideas and tests them over and over again. You probably already know and are comfortable with many of them, and even if you're not right now, you will be if you invest a little time in studying.

In addition to reviewing the grammar, you will use Process of Elimination and the Three-Pass System to beat this section. You'll supplement both of these with what may be your best friend on these questions: your ear. Remember how your ear could easily steer you wrong on vocabulary sentence completions because of the way the wrong answers sometimes sounded like the right one? Well, on this section, your ear, or how the answers sound, can actually help you eliminate answers right off the bat without using grammar at all. This won't work on all questions, but it certainly will on some, and you're going to take full advantage of this.

FIRST PASS: I'M SURE I'VE SEEN THIS SOMEWHERE BEFORE

First Pass

Remember—you don't have to do the questions in the order they're presented. Do the easiest ones first—no matter where they are numerically.

Again, the questions are not arranged in any particular order of difficulty, but the level of difficulty of the different questions varies tremendously. Your goal on the first pass is to locate the questions that test the verb tenses, pronouns, prepositions, and idioms that you know like the back of your hand. Find the easiest questions, and do them first. How do you tell whether a question is easy? Read it, and if the structure looks familiar, go for it. If it looks as if it's going to take a little POE to crack it, leave that question for the second pass.

SECOND PASS: HAVEN'T I SEEN THIS SOMEWHERE BEFORE?

If you read a question and the answer doesn't immediately jump off the page at you, don't be discouraged: Just because you don't immediately know what the answer *is* doesn't mean you can't tell what the answer *isn't*. Work backwards from the answer choices and eliminate answers that you know are wrong. If you understand some of the answer choices and know that they're wrong, it's just as effective as knowing which one is right.

THIRD PASS: I'VE NEVER SEEN THIS ANYWHERE

If the grammar in both the sentence and answers is a complete mystery to you, chances are you won't be able to back into the right answer using POE. Eliminate anything you can and guess. The most important thing about the third pass (on any section) is that you don't spend too much time on these really tough questions.

GRAMMAR REVIEW

Although we certainly can't lie to you by saying that reviewing grammar rules will be fun, we can promise you that a little time on this material will mean easy points for you on the day of the test. Grammar is merely a bunch of rules, and once you've learned the ones that are tested you'll be ready for this question type.

BASIC TERMS

The following terms, although you won't see them on the test, are important because they will come up later in the chapter. Knowing them will allow you to understand the rules of grammar that you're about to review.

Noun: a person, place, or thing.
EXAMPLES: Abraham Lincoln, New Jersey, a taco

Pronoun: a word that replaces a noun.
EXAMPLES: Abe Lincoln would be replaced by "he," New Jersey by "it," and a taco by "it." You'll see more about pronouns later.

Adjective: a word that describes a noun.
EXAMPLES: cold, soft, colorful

Verb: an action word. It is what is being done in a sentence.
EXAMPLE: Ron *ate* the huge breakfast.

Infinitive: the original, unconjugated form of a verb.
EXAMPLES: to eat, to run, to laugh

Auxiliary Verb: the verb that precedes the past participle in the perfect tenses.
EXAMPLE: He *had* eaten his lunch.

Past Participle: the appropriate form of a verb when it is used with the auxiliary verb.
EXAMPLE: They have *gone* to work.

Adverb: an adverb describes a verb, adjective, or another adverb, just like an adjective describes a noun.
EXAMPLES: slowly, quickly, happily (Adverbs often, but don't always, end in *-ly*.)

Subject: the thing (noun) in a sentence that is performing the action.
EXAMPLE: *John* wrote the song.

Compound: a subject that's made up of two or more subjects or nouns.
EXAMPLE: *John and Paul* wrote the song together.

Object: the thing (noun or pronoun) in the sentence that the action is happening to, either directly or indirectly.
EXAMPLES: Mary bought *the shirt*. Joe hit *him*. Mary gave a gift to *Tim*.

Direct Object: The thing that receives the action of the verb.
EXAMPLE: I see *the wall*. (The wall "receives" the action of seeing.)

Indirect Object: The person who receives the direct object.
EXAMPLE: I wrote the letter to *her*. (She receives the letter.)

Preposition: a word that marks the relationship (in space or time) between two other words.
EXAMPLES: He received the letter *from* her. The book is *below* the chair.

Article: a word (usually a very small word) that precedes a noun.
EXAMPLES: *a* watch, *the* room

That wasn't so bad, was it? Now let's put all those terms together in a couple of examples:

Dominic   spent   the   entire   night   here.
subject   verb   article   adjective   dir. obj.   adverb

Margaret   often   gives   me   money.
subject   adverb   verb   indir. obj.   dir. obj.

Alison and Rob   have   a   gorgeous   child.
compound subject   verb   article   adjective   dir. obj.

Once you've spent a little time with these terms, go on to review the grammar that you'll actually be tested on.

PRONOUNS

You already learned that a pronoun is a word that takes the place of a noun. Now you'll review what pronouns look like in Spanish, and learn how they are tested on the Spanish Subject Test.

If you can tell the difference between subject, direct object, and indirect object pronouns, you are in very good shape. Beyond those different types, there are a couple of odds and ends that may show up, but the majority of questions that test pronouns will focus on these three basic types.

SUBJECT PRONOUNS

These are the most basic pronouns, and probably the first ones you learned. Just take a moment to look them over to make sure you haven't forgotten them. Then spend some time looking over the examples that follow until you are comfortable with using them.

yo	I	**nosotros/nosotras**	we (mas./fem.)
tú/usted (Ud.)	you (familiar/ formal)	**vosotros/vosotras/ ustedes (Uds.)**	you (pl.) (mas./fem.)
ella/él	she/he	**ellas/ellos**	they

Note that "vosotros" is a form mainly used in Spain, and almost never appears on the Spanish Subject Test.

When to Use Subject Pronouns

A subject pronoun (like any other pronoun) replaces the noun that is the subject of the sentence.

Marco no pudo comprar el helado.
Marco couldn't buy the ice cream.

Who does the action of this sentence? Marco, so he is the subject. If we wanted to use a subject pronoun in this case, we'd replace "Marco" with "**él**":

Él no pudo comprar el helado.
He couldn't buy the ice cream.

Subject Pronouns

Subject pronouns aren't always necessary in Spanish sentences, because the form of the verb gives us a clue as to the subject's identity. They are used, however, for emphasis or clarification.

DIRECT OBJECT PRONOUNS

Direct object pronouns replace (you guessed it) the direct object in a sentence.

me	me	**nos**	us
te	you (*tú* form)	**os**	you (*vosotros* form)
lo/la	him, it (mas.)/her, it (fem.)/ you (*Ud.* form)	**los/las**	them (mas./fem.)/ you (*Uds.* form)

When to Use Direct Object Pronouns

Now let's see what it looks like when we replace the direct object in a sentence with a pronoun:

> *Marco no pudo comprar el helado.*

What couldn't Marco buy? Ice cream. Because ice cream is what's receiving the action, it's the direct object. To use the direct object pronoun, you'd replace "**helado**" with "**lo**":

> *Marco no pudo comprar**lo**.*   or   *Marco no **lo** pudo comprar.*

When the direct object pronoun is used with the infinitive of a verb, it can either be tacked on to the end of the verb (the first example) or it can come before the conjugated verb in the sentence (the second example). Another example:

> *Voy a ver**lo**.*   I'm going to see it.
>
> ***Lo** voy a ver.*   (Both sentences mean the same thing.)

The direct object pronoun also follows the verb in an affirmative command, for example:

> *¡Cóme**lo**!*   Eat it!
>
> *¡Escúchame!*   Listen to me!

Finding the Direct Object

I throw the ball.
What do I throw?
Ellen knew the answer.
What did she know?
We will see the bus.
What will we see?
What received the action of the verb?
The answer is always the direct object.

INDIRECT OBJECT PRONOUNS

These pronouns replace the indirect object in a sentence. The indirect object is easy to spot in English because a preposition often comes before it. However, *this is not the case in Spanish*. In Spanish, when the object is indirect, the preposition is often implied, not explicitly stated. So how can you tell the difference? In general, the indirect object is the person who receives the direct object.

me	me	**nos**	us
te	you (fam.)	**os**	you
le	him, her, you (for *Ud.*)	**les**	them, you (for *Uds.*)

When to Use Indirect Object Pronouns

This might seem a bit strange, but in Spanish the indirect object pronoun is often present in a sentence that contains the indirect object noun:

Juan le da el abrigo al viejo.

Juan gives the coat to the old man. or Juan gives the old man the coat.

Notice that the sentence contains the indirect object noun (**viejo**) and the indirect object pronoun (**le**). This is often necessary to provide clarification of the identity of the indirect object pronoun, or to emphasize that identity. Typically, an expression of clarification is needed with the pronouns "**le**" and "**les**" and "**se**" (see below), but is not obligatory with other pronouns:

*María **nos** ayudó.*	María helped us.
*Juan **me** trae el suéter.*	Juan brings me the sweater.

The identity of the indirect object is obvious with the choice of pronoun in these examples, and so it is not necessary for clarification. It may be used, however, to emphasize the identity of the indirect object:

*No **me** lo trajeron a **mí**; **te** lo trajeron a **ti**.*
They didn't bring it to **me**; they brought it to **you**.

We would change our intonation to emphasize these words in English. This doesn't happen in Spanish; the expressions "**a mí**" and "**a ti**" serve the same function.

"**Se**" is used in place of "**le**" and "**les**" whenever the pronoun that follows begins with "**l**":

¿Le cuentas la noticia a María?	Are you telling Maria the news?
*Sí, **se** la cuento **a María**.*	Yes, I'm telling it to her.
¿Les prestas los guantes a los estudiantes?	Do you lend gloves to the students?
*No, no **se** los presto **a ellos**.*	No, I don't lend them to them.

Notice that "**le**" changes to "**se**" in the first example and "**les**" to "**se**" in the second because the direct object pronoun that follows begins with an "**l**." Notice also the inclusion of "**a María**" and "**a ellos**" to clarify the identity of "**se**" in each example.

PREPOSITIONAL PRONOUNS

As we mentioned earlier, there are some pronouns that take an explicitly stated preposition, and they're different from the indirect object pronouns. The prepositional pronouns are as follows:

mí	me	**nosotros/as**	us
ti/Ud.	you (fam./formal)	**vosotros/vosotras/Uds.**	you (plural)
él/ella	him/her	**ellos/ellas**	them

Indirect Object
I will write a letter to her.
Who will get the letter?
We tell him the truth.
Who gets the truth?
He suggested changes to me.
Who got the changes?
Essentially, who gets the noun?
The answer is always the
Indirect Object.

When to Use Prepositional Pronouns

Consider the following examples:

1. *Cómprale un regalo de cumpleaños.*	Buy **him** a birthday present.
2. *Vamos al teatro sin él.*	We're going to the theater without **him**.

Notice that in the first example, "him" is translated as "**le**," whereas in the second, "him" is translated as "**él**." What exactly is the deal with that?! Why isn't it the same word in Spanish as in English? In Spanish, the different pronouns distinguish the different functions of the word within the sentence.

In the first example, "him" is the indirect object of the verb "to buy" (Buy the gift for whom? For him—"him" receives the direct object), so we use the indirect object pronoun "**le**." In the second example, however, "him" is the object of the preposition "without," so we use the prepositional pronoun "**él**." Here are some more examples that involve the prepositional pronouns. Notice that they all have explicitly stated prepositions.

*Las flores son **para** ti.*	The flowers are **for** you.
*Estamos enojados **con** él.*	We are angry **with** him.
*Quieren ir de vacaciones **sin** Uds.*	They want to go on vacation **without** you.

In two special cases, when the preposition is **con** and the object of the preposition is **mí** or **ti**, the preposition and the pronoun are combined to form "**conmigo**" (with me) and "**contigo**" (with you).

*¿Quieres ir al concierto **conmigo**?*	Do you want to go to the concert **with me**?
*No, no puedo ir **contigo**.*	No, I can't go **with you**.

When the subject is **él**, **ella**, **ellos**, **ellas**, **Ud.**, or **Uds.**, and the object of the preposition is the **same** as the subject, the prepositional pronoun is **sí**, and is usually accompanied by **mismo/a** or **mismos/as**:

*Alejandro es muy egoísta. Siempre habla de **sí mismo**.*

Alejandro is very egotistical. He always talks about **himself**.

*Ellos compran ropa para **sí mismos** cuando van de compras.*

They buy clothes for **themselves** when they go shopping.

POSSESSIVE ADJECTIVES AND PRONOUNS

Possessive adjectives and pronouns are used to indicate ownership. When you want to let someone know what's yours, use the following pronouns or adjectives:

STRESSED POSSESSIVE ADJECTIVES

mío/mía	mine	**nuestro/nuestra**	ours
tuyo/tuya	yours (fam.)	**vuestro/vuestra**	yours
suyo/suya	his, hers	**suyo/suya**	theirs, yours (for *Uds.*)
			yours (for *Ud.*)

UNSTRESSED POSSESSIVE ADJECTIVES

mi	my	**nuestro/nuestra**	our
tu	your (fam.)	**vuestro/vuestra**	yours
su	his/her/your (for *Ud.*)	**su**	their, your (for *Uds.*)

When to Use Possessive Adjectives

The first question is, "When do you use an unstressed adjective, and when do you use a stressed adjective?" Check out these examples, and then we'll see what the rule is:

*Esta es **mi** casa.*	*Esta casa es **mía**.*
This is **my** house.	This house is **mine**.
*Aquí está **tu** billetera.*	*Esta billetera es **tuya**.*
Here is **your** wallet.	This wallet is **yours**.

The difference between stressed and unstressed possessive adjectives is emphasis, as opposed to meaning. Saying "This is my house" puts emphasis on the house, while saying "This house is mine" takes the focus off the house and stresses the identity of its owner—me. In order to avoid getting confused, just remember that unstressed is the Spanish equivalent of "my" and stressed is the Spanish equivalent of "mine."

In terms of structure, there is an important difference between the two types of adjectives, but it's an easy one to remember: Stressed adjectives come after the verb, but unstressed adjectives come before the noun. Notice that neither type agrees with the possessor; they agree with the thing possessed.

If it's not clear to you why these are adjectives when they look so much like pronouns, consider their function. When you say "my house," the noun "house" is being described by "my." Any word that describes a noun is an adjective, even if that word looks a lot like a pronoun. The key is how it's being used in the sentence.

POSSESSIVE PRONOUNS

These look like stressed possessive adjectives, but they mean something different. Possessive pronouns *replace* nouns, they don't *describe* them.

When to Use Possessive Pronouns

This type of pronoun is formed by combining the article of the noun that's being replaced with the appropriate stressed possessive adjective. Just like stressed possessive adjectives, possessive pronouns must agree in gender and number with the nouns they replace.

Mi bicicleta es azul.   *La mía es azul.*
My bicycle is blue.   **Mine** is blue.

Notice how the pronoun not only shows possession, but also replaces the noun. Here are some more examples:

Mis zapatos son caros.   *Los míos son caros.*
My shoes are expensive.   **Mine** are expensive.

Tu automóvil es rápido.   *El tuyo es rápido.*
Your car is fast.   **Yours** is fast.

No me gustaban los discos que ellos trajeron.   *No me gustaban los suyos.*
I didn't like the records **they brought**.   I didn't like **theirs**.

REFLEXIVE PRONOUNS

Remember those reflexive verbs you saw in the vocabulary review (**ponerse**, **hacerse**, etc.)? Those all have a common characteristic, which is that they indicate that the action is being done to or for oneself. When those verbs are conjugated, the reflexive pronoun (which is always **se** in the infinitive) changes according to the subject:

> **Reflexives**
>
> Many reflexive verbs can be used non-reflexively. Ask yourself—is the person doing the action the one who is receiving it? If so, the verb is reflexive. If not, the verb is normal (or transitive).

me	myself		**nos**	ourselves
te	yourself (fam.)		**os**	yourselves (fam.)
se	him/herself/yourself (for *Ud.*)		**se**	themselves/yourselves (for *Uds.*)

Reflexive pronouns are used when the subject and indirect object of the sentence are the same. This may sound kind of strange, but after you see some examples it ought to make more sense.

Alicia se pone el maquillaje.
Alicia puts on makeup.

What does she put on? **Makeup**—direct object.
Who receives the makeup? **Alicia**—she's also the subject.

The action is thus *reflected* back upon itself: Alicia does the action and then receives it. No outside influences are involved.

Another meaning for reflexive verbs is literally that the person does something directly to or for him/herself:

*Rosa **se cortó** con el cuchillo.*
Rosa **cut herself** with the knife.

*Roberto tiene que **comprarse** una libreta nueva.*
Roberto has to **buy himself** a new notebook.

THE PRONOUN *QUE*

The pronoun **que** can mean *who*, *that*, or *which*, depending on the context of the sentence. In other words, it can take the place of a person or a thing. Fortunately, it isn't too tough to tell which meaning is correct.

*¿Cómo se llama la maestra **que** tuvimos ayer?*

What's the name of the teacher **(whom)** we had yesterday?

*Ese es el equipo **que** me gusta más que todos los demás.*

That's the team **(that)** I like more than all the others.

*¿Cuál es la revista **que** compraste ayer?*

Which is the magazine **(that)** you bought yesterday?

In the first example, **que** means "who," since you are talking about a person. In the other examples, **que** refers to things, so it means "that" or "which."

When to Use *Que*

Although in English we tend to leave out the pronouns *who*, *that*, and *which*, in Spanish you have to use **que**. **Que** always follows the noun (as in the examples above) because it begins a clause that further describes the noun.

When referring to people, **quien** (or **quienes**) replaces **que** if the pronoun follows a preposition:

*El maestro sin **quien** yo no pudiera haber aprendido español está aquí hoy.*
The teacher without **whom** I couldn't have learned Spanish is here today.

*Los tipos con **quienes** juego a la pelota son jugadores magníficos.*
The fellows with **whom** I play ball are magnificent players.

The Pronoun *Que*

Keep in mind that what follows *que* is generally an expression that further describes the noun just before it.

THE PRONOUN *CUÁL*

Cuál (meaning *which* or *what*) is used when a choice is involved. It's used in place of **que** before the verb **ser**, and it has only two forms: singular (**cuál**) and plural (**cuáles**). Both **cuál** and the verb **ser** must agree in number with the thing(s) being asked about:

> *¿Cuál es tu ciudad favorita?*   **What** is your favorite city?
> *¿Cuáles son nuestros regalos?*   **Which** presents are ours?

DEMONSTRATIVE PRONOUNS AND ADJECTIVES

Demonstrative pronouns have an accent on the first "e." The adjectives don't. First, learn the construction and meaning:

Demonstrative Adjectives

"This and these in Spanish have Ts."

este/esta	this (one)	**estos/estas**	these
ese/esa	that (one)	**esos/esas**	those
aquel/aquella	that (one over there)	**aquellos/aquellas**	those (over there)

Adjective or Pronoun — Which Is It?

If the demonstrative word comes before a noun, then it is an adjective:

> *Este plato de arroz con pollo es mío.*   **This** plate of chicken with rice is mine.
> *Ese edificio es de mi hermano.*   **That** building is my brother's.

If the demonstrative word takes the place of a noun, then it's a pronoun:

> *Dije que éste es mío.*   I said that **this one** is mine.
> *Sabemos que ése es de mi hermano.*   We know **that one** is my brother's.

When used as adjectives, these words mean *this, that,* etc. When used as pronouns, they mean *this one, that one,* etc. Don't worry about the use of **ese** versus **aquel**. No question on this exam will ask you to pick between the two.

PRONOUN SUMMARY

- The types of pronouns that you need to know are subject, object (direct and indirect), possessive, prepositional (which you'll see again later), reflexive, demonstrative, and a couple of odds and ends like **que** and **cuál**. We're not guaranteeing that only these types will appear, but, if you know these inside and out, you should feel confident that you'll be able to tackle most (if not all) of the pronoun questions.

- Don't just memorize what the different pronouns look like! Recognizing them is important, but it's just as important that you understand how and when to use them.

- Don't forget about POE. The folks at ETS love to try to trip you up on simple things (like the gender of a pronoun) that are easy to overlook if you're not on your toes. Before you start thinking about grammar on a pronoun question, eliminate answers that are wrong based on flagrant stuff like gender, singular vs. plural, etc.

- If all else fails, your ear can sometimes be your guide. In learning Spanish, you probably spoke and heard the language on a pretty regular basis, and so you have a clue as to what correct Spanish sounds like. You don't want to use your ear if you can eliminate answers based on the rules of grammar, but if you've exhausted the rules and you're down to two answers, one of which sounds a lot better than the other, guess the nice-sounding one. The fact is that many grammatical rules were born out of a desire to make the language sound good.

- Last (but not least), don't forget to pace yourself wisely and use the Three-Pass system. Look for questions that test the pronouns you're most comfortable with, and skip the tough ones. If you're stumped by a question, leave it for the third pass, eliminate what you can, and guess, but never spend too much time on a question that tests something you don't really know or like.

PRONOUN QUESTIONS

A Possible Scenario

First pass—1, 2, 4; Second pass—3, 5, 7; Third pass—6, 8. Get used to the process.

1. Si él puede hacerlo solo, yo no ------- tengo que ayudar.

   (A) la
   (B) lo
   (C) le
   (D) los

2. Pedimos asientos cerca de una ventana, pero ------- dieron éstos.

   (A) nos
   (B) les
   (C) nuestros
   (D) me

3. Cuando sus estudiantes se portan mal, la profesora ------- castiga.

   (A) las
   (B) los
   (C) les
   (D) le

4. ¿Son ------- aquellos guantes que están sobre la butaca?

   (A) mío
   (B) mía
   (C) míos
   (D) mías

5. Para tu cumpleaños ------- daré un caballo nuevo.

   (A) le
   (B) te
   (C) a ti
   (D) me

6. ¿ ------- es tu cantante favorito?

   (A) Quién
   (B) Cuál
   (C) Quiénes
   (D) Qué

7. ¿ ------- prefieres? ¿El azul o el rojo?

   (A) Qué
   (B) Cuál
   (C) Cuáles
   (D) Ese

ANSWERS AND EXPLANATIONS OF PRONOUN QUESTIONS

1. If he can do it alone, I don't have to help ------- .

    (A) her
    (B) him (direct object)
    (C) him (indirect object)
    (D) them

Whom do I have to help? **Him**, which is the direct object.

2. We asked for seats near a window, but they gave ------- these.

    (A) us
    (B) them (indirect object)
    (C) ours
    (D) me

Pedimos tells you that the subject of the sentence is **nosotros**. Since you are trying to say, "they gave us these," the correct pronoun is **nos**.

3. When her students misbehave, the professor punishes ------- .

    (A) them (f, direct object)
    (B) them (m, direct object)
    (C) to them (indirect object)
    (D) to him (indirect object)

Estudiantes is masculine and plural, so choices (A) and (D) are incorrect. (Remember that in Spanish the masculine pronoun is used whenever the gender of a group is mixed, even if the majority of the group is female. Also, when the gender of the people in the group is unknown [like in this question], the male pronoun is used.) Whom does the professor punish? **Them**, which is the direct object, therefore (B) is the answer.

4. Are those gloves that are on the armchair ------- ?

    (A) mine (m, sing.)
    (B) mine (f, sing.)
    (C) mine (m, pl.)
    (D) mine (f, pl.)

Guantes is a masculine plural word, so the correct form of the possessive adjective is **míos**, which is choice (C).

5. For your birthday, I'll give ------- a new horse.

   (A) him (indirect object)
   (B) you
   (C) to you
   (D) me

The person whose birthday it is in the sentence is **tú**, so **te** is the correct indirect object pronoun. It is indirect in this case because it receives the direct object "horse." (C) is incorrect because it is an expression of emphasis which complements an indirect object pronoun. However, there is no indirect object pronoun to complement, so it cannot be right. The indirect object pronoun itself is necessary, so (B) is the best answer.

6. ------- is your favorite singer?

   (A) Who
   (B) Which
   (C) Who (pl.)
   (D) What

Since the question refers to a single person (**el cantante**), **quién** is the correct pronoun.

7. ------- do you prefer? The blue one or the red one?

   (A) What
   (B) Which
   (C) Which (pl.)
   (D) That one

In this question a choice is being given, so **cuál** is used instead of **qué**. **Cuáles** is incorrect because the choice is between two singular things.

VERBS

You probably learned what felt like a zillion different verbs and tenses in Spanish class. For the purposes of this section, you only need to know a few of the tenses you learned. What's even better is that you don't need to know how to conjugate verbs in the different tenses, nor do you need to know the names for the different tenses. You do need to know how to recognize them. For example, you don't need to know how or why the conditional is used. All you need to know is what it looks like when a verb is in the conditional, and when the conditional should be used.

You should focus on recognizing clues in the sentences that suggest certain tenses, and then finding the answer in the appropriate tense. Remember, even if you don't know which answer is in the tense that corresponds with the sentence, you can still eliminate answers that definitely aren't in that tense. USE POE!! A brief review of the tenses that show up in the test is probably a good place to begin, so let's get right to it.

THE PRESENT TENSE (A.K.A. THE PRESENT INDICATIVE)

The present tense is the easiest, and probably the first, tense that you ever learned. It is used when the action is happening in the present, as in the following:

*Yo **hablo** con mis amigos cada día.*
I **speak** with my friends each day.

Since the present is the most basic, and probably the easiest, tense to deal with, it rarely shows up as the right answer to a question. So why go over it? Because it sometimes does show up as a right answer, and it often shows up as a wrong answer. You need to know how to recognize it in order to eliminate it if it's incorrect. Take a quick glance at the present tenses of the following verbs just to refresh your memory:

	trabajar	vender	escribir
yo	trabajo	vendo	escribo
tú (fam.)	trabajas	vendes	escribes
él/ella/Ud.	trabaja	vende	escribe
nosotros/nosotras	trabajamos	vendemos	escribimos
vosotros/vosotras (fam.)	trabajáis	vendéis	escribís
ellos/ellas/Uds.	trabajan	venden	escriben

Remember

Ud. and **Uds.** may have the same verb forms as **él/ella** and **ellos/ellas**, but they mean the same thing as **tú** and **vosotros** respectively.

THE PAST TENSE (A.K.A. THE PRETERITE)

The past tense is used to describe an action that had a *definite beginning and ending in the past* (as opposed to an action that may be ongoing), as in the following example:

*Ayer yo **hablé** con mis amigos.*
Yesterday I **spoke** with my friends. (The action began and ended.)

There are a bunch of different tenses that are past tenses that describe actions that took place at various points in the past. There are different tenses for saying "I spoke," "I was speaking," "I have spoken," etc. Let's start by reviewing the most basic of these, the plain past tense:

	trabajar	vender	escribir
yo	trabajé	vendí	escribí
tú (fam.)	trabajaste	vendiste	escribiste
él/ella/Ud.	trabajó	vendió	escribió
nosotros/nosotras	trabajamos	vendimos	escribimos
vosotros/vosotras	trabajasteis	vendisteis	escribisteis
ellos/ellas/Uds.	trabajaron	vendieron	escribieron

The easiest forms to spot are the first and third person singular (**yo** and **él/ella** forms) because of the accent.

THE FUTURE TENSE

The future tense is used to describe things that will *definitely* happen in the future. The reason we stress definitely is there is a different verbal mode (the dreaded subjunctive) used to describe things that *may* happen in the future. In Spanish, just as in English, there is a difference between being certain ("I will go") and being uncertain ("I might go"), and different forms are used for the different degrees of certainty. You'll see the fancier stuff later. First take a look at the regular future:

> *Mañana yo hablaré con mis amigos.*
> Tomorrow I **will speak** with my friends.

Notice that what takes two words to say in English (**will speak**) takes only one word to say in Spanish (**hablaré**). The future is a nice, simple tense (no auxiliary verb, only one word) which is easy to spot thanks to the accents and the structure. The future is formed by tacking on the appropriate ending to the infinitive of the verb *without dropping the -ar, -er, or -ir.*

	trabajar	vender	escribir
yo	trabajar**é**	vender**é**	escribir**é**
tú (fam.)	trabajar**ás**	vender**ás**	escribir**ás**
él/ella/Ud.	trabajar**á**	vender**á**	escribir**á**
nosotros/nosotras	trabajar**emos**	vender**emos**	escribir**emos**
vosotros/vosotras	trabajar**éis**	vender**éis**	escribir**éis**
ellos/ellas/Uds.	trabajar**án**	vender**án**	escribir**án**

THE FANCY STUFF

The Present Perfect

This is where it gets a little weird: If something happens in the very recent past, we can also use the present perfect to show its proximity to the present. We hardly ever do this in English.

The present perfect is used to refer to an action that began in the past and is continuing into the present (and possibly beyond). It is also used to describe actions which were completed very close to the present. Compare these sentences:

1. *Ayer hablé con mis amigos.*
   Yesterday **I spoke** with my friends.

   Decidiste no ir al cine.
   You decided not to go to the movies.

2. *He hablado mucho con mis amigos recientemente.*
   I have spoken a lot with my friends lately.

   Has decidido hacerte abogado.
   You have decided (recently) to become a lawyer.

The first examples are just the plain past tense: you started and finished talking with your friends yesterday, and you completed the process of deciding not to go to the movies. In the second examples, the use of the present perfect tense moves the action to the very recent past, instead of leaving it in the more distant past. The present perfect, then, is essentially a more precise verb form of the past, used when the speaker wants to indicate that an action happened very recently in the past.

Spotting the perfect tenses is rather easy. This is a compound tense, meaning that it is formed by combining two verbs: a tense of the auxiliary (or helping) verb **haber** (present, imperfect, future, conditional) and the past participle of the main verb.

	trabajar	vender	escribir
yo	he trabajado	he vendido	he escrito
tú (fam.)	has trabajado	has vendido	has escrito
él/ella/Ud.	ha trabajado	ha vendido	ha escrito
nosotros/nosotras	hemos trabajado	hemos vendido	hemos escrito
vosotros/vosotras	habéis trabajado	habéis vendido	habéis escrito
ellos/ellas/Uds.	han trabajado	han vendido	han escrito

Most past participles are formed by dropping the last two letters from the infinitive and adding **-ido** (for **-er** and **-ir** verbs) or **-ado** (for **-ar** verbs). **Escribir** has an irregular past participle, as do some other verbs, but don't worry about it. This is no problem, since the irregulars still look and sound like the regulars, and, with respect to this tense, you still know it's the present perfect because of **haber**.

THE IMPERFECT

The imperfect is yet another past tense used to describe actions that occurred continuously in the past, and exhibited no definitive end at that time. This is different from the preterite, which describes "one-time" actions that began and ended at the moment in the past that is being described. Look at the two together, and the difference between them will become clearer:

*Ayer **hablé** con mis amigos y entonces me fui.*
Yesterday **I spoke** with my friends and then left.
(The act of speaking obviously ended, because I left afterwards.)

*Yo **hablaba** con mis amigos mientras caminábamos.*
I spoke with my friends while we walked.
(The act of speaking was **in progress** at that moment, along with walking.)

The imperfect is also used to describe conditions or circumstances in the past, since these are obviously ongoing occurrences.

***Era** una noche oscura y tormentosa.*
It was a dark and stormy night.

*Cuando **tenía** diez años…*
When **I was** ten years old…

The Imperfect

This is a nightmare to understand. We have no distinction between the preterite and the imperfect in English, which is why it's so hard to figure out. How can we do either of these right in Spanish if we don't even do it in our own language?

In the first example, it didn't just start or just stop being a stormy night, did it? Was the dark and stormy night already a past event at that point? No. The dark and stormy night was **in progress** at that moment, so the imperfect is used, not the preterite.

In the second example, did I start or stop being ten years old at that point? Neither. Was being ten already a past event at the moment I am describing? No. I was simply in the process of being ten years old at that moment in the past, so the imperfect is the more precise tense to use.

Make sense? Good; now check out the formation:

	trabajar	vender	escribir
yo	trabaj**aba**	vend**ía**	escrib**ía**
tú (fam.)	trabaj**abas**	vend**ías**	escrib**ías**
él/ella/Ud.	trabaj**aba**	vend**ía**	escrib**ía**
nosotros/nosotras	trabaj**ábamos**	vend**íamos**	escrib**íamos**
vosotros/vosotras	trabaj**abais**	vend**íais**	escrib**íais**
ellos/ellas	trabaj**aban**	vend**ían**	escrib**ían**

Although the imperfect is similar to the other past tenses you've seen (i.e., the preterite and the present perfect), because it speaks of past actions, it looks quite different. That's the key since half of your job is just to know what the different tenses look like. The toughest part will be distinguishing the preterite from the imperfect.

BACK TO THE FUTURE: THE CONDITIONAL

Remember the future tense? (It's the one that's used to describe actions that are *definitely* going to happen in the future.) Well, now you'll learn the other future tense you will need to know, the one that's used to describe things that *might* happen in the future.

The conditional describes what could, would, or might happen in the future:

*Me **gustaría** hablar con mis amigos cada día.*
I **would like** to talk to my friends each day.

*Con más tiempo, **podría** hablar con ellos el día entero.*
With more time, I **could** speak with them all day long.

*Si gastara cinco pesos, solamente me **quedarían** tres.*
If I spent (were to spend) five dollars, I **would have** only three left.

It can also be used to make a request in a more polite way:

¿**Puedes** prestar atención?   ¿**Podrías** prestar atención?
Can you pay attention?   **Could you** pay attention?

The conditional is formed by taking the future stem of the verb (which is the infinitive) and adding the conditional ending:

	trabajar	vender	escribir
yo	trabajaría	vendería	escribiría
tú (fam.)	trabajarías	venderías	escribirías
él/ella/Ud.	trabajaría	vendería	escribiría
nosotros/nosotras	trabajaríamos	venderíamos	escribiríamos
vosotros/vosotras	trabajaríais	venderíais	escribiríais
ellos/ellas/Uds.	trabajarían	venderían	escribirían

To avoid confusing the conditional with the future, concentrate on the conditional endings. The big difference is the accented **í**, which is in the conditional, but not in the future:

Future	Conditional
trabajaré	trabajaría
venderán	venderían
escribiremos	escribiríamos

THE SUBJUNCTIVE

Don't give up now! Just two more verb modes (not tenses—the subjunctive is a different *manner* of speaking) and you'll be done with all this verb business (give or take a couple of special topics).

The Present Subjunctive

The present subjunctive is used in sentences that have *two distinct subjects* in *two different clauses*, generally (on this test, at least) in four situations:

1. When a *desire* or *wish* is involved:

   *Quiero que **comas** los vegetales.*
   I want you **to eat** the vegetables.

   *Ordenamos que Uds. nos **sigan**.*
   We order you (pl.) **to follow** us.

2. When *emotion* is involved:

   *Me alegro que **haga** buen tiempo hoy.*
   I am happy that the weather **is** nice today.

   *Te enoja que tu novio nunca te **escuche**.*
   It makes you angry that your boyfriend never **listens** to you.

3. When *doubt* is involved:

   *Ellos no creen que **digamos** la verdad.*
   They don't believe that **we are telling** the truth.

   *Jorge duda que su equipo **vaya** a ganar el campeonato.*
   Jorge doubts that his team **is going** to win the championship.

The Present Subjunctive

The key concept with the subjunctive is influence. When we say that we wish, prefer, deny, ask, or demand that someone else do something, or if we say that it is ridiculous, amazing, terrific, or terrible that something has happened, we are either directly influencing the action, or at least putting the influence of our opinion over the action. If we are happy, sad, scared, or excited that something has happened, it is the something that has happened that is influencing us and our emotions.

4. When an *impersonal, subjective commentary* is made:

> *Es ridículo que yo no **pueda** encontrar mis llaves.*
> It's ridiculous that I **can't** find my keys.

> *Es importante que los estudiantes **estudien** mucho.*
> It's important that students **study** a lot.

The subjunctive is formed by taking the **yo** form of the present tense, dropping the **-o**, and adding the appropriate ending:

	trabajar	vender	escribir
yo	trabaj**e**	vend**a**	escrib**a**
tú (fam.)	trabaj**es**	vend**as**	escrib**as**
él/ella/Ud.	trabaj**e**	vend**a**	escrib**a**
nosotros/nosotras	trabaj**emos**	vend**amos**	escrib**amos**
vosotros/vosotras	trabaj**éis**	vend**áis**	escrib**áis**
ellos/ellas/Uds.	trabaj**en**	vend**an**	escrib**an**

Commands also use the present subjunctive form, since they are an obvious attempt to tell someone what to do. The one exception to this happens in the **tú** form of affirmative commands, which have special endings—the same as the present indicative of **él/ella/Ud.**:

> *¡**Trabaja** con tu padre!*   *¡**Vende** el coche!*   *¡**Escribe** la carta!*
> **Work** with your father!   **Sell** the car!   **Write** the letter!

The present subjunctive is easy to spot because certain key phrases will tell you that a wish or desire, emotion, doubt, or an impersonal commentary is being made.

The Imperfect Subjunctive

The Imperfect Subjunctive

This follows the same rules as the present subjunctive, but it is in the past tense. Look for time clues and clues for the subjunctive.

Here we are, at the final verb form you'll need to know for the Spanish Subject Test! This version of the subjunctive is used with the same expressions as the present subjunctive (wish or desire, emotion, doubt, impersonal commentaries), but it's used in the *past tense*:

> *Quería que **comieras** los vegetales.*
> I wanted you **to eat** the vegetables.

> *Me alegré que **hiciera** buen tiempo ayer.*
> I was happy that the weather **was** nice yesterday.

> *No creían que **dijéramos** la verdad.*
> They didn't believe that **we told** the truth.

> *Era ridículo que yo no **pudiera** encontrar mis llaves.*
> It was ridiculous that **I couldn't** find my keys.

One very important thing to notice in the examples above is that because the *expression* is in the past, you use the imperfect subjunctive. If you're looking at a sentence that you know takes the subjunctive, but you're not sure whether it's present or imperfect, focus on the expression. If the expression is in the present, use the present subjunctive. If the expression is in the past, use the imperfect subjunctive.

The imperfect subjunctive is also always used after the expression **como si**, which means "as if." This expression is used to describe hypothetical situations:

*El habla como si **supiera** todo.*
He speaks as if **he knew** everything.

*Gastamos dinero como si **fuéramos** millonarios.*
We spend money as if **we were** millionaires.

The imperfect subjunctive is formed by taking the **ellos/ellas/Uds.** form of the preterite (which you already know, right?) and adding the correct ending:

	trabajar	vender	escribir
yo	trabaj**ara**	vend**iera**	escrib**iera**
tú (fam.)	trabaj**aras**	vend**ieras**	escrib**ieras**
él/ella/Uds.	trabaj**ara**	vend**iera**	escrib**iera**
nosotros/nosotras	trabaj**áramos**	vend**iéramos**	escrib**iéramos**
vosotros/vosotras	trabaj**arais**	vend**ierais**	escrib**ierais**
ellos/ellas/Uds.	trabaj**aran**	vend**ieran**	escrib**ieran**

Verbs that are in the imperfect subjunctive shouldn't be too tough to spot when they show up in the answer choices. The imperfect subjunctive has completely different endings from the preterite. It's not a compound tense, so you won't confuse it with the present perfect. The stems are different from the present subjunctive, so distinguishing between those two shouldn't be a problem.

Okay, there is some slightly bad news—it's almost exactly like the imperfect. There is a difference though, and it's in the stem. Don't try to tell the difference by looking at the endings, because there isn't one. Compare the same verb in the imperfect and the imperfect subjunctive:

imperfect	vs.	imperfect subjunctive
trabaj**aba**		trabaj**ara**
vend**ías**		vend**ieras**
escrib**íamos**		escrib**iéramos**

SPECIAL TOPICS

Ser vs. Estar

The verbs **ser** and **estar** both mean *to be* when translated into English. You might wonder, "Why is it necessary to have two verbs that mean exactly the same thing?" Good question. The answer is that in Spanish, unlike in English, there is a distinction between temporary states of being (e.g., "I am hungry") and fixed, or permanent states of being (e.g., "I am Cuban"). Although this difference seems pretty simple and easy to follow, there are some cases when it isn't so clear. Consider the following examples:

El señor González _____ mi doctor.
Cynthia _____ mi novia.

Would you use **ser** or **estar** in these two sentences? After all, Cynthia may or may not be your girlfriend forever, and the same goes for Mr. González's status as your doctor. You might get rid of both of them tomorrow (or one of them might get rid of you)! So which verb do you use?

In both cases, the answer is **ser**, because in both cases there is no *foreseeable* end to the relationships described. In other words, even though they may change, nothing in either sentence gives any reason to think they will. So whether you and Cynthia go on to marry or she dumps you tomorrow, you would be correct if you used **ser**. When in doubt, ask yourself, "does this action/condition have a definite end in the near or immediate future?" If so, use **estar**. Otherwise, use **ser**. Try the following drill:

Fill in the blank with the correct form of **ser** or **estar**.

1. Pablo _____ muy cansado.

2. El automóvil _____ descompuesto.

3. No puedo salir de casa esta noche porque _____ castigado.

4. Mi hermano _____ muy gracioso.

5. Mis profesores _____ demasiado serios.

6. Ayer salí sin abrigo, por eso hoy _____ enfermo.

7. Los tacos que mi madre cocina _____ ricos.

8. ¡No podemos empezar! Todavía no _____ listos.

9. _____ muy enojado con el tipo que me insultó.

Answers: 1. está 2. está 3. estoy 4. es 5. son 6. estoy 7. son 8. estamos 9. Estuve/Estaba

Don't assume that certain adjectives (like **enfermo**, for example) necessarily take **estar**. If you're saying someone is sick as in "ill," then **estar** is appropriate. If you're saying that someone is sick, as in, "a sickly person," then **ser** is correct.

Unfortunately, usage is not the only tough thing about these two verbs. They are both irregular, and they come up all over this exam. Spend a little time reviewing the conjugations of **ser** and **estar** before you move on.

estar	
present:	estoy, estás, está, estamos, estáis, están
preterite:	estuve, estuviste, estuvo, estuvimos, estuvisteis, estuvieron
pres. subj.:	esté, estés, esté, estemos, estéis, estén
imp. subj.:	estuviera, estuvieras, estuviera, estuviéramos, estuvierais, estuvieran

The other tenses of **estar** follow the regular patterns for **-ar** verbs.

ser	
present:	soy, eres, es, somos, sois, son
imperfect:	era, eras, era, éramos, eráis, eran
preterite:	fui, fuiste, fue, fuimos, fuisteis, fueron
pres. subj.:	sea, seas, sea, seamos, seáis, sean
imp. subj.:	fuera, fueras, fuera, fuéramos, fuerais, fueran

The other tenses of **ser** follow the regular patterns for **-er** verbs.

Conocer vs. Saber

We hate to do this to you again, but there is another pair of verbs that have the same English translation but are used differently in Spanish. However, don't worry; these two have (for the most part) regular conjugations, and knowing when to use them is really very straightforward.

The words **conocer** and **saber** both mean "to know." In Spanish, knowing a person or a thing (basically, a noun) is different from knowing a piece of information. Compare the uses of **conocer** and **saber** in these sentences:

¿Sabes cuánto cuesta la camisa?
Do you know how much the shirt costs?

¿Conoces a mi primo?
Do you know my cousin?

Sabemos que Pelé era un gran futbolista.
We know that Pelé was a great soccer player.

Conocemos a Pelé.
We know Pelé.

When what's known is a person, place, or thing, use **conocer**. It's like the English, "acquainted with." When what's known is a fact, use **saber**. The same basic rule holds for questions:

¿Saben a qué hora llega el presidente?
Do you know at what time the president arrives?

¿Conocen al presidente?
Do you know the president?

Hi Ho, Silver

Saber/conocer: Remember the Lone Ranger and Tonto? Well, there are some who claim that Tonto was not an American Indian, but a Mexican. We know that *tonto* means "stupid" or "dummy." But remember what Tonto called the Lone Ranger? Kemosabe? There are some who claim that this was not the Indian tongue, but Spanish: *Quien no sabe* —"He who knows nothing." So, instead of terms of endearment, the masked man and his faithful sidekick were trading insults!

Now that you know how they're used, take a look at their conjugations:

conocer

present:	conozco, conoces, conoce, conocemos, conocéis, conocen
pres. subj.:	conozca, conozcas, conozca, conozcamos, conozcáis, conozcan

The other tenses of **conocer** follow the regular **-er** pattern.

saber

present:	sé, sabes, sabe, sabemos, sabéis, saben
preterite:	supe, supiste, supo, supimos, supisteis, supieron
future:	sabré, sabrás, sabrá, sabremos, sabréis, sabrán
conditional:	sabría, sabrías, sabría, sabríamos, sabríais, sabrían
pres. subj.:	sepa, sepas, sepa, sepamos, sepáis, sepan
imp. subj.:	supiera, supieras, supiera, supiéramos, supierais, supieran

Try the following drill:

Fill in the blanks with the correct form of **conocer** or **saber**:

1. ¡Él _____ cocinar muy bien!

2. ¿ _____ el libro que ganó el premio? (tú)

3. Las mujeres _____ bailar como si fueran profesionales.

4. ¿Es verdad que _____ a Michael Jackson? (ustedes)

5. Es importante _____ nadar.

6. No _____ cómo voy a ganar la carrera.

7. ¿Cómo puede ser que tú no _____ la casa donde viviste?

8. Los dos abogados no se _____ el uno al otro porque nunca han trabajado juntos.

9. _____ que vamos a divertirnos en el circo esta noche. (yo)

Answers: 1. sabe 2. Conoces 3. saben 4. conocen 5. saber 6. sé 7. conozcas 8. conocen 9. Sé

VERB SUMMARY

- The tenses you need to know are the present, past, future, conditional, imperfect, and present perfect. You also need to know the subjunctive mode (both present and imperfect). In terms of memorizing and reviewing them, we think the best approach is to lump them together in the following way:

Present Tenses	Past Tenses	Future Tenses
Present	Preterite	Future
	Imperfect	Conditional
	Present Perfect	

  By thinking in terms of these groupings, you'll find that eliminating answers is a snap once you've determined the tense of the sentence. That is your first step on a question that tests your knowledge of verb tenses: Determine the tense of the sentence (or at least whether it's a past, present, or future tense), and eliminate.

- When memorizing the uses of the different tenses, focus on clues that point to one tense or another:

  - There are certain expressions (wish or desire, emotion, doubt, and impersonal commentaries) that tell you to use the subjunctive, and whether the expression is in the present or the past will tell you which subjunctive form to use.

  - To distinguish between future and conditional, focus on the certainty of the event's occurrence.

  - The three past tenses are differentiated by the end (or lack thereof) of the action and when that end occurred (or if it occurred). If the action had a clear beginning and ending in the past, use the regular past. If the action was a continuous action in the past, use the imperfect. If the action began in the past and is continuing into the present, or ended very close to the present, use the present perfect.

  - Recognizing the different tenses shouldn't be too tough if you focus on superficial characteristics.

  - The only compound tenses you're likely to see are the perfect tenses.

  - Certain tenses have accents, others do not.

- As far as pacing goes, apply the same principles that we outlined for pronoun questions: Spend time on the easy questions and use POE and guess on the tougher ones. Keep in mind that, although the simple tenses (present, past, and future) do appear, they are seldom the correct answer. Why? Because they're the first tenses you learned, they're the easiest to use, and the test writers know that you'll guess them if you're stuck on a question. They don't want you to guess successfully, so they use these basic tenses as trap answers. Careful now, we didn't say they were never right.

VERB QUESTIONS

No Time for Pride

Do you know the words or not? Fooling yourself into thinking you do will give you the wrong answer. Answer truthfully and quickly so you can use the best technique to find the answer.

1. Cuando tenga dinero, te ------- un automóvil de lujo.

   (A) compraré
   (B) compré
   (C) compraría
   (D) compraste

2. Quiero que ------- la tarea antes de acostarte.

   (A) hiciste
   (B) hace
   (C) haga
   (D) hagas

3. El año pasado nosotros ------- a México para las vacaciones.

   (A) iremos
   (B) fuimos
   (C) iríamos
   (D) vamos

4. Si tuvieran tiempo, ------- pasar el tiempo relajándose.

   (A) quieren
   (B) querían
   (C) quieran
   (D) querrían

5. Esperaba que Uds. ------- a construir el barco.

   (A) ayudarían
   (B) ayudaran
   (C) ayudaron
   (D) ayudan

6. Carlos ------- mucho tiempo estudiando la biología últimamente.

   (A) pasó
   (B) pasaría
   (C) pasaba
   (D) ha pasado

ANSWERS AND EXPLANATIONS OF VERB QUESTIONS

1. When I have money, I ------- you a luxury car.

   (A) **will buy (future)**
   (B) bought (past–*yo* form)
   (C) would buy (conditional)
   (D) bought (past–*tú* form)

The sentence refers to something that will happen in the future, so the correct answer will be in either the future or the conditional. In this case, the event is certain (I will buy you a luxury car); therefore, the future is correct.

You've already learned much of the grammar on the exam. Just remember how to use it.

2. I want you to ------- the homework before going to bed.

   (A) did (past–*tú* form)
   (B) does (present–*él* form)
   (C) do (present subjunctive–*él* form)
   (D) **do (present subjunctive–*tú* form)**

Quiero que is one of those expressions that tells you to use the subjunctive. In this case, the expression is in the present tense, so the present subjunctive is correct. If the expression were in the past (**quería que**), you'd use the imperfect subjunctive. The reason (D) is correct is that **te** is the direct object pronoun in the sentence, so you want the **tú** form of the verb.

3. Last year we ------- to Mexico for vacation.

   (A) will go (future)
   (B) **went (past)**
   (C) would go (conditional)
   (D) go (present)

El año pasado (last year) is a big hint that the answer will be in one of the past tenses. Since the event had a definite beginning and end in the past, the regular past tense is correct.

4. If they had (were to have) time, they ------- pass the time relaxing.

   (A) want to (present)
   (B) wanted to (imperfect)
   (C) want to (present subjunctive)
   (D) **would want to (conditional)**

Si tuvieran tells you to use the conditional (in fact, **si** often precedes use of the conditional because it introduces a condition that doesn't currently exist). The only answer that's in the conditional is **querrían**.

5. I hoped that you ------- build the boat.

    (A) would help (conditional)
    (B) would help (imperfect subjunctive)
    (C) helped (past)
    (D) help (present)

Esperaba que is another one of those expressions of desire that tell you to use the subjunctive, but this time the expression is in the past, so the correct tense is the imperfect subjunctive. Remember, the tense of the expression is what tells you whether to use the present or the imperfect subjunctive.

6. Carlos ------- much time studying biology lately.

    (A) spent (past)
    (B) would spend (conditional)
    (C) spent (imperfect)
    (D) has spent (present perfect)

POE + Three-Pass System +
your ear = success

"Lately" suggests the past tense, but a more recent past tense. Answers (A) and (C) place the action too far in the past, while (B) is not a past tense. Therefore, (D) is the answer.

PREPOSITIONS

Prepositions are those little words that show the relationship between two other words. In English, they're words like *to, from, at, for, about*, etc. In Spanish, they're words like **a, de, sobre,** etc.

Part of what you need to know about prepositions is what the different ones mean. That's the easy part. The other thing you need to know is how and when to use them. You need to know which verbs and expressions take prepositions and which prepositions they take. This isn't too difficult to learn either, but it can be tricky.

The good news is that ETS likes to test only a very small number of prepositions, so you can limit your study to those instead of trying to master every preposition in existence. Yes, it is a lot like doing vocabulary work, but, once again, you probably already know many of these expressions, so it shouldn't be too terrible.

Remember in the beginning of this chapter, when you learned that some of the sentence completion part of the exam would focus on grammar instead of meaning, and that because of this, answer choices on a given question would mean roughly the same thing? Well, we lied (sort of), but that's actually a good thing. What we're getting at is that, with preposition questions (unlike verb and pronoun questions), the answers sometimes do have different meanings, and this makes POE a lot easier.

COMMON PREPOSITIONS AND THEIR USES

a: to; at

¿Vamos a la obra de teatro esta noche?   *Llegamos a las cinco.*
Are we going to the play tonight?   We arrive at 5:00.

de: of; from

> *Son las gafas de mi hermano.*
> Those are my brother's glasses.
> (Literally, the glasses of my brother.)
>
> *Soy de la Argentina.*
> I am from Argentina.

con: with

> *Me gusta mucho el arroz con pollo.*
> I like chicken with rice a lot.

sobre: on; about; over

> *La chaqueta está sobre la mesa.*
> The jacket is on the table.

> *La conferencia es sobre la prevención del SIDA.*
> The conference is about AIDS prevention.

> *Los Yankees triunfaron sobre los Padres en la serie mundial.*
> The Yankees triumphed over the Padres in the World Series.

antes de: before

> *Antes de salir quiero ponerme un sombrero.*
> Before leaving I want to put on a hat.

después de: after

> *Después de la cena me gusta caminar un poco.*
> After dinner I like to walk a little.

en: in

> *Regresan en una hora.*
> They'll be back in an hour.

> *Alguien está en el baño.*
> Someone is in the bathroom.

entre: between

> *La carnicería está entre la pescadería y el cine.*
> The butcher shop is between the fish store and the movie theater.

> *La conferencia duró entre dos y tres horas.*
> The conference lasted between two and three hours.

Prepositions

Prepositions are often idiomatic, which means there are no rules for their use—they just sort of sound right. It's the same reasoning behind our use of prepositions in English.

durante: during

> *Durante el verano me gusta nadar todos los días.*
> During the summer I like to swim every day.

desde: since; from

> *He tomado vitaminas desde mi juventud.*
> I've been taking vitamins since my childhood.

> *Se pueden ver las montañas desde aquí.*
> The mountains can be seen from here.

PARA VS. POR

The prepositions **para** and **por** both mean "for" (as well as other things, depending on context), but they are used for different situations, and so they tend to cause a bit of confusion. Luckily, there are some pretty clear-cut rules as to when you use **para** and when you use **por**, because they both tend to sound fine even when they're being used incorrectly. Try to avoid using your ear when choosing between these two.

When to Use *Para*

The following are examples of the most common situations in which **para** is used. Instead of memorizing some stuffy rule, we suggest that you get a feel for what types of situations imply the use of **para**, so that when you see those situations come up on your test, you'll recognize them.

The preposition **para**, in very general terms, expresses the idea of *destination*, but in a very broad sense:

Destination in time

> *El helado es **para** mañana.*
> The ice cream is for tomorrow. (Tomorrow is the ice cream's destination.)

Destination in space

> *Me voy **para** el mercado.*
> I'm leaving for the market. (The market is my destination.)

Destination of purpose

> *Compraste un regalo **para** Luis.*
> You bought a gift for Luis. (Luis is the destination of your purchase.)

> *Estudiamos **para** sacar buenas notas.*
> We study to get good grades. (Good grades are the destination of our studies.)

When to Use *Para*

Para is almost always used to indicate some sort of destination—time, space, a person, an event, a resulting action (an effect)—so be on the lookout for this type of meaning in the sentence.

Destination of work

*Trabajo **para** IBM.*
I work for IBM. (IBM is the destination of my work.)

Two uses of *para* do not indicate a sense of destination:

To express opinion

***Para** mí, el lunes es el día más largo de la semana.*
For me, Monday is the longest day of the week.

To qualify or offer a point of reference

***Para** ser un niño joven, tiene muchísimo talento.*
For a young boy, he has a lot of talent.

When to Use *Por*

Chances are, if you're not discussing destination in any way, shape, or form, or the other two uses of **para**, then you'll need to use **por**. If this general rule isn't enough for you though, study the following possibilities and you should have all the bases covered.

To express a period of time

*Trabajé con mi amigo **por** quince años.*
I worked with my friend for fifteen years.

To express how you got somewhere (by)

*Fuimos a Italia **por** barco.*
We went to Italy by boat.

*Pasamos **por** esa tienda ayer cuando salimos del pueblo.*
We passed by that store yesterday when we left the town.

To describe a trade (in exchange for)

*Te cambiaré mi automóvil **por** el tuyo este fin de semana.*
I'll trade you my car for yours this weekend.

To lay blame or identify cause (by)

*Todos los barcos fueron destruidos **por** la tormenta.*
All the boats were destroyed by the storm.

To identify gain or motive (for; as a substitute for)

Ella hace todo lo posible por su hermana.
She does everything possible for her sister.

Cuando Arsenio está enfermo, su madre trabaja por él.
When Arsenio is ill, his mother works (as a substitute) for him.

IR A AND *ACABAR DE*

Ir a is used to describe what the future will bring, or, in other words, what is going to happen. The expression is formed by combining the appropriate form of **ir** in the present tense (subject and verb must agree) with the preposition **a**:

Mañana vamos a comprar el árbol de Navidad.
Tomorrow we are going to buy the Christmas tree.

¿Vas a ir a la escuela aun si te sientes mal?
You're going to go to school even if you feel ill?

Acabar de is the Spanish equivalent of "to have just," and is used to talk about what has just happened. It is formed just like **ir a**, with the appropriate form of **acabar** in the present tense followed by **de**:

Acabo de terminar de cocinar el pavo.
I have just finished cooking the turkey.

Ellos acaban de regresar del mercado.
They have just returned from the supermarket.

OTHER PREPOSITIONS TO REMEMBER

Other prepositions and prepositional phrases you should know follow. Notice that many of these are merely adverbs with a **de** tacked on to the end to make them prepositions.

hacia	towards
enfrente de	in front of
frente a	in front of
dentro de	inside of
fuera de	outside of
a la derecha de	to the right of
a la izquierda de	to the left of
debajo de	underneath
encima de	above, on top of
alrededor de	around, surrounding
en medio de	in the middle of

hasta	until
tras	behind
cerca de	near
lejos de	far from
detrás de	behind
delante de	in front of
al lado de	next to

PREPOSITION SUMMARY

- Much of your work with prepositions boils down to memorization: which expressions and verbs go with which prepositions, etc. Keep in mind that preposition questions account for less than fifteen percent of the questions on the sentence completion section of your exam, so don't drive yourself nuts trying to memorize every single one you've ever heard.

- You should concentrate on the bold-faced examples at the beginning of the preposition section since those are the most common. Once you're comfortable with them, the subsequent list should be a snap because many of those expressions are merely adverbs with **a** or **de** after them.

- Some verbs take prepositions all the time, some never do, and others sometimes do. This isn't as confusing as it may sound, though, because prepositions (or lack thereof) change the meaning of verbs. Consider the following:

> Voy a tratar ------- despertarme más temprano.
>
> (A) a
> (B) de
> (C) con
> (D) sin

Which one of these goes with **tratar**? Well actually, each of them does, depending on what you are trying to say. In this case you want to say "try to," so **de** is the appropriate preposition. **Tratar con** means "to deal with," and **tratar sin** means "to try/treat without," while **tratar a** doesn't mean anything unless a person is mentioned afterwards, in which case it means "to treat." None of them makes sense in this sentence. The moral of the story is don't try to memorize which verbs go with which prepositions; concentrate on meaning.

- Just like you did with the vocabulary list, scan the prepositional phrase list and check off the expressions you are comfortable with and certain that you'll remember on the day of the exam. You may want to review them briefly as you approach the date of the test, but for now focus your efforts on the ones you have trouble with.

PREPOSITION QUESTIONS

First Pass

Easy vocabulary; present, past, and future tenses; simple prepositions that you've already memorized

1. Quiero llegar a la fiesta antes ------- María.

   (A) de
   (B) de que
   (C) a
   (D) sin

2. Todos mis alumnos estuvieron ------- acuerdo conmigo.

   (A) entre
   (B) en
   (C) con
   (D) de

3. Estamos apurados, y por eso tenemos que viajar ---- el camino más corto.

   (A) dentro de
   (B) por
   (C) alrededor de
   (D) para

Second Pass

Not so obvious vocabulary; subjunctive and conditional tenses; harder prepositions

4. Los paraguas se usan ------- parar la lluvia.

   (A) en medio de
   (B) hacia
   (C) para
   (D) por

5. La próxima semana ellos van ------- tocar aquí.

   (A) a
   (B) de
   (C) con
   (D) por

Third Pass

More obscure vocabulary and grammar, and the imperfect subjunctive tense

6. No me gusta ver las películas de horror ------- la noche.

   (A) tras de
   (B) sobre
   (C) en
   (D) durante

7. Salieron hace un rato, así que deben regresar ------- cinco minutos.

   (A) alrededor de
   (B) en vez de
   (C) en
   (D) después de

ANSWERS AND EXPLANATIONS OF PREPOSITION QUESTIONS

1. I want to arrive at the party ------- María.

   (A) before
   (B) before (preceeding a verb)
   (C) at
   (D) without

In the original sentence, you're given **antes** followed by a blank, leaving it up to you to fill in the correct preposition. **Antes** tells you that you're going for "before," so **de** is the correct preposition. Choice (B) (**de que**) is one of those expressions that needs to be followed by a verb (in the subjunctive) because the word **que** always begins a new clause. The others are way off in terms of meaning.

2. All of my students were ------- agreement with me.

   (A) between
   (B) in
   (C) with
   (D) in

This is a tough question, especially if you haven't seen the expression **estar de acuerdo**. In English we say that two people are "in agreement" with each other, but unfortunately the Spanish translation isn't the literal equivalent of the English expression. In Spanish two people **están de acuerdo**. (We know this isn't on your list, but that list is only a start: if you find new expressions that you don't know, add to your list!)

3. We're in a rush, so we must travel ------- the shortest route.

   (A) inside of
   (B) by
   (C) around
   (D) for

This is the old **para** vs. **por** trap, which is definitely tricky. In this case you want to say "travel by," and **por** is the preposition that sometimes means "by." **Para** is never used to mean "by."

4. Umbrellas are used ------- stopping the rain.

   (A) in the middle of
   (B) towards
   (C) for
   (D) for

Here it is again, **para** vs. **por**. The other choices are pretty clearly wrong based on meaning, which leaves us with (C) and (D). In what sense are we saying "for" in this sentence? Is it "for the purpose of" (which would tell you to use **para**) or "for," as in a period of time or cause of action (which would tell you to use **por**)? In this case, "for the purpose of" fits pretty neatly, and so **para** is correct.

5. Next week they are going ------- play here.

    (A) to
    (B) of
    (C) with
    (D) for

Nice and easy, no tricks or traps, and it translates straight from English. This is an example of the use of **ir a**. Notice that **ir** is conjugated to agree with the subject of the sentence (**ellos**).

6. I don't like to see horror films ------- the night.

    (A) behind
    (B) on
    (C) in
    (D) during

Pretty tough call between (C) and (D) because both sound fine in the blank, but one of them makes a little more sense than the other if you think carefully about the difference in meaning between the two. Do you see films in (as in, "inside") the night, or during the night? They're sort of close, and the exact English would be "at night," but "during" makes a bit more sense.

7. They left a while ago, so they should return
   ------- five minutes.

    (A) around
    (B) instead of
    (C) in
    (D) after

Basically what you're trying to say is that they'll be back soon, and "in five minutes" says that. "Around" would be fine if it were preceded by "in," or if "from now" were tacked on to the end of the sentence, but neither is the case here. Choices (B) and (D) don't really make sense.

Paragraph Completion

PARAGRAPH COMPLETION BASICS

In this chapter we are going to take a look at the paragraph completion questions that will appear in Part B of the Spanish Subject Test and Part B of the Reading section of the Spanish with Listening Subject Test. To simplify things, we're simply going to refer to this section of each respective exam as Part B.

If you've made it this far, you've completed the review of all the grammar and vocabulary that's likely to appear on your Spanish Subject Test! No more new material (although it would probably be wise to continue reviewing anything that gave you trouble up to now). Just as you did in the last chapter, the first thing you should do is memorize the directions:

Part B

Directions: In each of the following passages, there are numbered blanks indicating that words or phrases have been omitted. For each numbered blank, four completions are provided. First read through the entire paragraph. Then, for each numbered blank, choose the completion that is most appropriate given the context of the entire paragraph and fill in the corresponding oval on the answer sheet.

Part B is a lot like a combination of the vocabulary and grammar sentence completion parts. You're given two to four (most likely three) brief paragraphs (roughly five to seven sentences each) with several words or phrases replaced by blanks. Your job is to fill the blanks with the answers that are appropriate based on either meaning or grammar. How do you know whether it's a "meaning" blank or a "grammar" blank? Well, if it's a grammar blank the answers will all have the same (or very similar) meanings and you'll have to choose based on form or verb tense. Sound familiar? It should, since it's the same as in Part A. The meaning-blank answers will have different meanings, only one of which will make sense in the context of the passage. These questions are just like those in Part A.

So what's the difference between Parts A and B? In Part A, if a sentence makes no sense you just skip it and go on to the next one—no sweat. In Part B, missing a sentence is a bit more important, since it can make understanding the overall passage difficult. You don't need to get every single word, but getting at least the main idea of each of the sentences is definitely helpful.

As we mentioned earlier, you've already covered the material necessary to answer the questions in Part B. The vocabulary is all you need for the meaning questions, and the grammar (especially verb tenses) is all you need for the grammar questions. This does not mean you're ready to do drills! First, you need to learn the best way to approach the overall section.

PACING

Since the passages in Part B have different degrees of difficulty, but are in no particular order, your first decision is the order in which to attack these questions. As in Part A, you want to start with the easiest questions and finish up with the toughest ones. In Part B this decision will be more involved and more important, because if you choose a really tough passage first, you will probably waste time and throw off your pacing for the remainder of the section. We're not trying to make it sound like life or death. We're just saying that by taking on these passages in a certain order you can make the section easier for yourself. You're eventually going to do all three, but you're going to do them in the order that you like, *not* the order that ETS likes.

Your decision should be based on a brief skim of the first couple of sentences of the passage. If these sentences make sense, and the writing style strikes you as being pretty clear, go for it. If you have any doubt as to whether the passage is going to be easy, go on and see what the next one looks like. Your goal is to find the easiest one and to do it first.

Don't base your decision on subject matter. The fact that a passage pertains to something you know about or find interesting doesn't mean much if you can't understand every third word. You're not going to be asked about content (that comes later in the reading comprehension section); you'll only be asked to fill in blanks. You don't need to retain the information in the passage, but you need to understand the tense that it's in and the meaning of individual sentences. In other words, topic doesn't count for much. Base your decision on writing style and vocabulary.

THREE-PASS SYSTEM

Once you've decided which passage you're doing first, what next? Answer the questions in the order that's best for you.

First Pass

The questions on each of the Part B passages should be done in order. Starting at the beginning will give you some sense of the passage's structure, which will probably make you more comfortable with it overall. On the other hand, on your first pass through the passage you should skip any question that looks like it *might* be tricky. Attempt only the very easiest questions on this pass. Focus on the ones you know the answer to without using POE or anything but your knowledge of grammar or vocabulary.

Second Pass

On the second pass you'll start using POE to eliminate and guess. Go back to the questions you left blank on the first pass and see if there are any answers that can be eliminated. Look to cancel wrong answers. You'll find (just as you did on Part A) that some of the wrong answers are pretty obviously wrong, and in some cases you'll be able to cancel all but one—the right one.

Don't be intimidated if the sentence that contains a certain blank is difficult. You can determine what tense a verb is even if you don't understand the verb's meaning! The same goes for pronouns and prepositions. If you are pretty sure that the noun being replaced is feminine, then eliminate the masculine pronouns! You have to be aggressive if you want to take advantage of POE.

As far as *meaning* blanks are concerned, use the same technique you learned for second-pass questions on Part A. Piece together any words in the sentence that you know to try to get some sense of the context. See if any of the answers are completely wacky based on that context. This is where a general knowledge of the passage can be helpful to you as well. Any sentence in the passage, even if you don't understand it, has to make sense within the topic and intention of the overall passage. In other words, there won't be a sentence about the history of the toothpick in a passage about military strategies. Answer choices that seem to stray off the subject of the overall passage are probably wrong.

Third Pass

As before, spend very little time, eliminate what you can based on whatever clues the sentence or passage has to offer, use your ear if necessary, and guess. The same rule about not guessing holds here as well. If you can't cancel any of the answers, then it's fine to leave a question blank.

It's very easy to fall into a mindset that says you're not done with a passage until every single question is answered, but this is a dangerous mindset. Just because a passage is easy overall, doesn't mean every single question in that passage is a gift.

Don't waste your time: If you've answered all the questions that you can and there are still one or two blanks, move on to the next passage. You may never have to, but you should be prepared to skip some questions.

SUMMARY

- This section is a combination of the two that preceded it. No new information, just a different format. You should be warmed up and confident going in.

- The majority of the blanks will test you on meaning. If the answer to a meaning question isn't immediately apparent, leave it for the second pass. When you come back to it, try to determine the context of the sentence and use POE.

- Determine the best order for you to attack the passages—this could make the difference between smooth sailing and a really big headache, so don't rush your decision.

- Use the Three-Pass System: Do easy questions first, tougher questions second, eliminate what you can, and guess on whatever's left.

- Don't feel as if you have to answer every single question on a given passage. Sometimes your best move is to go on to the next passage.

PRACTICE QUESTIONS

Part B

<u>Directions:</u> In each of the following passages, there are numbered blanks indicating that words or phrases have been omitted. For each numbered blank, four completions are provided. First read through the entire paragraph. Then, for each numbered blank, choose the completion that is most appropriate given the context of the entire paragraph and fill in the corresponding oval on the answer sheet.

Parecía que el pasado 6 de abril todo (1) listo para el despegue del transbordador Discovery cuya misión era la de realizar investigaciones atmosféricas y (2) solares, pero una (3) de última hora obligó a la Agencia Nacional de Aeronáutica y el Espacio (NASA) a abortar por (4) vez consecutiva el lanzamiento de la nave.

Al cierre de esta edición, la causa del incidente aún era desconocida y se esperaba que el viaje espacial pudiera concretarse (5) cualquier momento.

El apagado del motor ocurrió (6) antes de que los tres motores principales de la nave, alimentados por hidrógeno, fueron activados a las 2:32 de la (7) del pasado 6 de abril, unos 6.6 segundos antes del lanzamiento.

1. (A) estaba
   (B) esté
   (C) estaría
   (D) está

2. (A) clases
   (B) estudios
   (C) cuentos
   (D) lecturas

3. (A) negocio
   (B) testigo
   (C) retrato
   (D) dificultad

4. (A) nueva
   (B) tremenda
   (C) segunda
   (D) dos

5. (A) de
    (B) sobre
    (C) en
    (D) antes de

6. (A) año
    (B) días
    (C) segundos
    (D) lugares

7. (A) hora
    (B) madrugada
    (C) tiempo
    (D) reloj

ANSWERS AND EXPLANATIONS OF PRACTICE QUESTIONS: PART B

TRANSLATION

The Basics

Pay attention to "time words"—all sentences have clues which put us in a particular tense.

It seemed that last April 6 everything was ready for the launching of the shuttle Discovery, whose mission was to conduct atmospheric investigations and solar studies, but a last-minute difficulty forced the National Aeronautics and Space Administration (NASA) to abort for the second time the launching of the ship.

At the closing of this edition, the cause of the incident was still unknown and it was hoped that the space voyage could take place at any moment.

The shutdown of the motor occurred seconds before the three principal engines of the ship, fed by hydrogen, were activated at 2:32 in the morning last April 6, some 6.6 seconds before takeoff.

1. **(A) was**
    (B) is (pres. subjunctive)
    (C) would be
    (D) is (present)

The aborted launching of the shuttle already happened, so you need to use some kind of past tense. Since there is only one choice that's a past tense, you don't really need to think about which past tense applies. If you had trouble determining whether the event was in the past, present, or future, don't forget to look forward—the word **obligó** later in the sentence tells you that it's in the past. There are always clues in the passage that help you fill in the blanks, but it's up to you to find them.

2. (A) classes
    (B) studies
    (C) stories
    (D) lectures

The adjective **solares** that follows the blank is a big help on this question, because the expressions "solar classes," "solar stories," and "solar lectures" are all awkward in this context when compared with "solar studies."

3. (A) business
    (B) witness
    (C) portrait
    (D) difficulty

Abortar, which means the same thing in English as it does in Spanish (to abort), tells you that something went wrong with the launch, so you want a negative word for the blank. This leaves you with only choice (D). In addition, and even more simply, the word **una** tells us that we need a feminine word. Only (D) is feminine.

4. (A) new
    (B) tremendous
    (C) second
    (D) two

It's easiest to think of this blank as part of the larger phrase **abortar por . . . vez**. In this context, only **segunda** makes any sense in the blank.

5. (A) of
    (B) on
    (C) at
    (D) before

This question asks which preposition is correct before **cualquier momento**. This is purely idiomatic (no real rule—it's just the way it's done), and is much easier to do if you've seen the expression before. Choice (C) is the proper answer.

6. (A) years
    (B) days
    (C) seconds
    (D) places

If you think about the situation described in the passage, and read ahead in the last paragraph, you realize that the period of time you're looking for is very brief. Also, there is a clue earlier in the passage that helps you out on this question. **De última hora**, which appears in the first sentence, means "at the last moment."

7. (A) hour
    (B) morning
    (C) time
    (D) clock

When you discuss the time in Spanish, you often give the hour followed by an expression that tells you what part of the day you're talking about. These expressions are **de la noche** (at night), **de la tarde** (in the afternoon), **de la mañana** (in the morning), etc. **De la madrugada** is used for the very early morning, generally between midnight and 6 A.M.

Reading Comprehension

Welcome to Part C, reading comprehension. Reading comprehension is the last question type you will see on the exam. It is also probably the most difficult to see improvement on in a short period of time. Despite this, there are two good reasons you shouldn't worry. The first is that you can afford to leave some (or most) of the reading comprehension questions blank and still come away with a great score. The second is that, by carefully choosing the right passage(s) to leave blank, you can make the reading comprehension section much easier. As usual (and for the last time), the first step is to acquaint yourself with the directions:

Part C

Directions: Read the following texts carefully for comprehension. Each passage is followed by a number of questions or incomplete statements. Select the answer or completion that is best according to the text and fill in the corresponding oval on the answer sheet.

This section will contain approximately 28 questions on the Spanish Subject Test and approximately 17 questions on the Spanish with Listening Subject Test. On each test you will have between four and six passages or pictures (ads, announcements, menus, etc.) that contain between two and six questions each. The longer passages are usually followed by more questions. We'll get into how to choose which passages to do later, but for now realize that the length of the passage tells you nothing about its difficulty, so don't assume that the long passages are the hardest ones.

One of the nicest things about reading comprehension is that you really don't need to do very much of it in order to get your desired score. In terms of the big picture, you should not rush through Parts A and B in order to get to Part C. In fact, since the other two parts lend themselves to POE and guessing accurately, you should do the opposite. Take your time on the questions that are the most "technique-able" (Parts A and B), and if this means leaving some of the reading blank, then that's just fine. It's not that the reading comprehension is impossible, it's just that it lends itself less to shortcuts and techniques.

HOW TO CRACK THE SECTION

The first and most important step in beating the reading comprehension section is choosing which passages to do and which passages to skip. Luckily, you've already had an introduction to this type of decision in Part B of the exam. The idea is very similar: If the writing style is familiar (i.e., you can understand it without a major struggle) and there isn't too much tough vocabulary, then you're probably looking at a passage that you should do. This doesn't mean that you must know every single word in the passage. In fact, most passages will have some words (if only one or two) that you don't know. If you can understand the gist of the overall passage, then you can answer the questions that follow.

How to Read

Over the years, you've probably developed a reading style that includes a pace at which you're comfortable reading, a certain level of attention to detail, etc. When you know that someone is going to ask you questions about what you've read, you usually change your reading style to match the situation. You read much more slowly, and you pay much more attention to detail than you would if you were reading, say, an article in a newspaper. The reason for this is simple: You assume that by reading more slowly and carefully you will better understand what you've read. Makes sense, right? Unfortunately, even though it seems logical, this approach can be disastrous when it comes to the reading comprehension section of the SAT Spanish Subject Test.

What usually happens when you try to read ultra-slowly and virtually memorize the passage is that you finish reading with no sense of what the overall passage is about. You may have picked up a few details, but who knows if those particular details will be asked of you? What eventually happens is that on each question (or at least on most questions) you end up going back to the passage and rereading what you just read a minute ago. This approach is time-consuming and can be very frustrating. There is a better way.

Looking back at the passage in order to find the answer to a question is a very good idea. The problem is the initial time wasted in trying to memorize the passage in one reading. If you're going to refer to the passage anyway, then what's the point? It doesn't make sense to read the passage slowly and carefully twice, especially if one of those two readings doesn't help you answer questions.

Reading Comprehension, or Treasure Hunt?

We know that the instructions to the section ask you to read for comprehension, but we also know that those same instructions are written by the folks at ETS. Is this section really about reading for comprehension, or is it about answering a few silly questions? Not suprisingly, it's about answering a few silly questions. Treat the reading comprehension like a treasure hunt; the answers to the individual questions are hidden somewhere in the passage and your job is to find them. Here's the best way to approach that task.

Get the Big Picture

You've already seen that it's a waste of time to try to memorize the passage in one reading. Instead of trying to memorize the entire thing, your first reading should be dedicated to finding the *topic* and the *structure* of the passage. This means that if you finish your initial read and you know what the overall passage is about, and you know the main point of each paragraph, you've read the passage properly. Don't worry about facts or details (like names, dates, places, titles, etc.). Focus on what the whole passage is about and, in a very general sense, what each paragraph is about. A good way to test whether you've done this well is to try to summarize the passage in a few words (no more than five or six), and summarize the content of each paragraph in even fewer words. If you can do both of these things, you've definitely got a handle on the big picture, and that's going to be a big help in answering the questions.

There's no way we can tell you how long this initial reading should take, simply because everyone reads at a different pace. We can tell you that if you're stopping to try to decipher the meaning of every unknown word you come across, or if you're reading the same difficult sentence again and again, you've missed the boat. Focus on ideas, not on particular words or facts.

The point of reading this way is not to enable you to answer all the questions without looking back (we wish it were that easy, too). The point is to give you a sense of where things are, so that when a question asks about a particular fact or detail, even if you don't know the answer, you *will* know where to look to find it.

ANSWERING QUESTIONS

Although there are some general questions (main idea, or what the passage is about), most of the questions ask you about more specific things that come from a particular place in the passage. These two types of questions should be dealt with separately.

GENERAL QUESTIONS

Once you've finished your first reading, you should go right to the questions to see if there are any general ones. Why? Because if you know the topic and structure of the passage, you can answer any general question without looking back to the passage. The general questions (when they appear) ask you for precisely what you just read for: general ideas. Here are some examples of general questions:

> *¿De qué se trata este artículo?*
> What is this passage about?

> *¿Quién narra este pasaje?*
> Who narrates this passage?

Very few of these appear on a given Reading section, but when they do appear they are very easy. Make sure to do the general questions first if you choose a passage that contains any.

SPECIFIC QUESTIONS

The vast majority of reading comprehension questions require you to refer to the passage to find the answer. This is why it's so important to get a sense of structure before you attempt to answer them. Otherwise you waste lots of time looking for the part of the passage the question came from. The approach to these questions is simple:

- Read the question.

- Locate the source of the question by using guide words (we'll discuss guide words in a bit).

- Carefully read the section of the passage where the question came from.

- Go to the answers and find the one that matches what you just read.

How Do You Know Where to Look?

Any specific question will have a word or words that tell you what the question is about. We call these *guide words* because they guide you to the place in the passage where the question originated. If you can determine the subject of the question, you should be able to tell (at least roughly) where it came from. Now all that's left is for you to read the source of the question carefully, and match it up with one of your answer choices.

POE AND AVOIDING TRAP ANSWERS

There will be times on the reading comprehension questions when the correct answer is so obvious that it practically jumps off the page at you. Some of the time, however, it probably won't be quite that easy. If you know how to work through the answer choices efficiently, and know how they might try to stump you, even the hardest questions can be tamed.

PROCESS OF ELIMINATION

One of the biggest problems students have with this section is that they don't like any of the answer choices to some questions. It's as if on some questions the test writers forgot to include the correct answer in the choices. The key to using Process of Elimination on Part C is that, when you're stuck, you should forget about finding the right answer and concentrate on finding wrong answers. If you read all four choices and none of them looks good to you, don't panic. A couple of them probably look pretty bad to you, and those are just as helpful as the answers that look good. Eliminate the ones you know are wrong, and choose from whatever is left.

We know this is a bitter pill to swallow, but the fact is that sometimes you'll end up choosing an answer that you don't like or even understand. That's fine, though, because if you're sure that three of the answers are incorrect, then you must have confidence that the last one is the right one. Too often students shy away from answers they don't understand or don't like. Unfortunately, this section has little to do with what you like or understand. You're looking for the answer that will earn you a point, not the one you agree with.

TRAP ANSWERS

On *general questions*, the main thing to be on the lookout for is an answer that is too specific. Unlike the answer to a specific question, the answer to a general question can't be located in one particular place in the passage. This makes sense because the answer to a general question should encompass the contents of the entire passage.

The test writers try to trip you up by providing answers that come from one part of the passage or another, but are not general enough to be correct. These answers tend to be very tempting, because they are in the passage that you just finished reading and you recognize them. If the answer to a general question is about a specific part of the passage, it's probably a trap.

On *specific questions*, the most important thing to remember is that the correct answer must come from the passage. We know this seems obvious, but one of ETS's favorite tricks on these questions is to provide answers that are reasonable, logical, and gel with the contents of the passage, but are not *in* the passage. For this reason it's important that you stick to what you read when you refer to the passage. Don't think in terms of what the author might think or what you think. What's on the page in black and white is all you should go by to answer these questions.

Correct answers to specific questions won't be exact quotes from the passage, but they'll be pretty darn close. They'll have the same exact meaning as the corresponding words in the passage, with maybe a couple of the words moved around or changed so that it looks a little different. In other words, the right answers are *close* paraphrases of the passage.

QUESTION ORDER

The specific questions are best done in the order in which they appear (although you want to follow the golden rule of skipping any question that looks really difficult). This is because the order of the questions usually follows the progression of the passage—early questions come from the beginning of the passage, and subsequent questions come from the middle of the passage. Something that you read in the early part of the passage can sometimes help on a later question.

As with Part B of the exam, there is a tendency on Part C to feel as if you're not done until you've answered every question that pertains to a certain passage. You're done whenever you want to be done. In other words, if you've done all the questions that you understand and can easily find the answers to, then move on to the next passage and see if you can find a couple of easy questions there. To a certain extent, reading comprehension will be as easy (or as difficult) as you want to make it.

TYPES OF PASSAGES

In this section you will primarily encounter passages based on fictional events or characters, history, or current events. However, you may also come across ads, announcements, or menus. Although subject matter has nothing to do with the difficulty of a passage, you may find that a certain passage, because it's about a familiar topic, has vocabulary that you understand. Don't take this on faith. Read a few sentences to make sure.

READING COMPREHENSION SUMMARY

- Choose the order in which you want to do the passages. Read a couple of sentences to see if the writing style is easy to follow and the vocabulary is manageable. If so, go for it. If not, look ahead for something easier.

- Read the passage for topic and structure only. Don't read for detail, and don't try to memorize the entire thing. The first read is for you to get a sense of the subject and the overall structure—that's all.

- Go straight to the general questions. If you read correctly, you should be able to answer any general questions without looking back to the passage. Very few passages have general questions, so don't expect to find many.

- Now, do the specific questions in order. For these, you're going to let the guide words in the question tell you where to look in the passage. Then slowly and carefully read the area that the question comes from. Find an answer choice that basically says the same thing in slightly different language. These questions are about paraphrasing, not about comprehension.

- Avoid specific answers on general questions, and on specific questions avoid answers that are reasonable but aren't from the passage.

- Don't be afraid to leave blanks if there are questions that stump you. You're done with a passage whenever you've answered all the questions that you can answer. Instead of banging your head against a wall trying to do the last remaining question on a passage, go on to the next passage and find something easier.

PRACTICE QUESTIONS

Part C

Directions: Read the following texts carefully for comprehension. Each passage is followed by a number of questions or incomplete statements. Select the answer or completion that is best according to the text and fill in the corresponding oval on the answer sheet.

Pacing
If the passage sort of makes sense to you in the first couple of lines, go for it. If not, see if another is easier.

España, con una superficie aproximada de dos veces la del estado de Wyoming y una población de una vez y media la de California, está situada en el suroeste de Europa, separada de Francia por las montañas de los Pirineos y de África por el estrecho de Gibraltar. Su territorio está formado por la Península Ibérica, excepto Portugal, y los archipiélagos de las Islas Baleares, en el Mar Mediterráneo, y de las Islas Canarias, en el Océano Atlántico. Además, ejerce su soberanía en dos ciudades de la costa de Marruecos, Ceuta y Melilla, y no la ejerce en un peñón, en su propia costa, el Peñón de Gibraltar, que es una posesión inglesa.

El español, aunque tiene muy poco que ver en muchos aspectos con los habitantes del norte y centro de Europa, es europeo y latino, por su historia y por su cultura. A pesar de todo, algunos dicen que "África empieza en los Pirineos," y esto se debe a la influencia que tuvieron los casi ocho siglos de dominación árabe.

Para mucha gente, los españoles son personas pequeñas, morenas, que pasan la vida cantando y bailando flamenco, muy aficionadas a las corridas de toros, que les gusta mucho perder el tiempo hablando de todo en las tertulias y en la sobremesa y que cuando están contentas, que es muy frecuente, dicen "olé." Esta idea es tan falsa como la que en España mucha gente también tiene de los americanos. El estadounidense típico, para ellos, es el *cowboy*, el gangster o el artista de Hollywood. Sin embargo hay españoles en los Estados Unidos que han visto, oído, cantado y bailado más flamenco aquí que en España, lo mismo que la mayoría de los estadounidenses no tienen nada que ver ni con un *cowboy*, ni con un gangster ni con Hollywood.

Second Pass

POE is very important here. Eliminate the answers that can't possibly be right and focus on the only logical ones that are left.

1. El pasaje se trata de

   (A) la geografía de España y los españoles
   (B) los *cowboys* estadounidenses
   (C) la influencia de la dominación árabe en España
   (D) la manera en cual los españoles verdaderamente viven

2. La superficie de España es de un tamaño

   (A) dos veces el tamaño de los Estados Unidos
   (B) dos veces el tamaño del estado de Wyoming
   (C) una vez y media el tamaño de California
   (D) igual al tamaño del Peñón de Gibraltar

3. ¿Qué dice el autor sobre la historia y cultura del español?

   (A) tienen mucho en común con la historia y la cultura del centro de Europa
   (B) son adoptadas de la cultura africana
   (C) tienen muchos aspectos de la cultura estadounidense
   (D) son una combinación de influencias latinas y europeas

4. ¿Cuál de las ideas siguientes tienen muchos estadounidenses de los españoles?

   (A) que los españoles típicos son gangsters
   (B) que las mujeres españolas están enamoradas de los *cowboys* estadounidenses
   (C) que todos pasan el día bailando y cantando flamenco
   (D) que quisieran vivir en Hollywood

ANSWERS AND EXPLANATIONS OF READING COMPREHENSION QUESTIONS

HERE'S A TRANSLATION OF THE PASSAGE

Spain, with an approximate area of two times that of the state of Wyoming, and a population one and a half times that of California, is situated in the southwest of Europe, separated from France by the Pyrenees Mountains and from Africa by the Strait of Gibraltar. Its territory is formed by the Iberian Peninsula, except for Portugal, and the archipelagos of the Balearic Islands, in the Mediterranean Sea, and the Canary Islands, in the Atlantic Ocean. It also exercises its sovereignty over two cities on the coast of Morocco, Ceuta and Melilla, but does not exercise it over a rock on its own coast, the Rock of Gibraltar, which is an English possession.

Spaniards, although they have very little to do in many ways with the inhabitants of northern and central Europe, are European and Latin, in their history and their culture. All the same, some say that "Africa begins in the Pyrenees," and this is due to the influence that almost eight centuries of Arab domination had.

For many people, Spaniards are small, dark people who spend life singing and dancing flamenco, who are very fond of bullfights, who love to spend time talking at social gatherings or at the dinner table and who, when they're happy, which is very frequently, say *"olé."* This idea is as false as the one that many people in Spain also have of Americans. The typical American, for them, is the cowboy, the gangster, or the Hollywood artist. However, there are Spaniards in the United States that have seen, heard, sung, and danced more flamenco here than in Spain, just as the majority of Americans have nothing to do with cowboys, gangsters, or Hollywood.

> **Yes!**
> You can skip entire passages! If it makes no sense to you, how are you going to get anything right? Do the easy passages first to make your work less difficult.

1. The passage is about

   (A) the geography of Spain and the Spaniards
   (B) American cowboys
   (C) the influence of Arab domination in Spain
   (D) the way in which the Spaniards truly live

This is a general question, so its answer won't be located in any one specific place in the passage. Instead, the answer is a brief, general summary of the content of the three paragraphs.

2. The area of Spain is of a size

   (A) twice the size of the United States
   (B) twice the size of the state of Wyoming
   (C) one and a half times the size of California
   (D) equal to the size of the Rock of Gibraltar

The answer to this question is located in the beginning of the first paragraph. The lead word **superficie** is located only in that one area of the passage, and that's a big hint that that's where they took the question from.

Don't Be Intimidated

Reading in Spanish freaks most students out—all those words coming at you at the same time is a little intimidating. Instead of trying to make sense of every bit of the entire passage, read it once, ignoring words and phrases you don't know, to get the gist. Try to answer some questions with this limited information. Next, look at the individual questions (easiest first!) and use guide words to search for the answer in the passage.

3. What does the author say about the history and culture of Spaniards?

   (A) They have much in common with the history and culture of central Europe.
   (B) They are borrowed from African culture.
   (C) They have many aspects of American culture.
   (D) They are a combination of Latin and European influences.

The answer to this one is in the middle paragraph, which talks about the origins of Spaniards. The guide words in the question are **historia y cultura**, which are found only in that middle paragraph.

4. Which of the following ideas do many Americans have about Spaniards?

   (A) That typical Spaniards are gangsters.
   (B) That Spanish women are in love with American cowboys.
   (C) That they all spend the day dancing and singing flamenco.
   (D) That they'd like to live in Hollywood.

This question doesn't have guide words, but since the entire third paragraph is about the mutual stereotypes that Americans and Spaniards subscribe to, it isn't too tough to locate the source of the question. You *do* have to read the question carefully, though, because some of the wrong answers are misconceptions Spaniards have about Americans and the question asks for the opposite.

PART III

The Princeton Review Practice SAT Spanish Subject Tests and Explanations

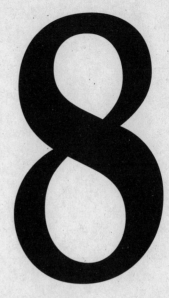

Practice Test 1

SPANISH SUBJECT TEST 1

Your responses to Spanish Subject Test 1 questions must be filled in on Test 1 of your answer sheet (at the back of the book). Marks on any other section will not be counted toward your Spanish Subject Test score.

When your supervisor gives the signal, turn the page and begin the Spanish Subject Test.

SPANISH SUBJECT TEST

PLEASE NOTE THAT YOUR ANSWER SHEET HAS FIVE ANSWER POSITIONS MARKED A, B, C, D, E, WHILE THE QUESTIONS THROUGHOUT THIS TEST CONTAIN ONLY FOUR CHOICES. BE SURE <u>NOT</u> TO MAKE ANY MARKS IN COLUMN E.

Part A

<u>Directions:</u> This part consists of a number of incomplete statements, each having four suggested completions. Select the most appropriate completion and fill in the corresponding oval on the answer sheet.

---

1. Si quieres ver el principio de la película, llega al teatro ------- .

   (A) más tarde
   (B) sin dinero
   (C) a tiempo
   (D) por la noche

2. Cuando vivía en Nueva York, ------- mucho tiempo escuchando conciertos y visitando los museos.

   (A) pasaba
   (B) pasé
   (C) he pasado
   (D) pasaré

3. Mi abuelo quiere vivir en un sitio bien tranquilo porque no le gusta el ruido. Por eso se ha mudado ------- .

   (A) a una calle muy ruidosa
   (B) fuera de la ciudad
   (C) al centro del mundo
   (D) sin querer

4. ¿ ------- museo prefieres, el de ciencia o el de arte?

   (A) Cuál
   (B) Qué
   (C) Cuánto
   (D) Quién

5. ¿Qué ------- cuando me llamaste al móvil esta tarde?

   (A) quisieras
   (B) querrían
   (C) querías
   (D) quieres

6. No lo conozco muy bien, pero la gente dice que ------- un tipo muy sincero e inteligente.

   (A) estamos
   (B) son
   (C) está
   (D) es

7. Consuelo no pudo tomar la taza de café porque estaba ------- .

   (A) bastante seco
   (B) demasiado rico
   (C) muy caliente
   (D) falta de aceite

8. Vamos a tomar el viaje en dos días en vez de uno porque nuestro destino está muy ------- aquí.

   (A) cerca de
   (B) lejos de
   (C) junto a
   (D) en frente de

9. Mi hermano nació tres años antes que yo; por eso es ------- .

   (A) mayor
   (B) más alto
   (C) mi hermano favorito
   (D) muy aburrido

10. Si no te gusta la ley, ¿por qué ------- los cuatro últimos años trabajando como abogado?

    (A) pasas
    (B) has pasado
    (C) pasarías
    (D) pasarás

11. En la biblioteca se encuentran ------- .

    (A) plumas
    (B) esperanzas
    (C) preguntas
    (D) libros

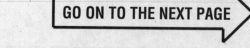

12. La bandera que ondea sobre el estadio
    es ------- .

    (A) nuestro
    (B) nuestras
    (C) nuestra
    (D) mío

13. La sopa caliente me dio dolor de muelas.
    Necesito ------- .

    (A) una silla
    (B) una mesa
    (C) un dentista
    (D) un tornillo

14. Si tuviera la oportunidad de conocer al presidente,
    le ------- miles de sugerencias.

    (A) he dado
    (B) daba
    (C) daría
    (D) daré

15. Para ir a México el ------- más rapido es éste.

    (A) camino
    (B) cielo
    (C) paseo
    (D) suelo

16. Ayer tenía mucho dolor de espalda, pero hoy no
    ------- ninguno.

    (A) tienen
    (B) tenemos
    (C) tienes
    (D) tengo

17. Como Gustavo se rompió la pierna en el partido de
    fútbol, tuve que jugar ------- él al día siguiente.

    (A) para
    (B) por
    (C) con
    (D) contra

18. García es nuestro cliente más estimado; siempre
    ------- damos a él lo que quiera.

    (A) la
    (B) le
    (C) lo
    (D) les

19. Alberto se sienta y pide arroz con pollo y una copa
    de vino. El está en ------- .

    (A) un restaurante
    (B) un circo
    (C) un banco
    (D) una zapatería

20. ¿ ------- cuándo han estudiado la historia española?

    (A) Hasta
    (B) Durante
    (C) Desde
    (D) En

21. En abril las flores crecen rápidamente porque
    ------- bastante.

    (A) duran
    (B) llora
    (C) llueve
    (D) llega

22. Mi tío sabe cocinar los frijoles negros
    bastante ------- .

    (A) bien
    (B) bueno
    (C) buenos
    (D) baños

23. El concierto que vimos anoche fue estupendo.
    ¡Esa ------- de verdad sabe tocar!

    (A) partido
    (B) novela
    (C) comida
    (D) orquesta

24. Tengo miedo de que la tormenta ------- durante la
    boda que vamos a tener en el patio.

    (A) llegue
    (B) llega
    (C) llegaría
    (D) llegara

GO ON TO THE NEXT PAGE

25. Carlos es un muchacho muy pesado que siempre
    está metido en algún lío. No es milagro que todo el
    mundo lo ------- .

    (A) quiera
    (B) rechace
    (C) ayude
    (D) conozca

26. Yo manejé por dos horas para encontrar esa
    medicina—si no te ------- tomas ¡te mataré!

    (A) lo
    (B) le
    (C) las
    (D) la

27. Después de dos años de investigaciones, el médico
    por fin ------- la causa de la enfermedad.

    (A) descubrió
    (B) dirigió
    (C) abrió
    (D) buscó

28. Jamás hemos bailado la samba, pero sí ------- bailar la
    lambada.

    (A) conocemos
    (B) conozca
    (C) sabrán
    (D) sabemos

29. Se dice que José Martí, el famoso autor cubano,
    empezó a escribir ------- cuando tenía solamente
    seis años.

    (A) lápices
    (B) alfabetos
    (C) idiomas
    (D) poemas

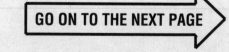

GO ON TO THE NEXT PAGE

Part B

Directions: In each of the following passages, there are numbered blanks indicating that words or phrases have been omitted. For each numbered blank, four completions are provided. First read through the entire paragraph. Then, for each numbered blank, choose the completion that is most appropriate given the context of the entire paragraph and fill in the corresponding oval on the answer sheet.

Emma dejó caer el papel. Su primera (30) fue de malestar en el vientre y en las rodillas; luego, de ciega culpa, de irrealidad, de frío, de (31) ; luego, quiso ya (32) en el día siguiente. Acto seguido comprendió que ese deseo era inútil porque (33) muerte de su padre era lo único que (34) en el mundo, y (35) sucediendo sin fin. Recogió el papel y se fue a su cuarto. Furtivamente lo (36) en un cajón, como si de algún modo ya (37) los hechos ulteriores.

30. (A) tiempo
    (B) vista
    (C) puesto
    (D) impresión

31. (A) juventud
    (B) temor
    (C) alegría
    (D) hambre

32. (A) estar
    (B) ser
    (C) estaré
    (D) ir

33. (A) lo
    (B) el
    (C) la
    (D) las

34. (A) entraba
    (B) crecía
    (C) había terminado
    (D) había sucedido

35. (A) seguiría
    (B) pararía
    (C) cambiaría
    (D) sentiría

36. (A) sacó
    (B) guardó
    (C) encontró
    (D) quitó

37. (A) sabe
    (B) sabía
    (C) supiera
    (D) sabría

Después (38) haber mandado dos expediciones a explorar la costa de México, el gobernador de Cuba (39) otra expedición bajo el mando de Hernán Cortés en 1519. En las tres expediciones (40) parte un soldado que se (41) Bernal Díaz del Castillo. (42) soldado, cuando ya era casi un viejo y (43) retirado en Guatemala, (44) sus recuerdos de las guerras mexicanas, que forman la mejor narración (45) la conquista de México y que se titula "Historia verdadera de la conquista de la Nueva España."

La expedición de Cortés constaba de once navíos que (46) poco más de seiscientos hombres y dieciséis (47). Cuando Cortés estaba listo (48) salir, el gobernador trató de quitarle el mando, pero él decidió hacerse a la mar.

38. (A) que
    (B) de
    (C) a
    (D) por

39. (A) puso fin a
    (B) ensayó
    (C) preguntó
    (D) organizó

40. (A) hizo
    (B) dio
    (C) dejó
    (D) tomó

41. (A) llamó
    (B) llama
    (C) llamaba
    (D) había llamado

42. (A) Este
    (B) Esa
    (C) Un
    (D) La

43. (A) paraba
    (B) pensaba
    (C) oía
    (D) vivía

44. (A) escribió
    (B) corrió
    (C) perdió
    (D) pidió

45. (A) encima de
    (B) junto a
    (C) sobre
    (D) en vez de

46. (A) llevaba
    (B) llevaron
    (C) llevaban
    (D) llevan

47. (A) automóviles
    (B) aviones
    (C) caballos
    (D) guantes

48. (A) por
    (B) para
    (C) en
    (D) de

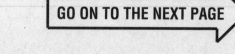
GO ON TO THE NEXT PAGE

Pero hoy, esta mañana fría, en que tenemos más prisa que nunca, la niña y yo (49) de largo delante de la fila tentadora de autos parados. Por (50) vez en la vida vamos al colegio . . . Al colegio, le digo, no (51) ir en taxi. Hay que correr un poco por las calles, hay que tomar el metro, hay que (52) luego, en un sitio determinado, a un autobús . . . Es que yo he escogido un colegio muy (53) para mi niña, ésa es la verdad; un colegio que (54) mucho, pero está muy lejos . . . Sin embargo, yo no estoy impaciente hoy, ni (55), y la niña lo sabe. Es ella ahora la que inicia una caricia tímida con su manita (56) la mía; y por primera vez me doy cuenta de que su mano de cuatro años es (57) mi mano grande: tan decidida, tan suave, tan nerviosa como la mía.

49. (A) pasamos
    (B) entramos
    (C) dábamos
    (D) pagamos

50. (A) ninguna
    (B) primera
    (C) siempre
    (D) costumbre

51. (A) se engaña
    (B) conocemos
    (C) se puede
    (D) sobran

52. (A) dormir
    (B) tocar
    (C) jugar
    (D) caminar

53. (A) cerrado
    (B) lejano
    (C) oscuro
    (D) difícil

54. (A) me gusta
    (B) odio
    (C) no conozco
    (D) dudamos

55. (A) vieja
    (B) alta
    (C) cansada
    (D) fresca

56. (A) dentro de
    (B) fuera de
    (C) cerca de
    (D) sin

57. (A) diferente a
    (B) igual a
    (C) cerca de
    (D) encima de

GO ON TO THE NEXT PAGE

Part C

Directions: Read the following texts carefully for comprehension. Each passage is followed by a number of questions or incomplete statements. Select the answer or completion that is best according to the text and fill in the corresponding oval on the answer sheet.

Al pasar ante una granja, un perro mordió a mi amigo. Entramos a ver al granjero y le preguntamos si era suyo el perro. El granjero, para evitarse complicaciones, dijo que no era suyo.

—Entonces—dijo mi amigo—présteme una hoz para cortarle la cabeza, pues debo llevarla al Instituto para que la analicen.

En aquel momento apareció la hija del granjero y le pidió a su padre que no permitiera que le cortáramos la cabeza al perro.

—Si es suyo el perro—dijo mi amigo—enséñeme el certificado de vacunación antirrábica.

El hombre entró en la granja, y tardó largo rato en salir. Mientras tanto, el perro se acercó y mi amigo dijo:

—No me gusta el aspecto de este animal.

En efecto, babeaba y los ojos parecían arderle en las órbitas. Incluso andaba dificultosamente.

—Hace unos días—dijo la joven—le atropelló una bicicleta.

El granjero nos dijo que no encontraba el certificado de vacunación.

—Debo haberlo perdido.

—La vida de un hombre puede estar en juego—intervine yo. Díganos, con toda sinceridad, si el perro está vacunado o no.

El hombre bajó la cabeza y murmuró:

—Está sano.

58. ¿Qué les pasó a los tipos cuando pasaron por la granja?

(A) a uno de ellos lo mordió un perro
(B) un granjero les pidió direcciones
(C) se evitaron complicaciones
(D) perdieron su perro

59. ¿Por qué el granjero les dijo que el perro no era suyo?

(A) no sabía de quien era el perro
(B) no conocía a los tipos que vinieron a la puerta
(C) no quería echarse la culpa de lo que había hecho el perro
(D) no le gustaban los perros

60. ¿Qué le pidió su hija al granjero?

(A) que le permitiera comprar caramelos
(B) que llevara el perro al médico
(C) que le diera comida al perro
(D) que no dejara que los hombres dañaran al perro

61. ¿Qué le pidieron los tipos al granjero?

(A) un vaso de agua
(B) el certificado de vacunación antirrábica
(C) un teléfono para llamar a la policía
(D) prueba de que verdaderamente era granjero

62. ¿Cómo parecía el perro del granjero?

(A) sano y de buen humor
(B) enfermo, como si tuviera rabias
(C) joven y lleno de energía
(D) serio y pensativo

63. ¿Qué razón dio la niña por la manera en que el perro se portaba?

(A) tuvo un accidente con una bicicleta
(B) acaba de recibir su vacuna antirrábica
(C) es un perro muy feroz
(D) tenía mucha hambre

64. En fin, ¿que les dice el granjero a los tipos?

(A) que vayan al hospital
(B) que adopten un perro
(C) que se vayan de la granja ahora mismo
(D) que el perro no tiene ninguna enfermedad

GO ON TO THE NEXT PAGE

En nuestra oficina regía el mismo presupuesto desde el año mil novecientos veintitantos, o sea desde una época en que la mayoría de nosotros estábamos luchando con la geografía y con los quebrados. Sin embargo, el Jefe se acordaba del acontecimiento y a veces, cuando el trabajo disminuía, se sentaba familiarmente sobre uno de nuestros escritorios, y así, con las piernas colgantes que mostraban después del pantalón unos inmaculados calcetines blancos, nos relataba con la misma emoción de antes y las quinientas noventa y ocho palabras de costumbre, el lejano y magnífico día en que su Jefe—él era entonces Oficial Primero—le había palmeado el hombro y le había dicho: "Muchacho, tenemos presupuesto nuevo", con la sonrisa amplia y satisfecha del que ya ha calculado cuántas camisas podrá comprar con el aumento.

65. ¿Por más o menos cuánto tiempo han tenido el mismo presupuesto?

(A) por varias décadas
(B) por varios siglos
(C) por unas cuantas semanas
(D) desde ayer

66. El Jefe hacía el cuento cuando

(A) estaba triste
(B) había tomado demasiado cerveza
(C) el trabajo era menos de lo corriente
(D) tenían una fiesta

67. El cuento del presupuesto nuevo que hacía el Jefe

(A) tenía calcetines blancos
(B) siempre era diferente
(C) era interesante
(D) siempre era el mismo

68. ¿Cuál fue la reacción del Jefe cuando su jefe le contó del presupuesto nuevo?

(A) se fue de la compañía
(B) se puso muy contento
(C) le dio un abrazo a su jefe
(D) compró camisas nuevas

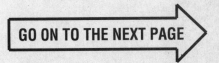

GO ON TO THE NEXT PAGE

Para los arqueólogos y los historiadores, la civilización maya es, sin duda ninguna, la que alcanzó un mayor nivel de desarrollo entre todas las civilizaciones que existían antes de la llegada de Colón. Aunque todavía hay muchos secretos que no se han descifrado con relación a los mayas parece que esta civilización empezó varios siglos antes del nacimiento de Cristo. Sin embargo se sabe que los mayas abandonaron los grandes centros ceremoniales en el siglo X de nuestra era.

Los primeros templos que construyeron son de forma de pirámide de cuatro lados con una gran escalinata. Sobre la pirámide hay un edificio de un piso normalmente, y en algunos casos de dos, y en ellos podemos ver relieves de arcilla y esculturas de madera y piedra caliza. Las figuras son siempre de perfil y en ellas se puede apreciar los adornos y joyas que usaban. En la clasificación que se ha hecho de las épocas de esta civilización, se llama preclásica a la época primera, que se desarrolla en Guatemala y Honduras, y que según los arqueólogos duró hasta el fin del siglo III de nuestra era.

69. ¿Qué piensan los arqueólogos y los historiadores de la civilización maya?

(A) que era una civilización muy avanzada
(B) que los maya escribieron libros magníficos
(C) que conocieron a Colón
(D) que tenían muchos secretos

70. ¿Cuándo empezó la civilización maya?

(A) en el siglo X de nuestra era
(B) inmediatamente antes de la llegada de Colón
(C) varios siglos antes del nacimiento de Cristo
(D) varios siglos después del nacimiento de Cristo

71. ¿Cómo parecían los primeros templos de los mayas?

(A) eran edificios muy bajos
(B) eran hechos de madera y piedra caliza
(C) eran pirámides de cuatro lados
(D) eran casas corrientes, como las que tenemos hoy

72. ¿Qué se puede decir de las esculturas que hicieron los mayas?

(A) tenían escalinatas grandes
(B) dan información sobre las joyas y adornos que usaban
(C) cuesta mucho comprarlas
(D) se puede encontrarlas en los museos famosos

73. ¿Dónde empezó y se desarrolló la época preclásica?

(A) en Nicaragua
(B) en México
(C) en la época preclásica
(D) en Honduras y Guatemala

74. El pasaje se trata de

(A) la civilización y arquitectura maya
(B) la influencia de Cristo sobre la civilización maya
(C) las diferencias entre nuestra civilización y la de los mayas
(D) los adornos y las joyas que usaban los mayas

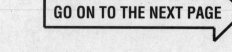

GO ON TO THE NEXT PAGE

En 1992 se cumplieron cinco siglos ya del encuentro de Europa con América. Fue poco después de la medianoche del 11 al 12 de octubre de 1492, cuando Rodrigo de Triana, un tripulante de la carabela "La Niña", la cual se había adelantado a "La Santa María", donde iba Colón, dio el grito de "¡Tierra! ¡Tierra!" El lugar estaba muy cercano a la Florida, era una pequeña isla llamada Guanahaní que Colón llamó San Salvador y que pertenece al archipiélago de las Lucayas o Bahamas.

Lo que Colón encontró y describe en sus cartas a los Reyes Católicos fue mucha pobreza y gente que iba desnuda, como su madre los parió, todos jóvenes, con hermosos cuerpos, cabellos gruesos como los de los caballos y cortos, que les caían por encima de las cejas y otros largos por detrás.

Pocos días después, descubrió la costa de Cuba, que llamó Juana, por la hija de los reyes. Por entonces, Martín Alonso Pinzón, que mandaba "La Pinta", se separó de la expedición, lo cual consideró Colón como una deserción, aunque lo disimuló por mantener la unidad de la expedición. Al cabo de unos días llegó a Haití, que llamó la Hispaniola, pero debido a los muchos bajos y arrecifes que había, "La Santa María" encalló.

75. ¿Quién fue el primero que vio tierra en la expedición?

   (A) un tripulante que se llamaba
       Rodrigo de Triana
   (B) Colón
   (C) La Niña
   (D) Guanahaní, el mejor amigo de Colón

76. ¿Cómo era la gente que Colón encontró?

   (A) muy pobre, pero también hermosa
   (B) violenta y agresiva
   (C) más inteligente que los tripulantes
   (D) muy miedosa y confundida

77. ¿Qué descubrió Colón unos días después de que descubrió San Salvador?

   (A) el archipiélago de las Bahamas
   (B) la isla que hoy se llama Cuba
   (C) Haití
   (D) cabellos gruesos

78. ¿Cuál fue la reacción de Colón cuando Martín Alonso Pinzón se separó de la expedición?

   (A) se puso furioso
   (B) empezó a llorar
   (C) dio la impresión de que no sabía
       lo que había pasado
   (D) mandó otra carabela tras él

79. ¿Cómo terminó "La Santa María"?

   (A) regresó a España
   (B) se perdió y nunca la han encontrado
   (C) fue hundida
   (D) encalló como resultado de los arrecifes y bajos

GO ON TO THE NEXT PAGE

Si no fuera por el gusto exigente de los bebedores de café de Arabia Saudita, el pueblo guatemalteco de Cobán, al otro lado del mundo, estaría en problemas.

Cobán, capital de la región montañosa de Alta Verapaz, en Guatemala, es la fuente de la mayor parte del cardamomo que consume el mundo árabe: una especia dulce, picante y sumamente aromática que se emplea en la cocina de la India. De hecho, el café de cardamomo, conocido en el mundo árabe como *kahwe hal*, es considerado un símbolo de hospitalidad en todo el Cercano Oriente.

En Cobán, famoso por su iglesia católica del siglo XVI y las ruinas mayas que se encuentran en los alrededores, prácticamente nadie habla árabe y ninguno de sus 125.000 habitantes pone cardamomo en el café. Sin embargo, todos conocen perfectamente la conexión que existe entre la especia y el mundo árabe. "El cardamomo es la base de nuestra economía, y Guatemala es el principal exportador del mundo."

80. ¿En qué país en particular toman el café de cardamomo?

(A) en Guatemala
(B) en Arabia Saudita
(C) en la Alta Verapaz
(D) en el Cercano Oriente

81. ¿Qué es el cardamomo?

(A) un tipo de café raro
(B) una especia
(C) un estilo de cocinar indio
(D) un tipo de árbol

82. ¿Cómo sabe el cardamomo?

(A) picante, pero también dulce
(B) un poco amargo
(C) casi no tiene sabor
(D) sabe como el café colombiano

83. ¿Por qué es conocida la ciudad de Cobán?

(A) por el cardamomo
(B) por el mejor café en el Norte América
(C) por sus ruinas, y por su iglesia del siglo XVI
(D) por la comida india

84. ¿Cuál es la conexión entre el mundo árabe y Guatemala?

(A) en Guatemala todos hablan árabe
(B) en los dos lugares les encanta el café de cardamomo
(C) Guatemala exporta mucha especia al mundo árabe
(D) de verdad no hay conexión entre los dos lugares

85. ¿Cuál sería un buen título para el pasaje?

(A) "Cobán: la ciudad en las montañas"
(B) "La economía de Guatemala"
(C) "Los cafés del mundo"
(D) "Cardamomo: lo que une a Guatemala con el mundo árabe"

STOP
IF YOU FINISH BEFORE TIME IS CALLED, YOU MAY CHECK YOUR WORK ON THIS TEST ONLY.
DO NOT TURN TO ANY OTHER TEST IN THIS BOOK.

HOW TO SCORE THE PRINCETON REVIEW SPANISH SUBJECT TEST

When you take the real exam, the proctors take away your exam and your bubble sheet and send it to New Jersey where a computer looks at the pattern of filled-in ovals on your exam and gives you a score. We couldn't include even a small computer with this book, so we are providing this more primitive way of scoring your exam.

DETERMINING YOUR SCORE

STEP 1 Using the answers on the next page, determine how many questions you got right and how many you got wrong on the test. Remember, questions that you do not answer do not count as either right answers or wrong answers.

STEP 2 List the number of right answers here.

(A) _____

STEP 3 List the number of wrong answers here. Now divide that number by 3.

(B) _____ ÷ 3 _____ = (C) _____

STEP 4 Subtract the number of wrong answers divided by 3 (C) from the number of correct answers (A). Round this score to the nearest whole number. This is your raw score.

(A) – (C)=____

STEP 5 To determine your real score, take the number from Step 4 above and look it up in the left column of the Score Conversion Table on page 121; the corresponding score on the right is your score on the exam.

ANSWERS TO SPANISH SUBJECT TEST 1

Question Number	Correct Answer	Right	Wrong	Question Number	Correct Answer	Right	Wrong	Question Number	Correct Answer	Right	Wrong
1	C	_____	_____	33	C	_____	_____	65	A	_____	_____
2	A	_____	_____	34	D	_____	_____	66	C	_____	_____
3	B	_____	_____	35	A	_____	_____	67	D	_____	_____
4	A	_____	_____	36	B	_____	_____	68	B	_____	_____
5	C	_____	_____	37	C	_____	_____	69	A	_____	_____
6	D	_____	_____	38	B	_____	_____	70	C	_____	_____
7	C	_____	_____	39	D	_____	_____	71	C	_____	_____
8	B	_____	_____	40	D	_____	_____	72	B	_____	_____
9	A	_____	_____	41	C	_____	_____	73	D	_____	_____
10	B	_____	_____	42	A	_____	_____	74	A	_____	_____
11	D	_____	_____	43	D	_____	_____	75	A	_____	_____
12	C	_____	_____	44	A	_____	_____	76	A	_____	_____
13	C	_____	_____	45	C	_____	_____	77	B	_____	_____
14	C	_____	_____	46	C	_____	_____	78	C	_____	_____
15	A	_____	_____	47	C	_____	_____	79	D	_____	_____
16	D	_____	_____	48	B	_____	_____	80	B	_____	_____
17	B	_____	_____	49	A	_____	_____	81	B	_____	_____
18	B	_____	_____	50	B	_____	_____	82	A	_____	_____
19	A	_____	_____	51	C	_____	_____	83	C	_____	_____
20	C	_____	_____	52	D	_____	_____	84	C	_____	_____
21	C	_____	_____	53	B	_____	_____	85	D	_____	_____
22	A	_____	_____	54	A	_____	_____				
23	D	_____	_____	55	C	_____	_____				
24	A	_____	_____	56	A	_____	_____				
25	B	_____	_____	57	B	_____	_____				
26	D	_____	_____	58	A	_____	_____				
27	A	_____	_____	59	C	_____	_____				
28	D	_____	_____	60	D	_____	_____				
29	D	_____	_____	61	B	_____	_____				
30	D	_____	_____	62	B	_____	_____				
31	B	_____	_____	63	A	_____	_____				
32	A	_____	_____	64	D	_____	_____				

THE PRINCETON REVIEW SPANISH SUBJECT TEST
SCORE CONVERSION TABLE

Raw Score	Scaled Score	Raw Score	Scaled Score	Raw Score	Scaled Score
85	800	47	590	9	360
84	800	46	580	8	360
83	800	45	570	7	350
82	800	44	570	6	350
81	790	43	560	5	340
80	790	42	550	4	340
79	780	41	550	3	330
78	780	40	540	2	320
77	770	39	530	1	320
76	770	38	530	0	310
75	760	37	520	−1	310
74	760	36	520	−2	300
73	750	35	510	−3	290
72	750	34	500	−4	290
71	740	33	500	−5	280
70	730	32	490	−6	270
69	730	31	490	−7	260
68	720	30	480	−8	260
37	720	29	470	−9	250
66	710	28	470	−10	240
65	700	27	460	−11	230
64	700	26	460	−12	220
63	690	25	450	−13	220
62	680	24	450	−14	220
61	680	23	440	−15	210
60	670	22	430	−16	210
59	670	21	430	−17	210
58	660	20	420	−18	200
57	650	19	420	−19	200
56	650	18	410	−20	200
55	640	17	410	−21	200
54	630	16	400	−22	200
53	630	15	400	−23	200
52	620	14	390	−24	200
51	620	13	390	−25	200
50	610	12	380	−26	200
49	600	11	380	−27	200
48	590	10	370	−28	200

Practice Test 1:
Answers and
Explanations

PART A

1. If you want to see the beginning of the film, arrive at the theater ------- .

   (A) later
   (B) without money
   (C) on time
   (D) at night

   The key phrase in this sentence is **si quieres ver el principio**. If you were able to get this much, you could determine that time had something to do with the answer, and that would eliminate (B) and (D). What would make more sense in terms of seeing the beginning of something: arriving later, or arriving on time? On time makes more sense, and (C) is the correct answer.

2. When I lived in New York I ------- a lot of time listening to concerts and visiting the museums.

   (A) spent (imperfect)
   (B) spent
   (C) have spent
   (D) will spend

   Since the sentence refers to the past, the answer must be some kind of past tense, and since **pasaré** is the future you can immediately scratch (D). The other three choices are all past tenses, but since the action described was an ongoing one during the time the person lived in New York the answer must be in the imperfect tense.

3. My grandfather wants to live in a peaceful place because he doesn't like noise. That's why he's moved ------- .

   (A) to a noisy street
   (B) outside of the city
   (C) to the center of the Earth
   (D) unintentionally

   If you understood either the part about not liking noise or the part about wanting to live peacefully you could eliminate (A). Choices (C) and (D) are sort of ridiculous, and so (B) is your best bet.

4. ------- museum do you prefer, science or art?

   (A) Which
   (B) What
   (C) How much
   (D) Who

   Quién is used to refer to people, and since we're talking about museums you can eliminate (D). **Cuánto** is used to inquire about quantities, so we're down to (A) and (B). **Qué** is often used in questions (¿**Qué hora es?**), but since a choice is asked for, **cuál** is used instead of **qué**.

5. What ------- when you called my cell phone this
afternoon?

    (A) would you have wanted
    (B) would they have wanted
    (C) did you want
    (D) do you want

Choice (B) can be eliminated because **me llamaste** tells us that we need a second person verb. The preterite, along with **cuando**, clues us into the need for the imperfect to express an action that was ongoing when something else occurred.

6. I don't know him well, but people say that he
------- a sincere and intelligent guy.

    (A) are
    (B) are
    (C) is
    (D) is

Since we're talking about one person (**lo** is a singular pronoun), (A) and (B) can be easily eliminated. Now for the subtle part. If you know when to use **ser** and when to use **estar**, this question is a piece of cake. Does the sentence give us any reason to suspect that this person's admirable qualities are going to change or disappear in the near future? No, therefore (D) is correct.

7. Consuelo couldn't drink the cup of coffee because it
was -------.

    (A) dry enough
    (B) too tasty
    (C) very hot
    (D) lacking oil

This one is a bit tricky, but if you understood the first part of the sentence, you can definitely tackle it (probably a second-pass question). What would keep someone from drinking something? The only choice that makes any sense is (C).

8. We're going to make the trip in two days instead of
one because our destination is ------- here.

    (A) near
    (B) far from
    (C) next to
    (D) in front of

The meaning of this sentence gives some helpful clues. In fact, since the duration of the trip is going to be twice what was expected, the only answer that makes any sense is **lejos de**.

9. My brother was born three years before I was; that's
why he's -------.

    (A) older
    (B) taller
    (C) my favorite brother
    (D) very boring

Although each of the answers is something a brother could be, "born three years before" clearly suggests choice (A), which is correct.

10. If you don't like the law, why ------- the past four
    years working as a lawyer?

    (A) do you spend
    (B) have you spent
    (C) would you spend
    (D) will you spend

"The past four years" tells you that we need some type of past tense, so eliminate (A), (C), and (D).

11. In the library one finds -------.

    (A) pens
    (B) hopes
    (C) questions
    (D) books

This is a very straightforward question, that is, if you know the word for library. The correct answer is (D). Be careful not to confuse **biblioteca** with **librería**, which means bookstore.

12. The flag that flies over the stadium is -------.

    (A) ours (masculine)
    (B) ours (feminine, plural)
    (C) ours (fem. sing.)
    (D) mine (masculine)

The wrong answers here (as on many SAT Spanish Subject Test questions) are incorrect because they don't agree with what they're replacing, either in gender or in number. Since **la bandera** is singular and feminine, **nuestra** is the correct pronoun.

13. The hot soup gave me a toothache. I need -------.

    (A) a chair
    (B) a table
    (C) a dentist
    (D) a screw

"Toothache" is the key word in this example. If you understood that much, you could easily have guessed (C), which is correct.

14. If I had the chance to meet the president, I ------- him
    thousands of suggestions.

    (A) have given
    (B) gave
    (C) would give
    (D) will give

Si is your big clue that the conditional is used. The only choice that's in the conditional is (C).

15. To go to Mexico, the fastest ------- is this one.

    (A) road
    (B) sky
    (C) stroll
    (D) ground/floor

Only one of the answers is something that would be involved in going to Mexico, and that answer is (A). "Stroll" is a tricky choice because it sort of goes with "fastest," but it makes no sense with the first part of the sentence.

16. Yesterday I had a lot of back pain, but today I don't ------- any.

    (A) have (ellos)
    (B) have (nosotros)
    (C) have (tú)
    (D) have (yo)

Somewhere on your exam you will probably see a question whose answer is the plain present tense, like this one. All four answers are in the present, so you have to pay special attention to the subject (**yo**).

17. Since Gustavo broke his leg in a soccer game, I had to play ------- him on the following day.

    (A) for
    (B) for (instead of)
    (C) with
    (D) against

This is a fairly nasty example of the **para/por** dilemma. Since Gustavo broke his leg, he is incapable of playing soccer the day after, so cross out (C) and (D). Since the sentence points to the need for replacing someone, (B) is the answer.

18. García is our most respected client; we always give ------- what he wants.

    (A) it (feminine)
    (B) him
    (C) it (masculine)
    (D) them

Direct object or indirect object; that is the question. What do we give? *What he wants*—that's the direct object. To whom? To *him*—the singular indirect pronoun is needed, which is (B).

19. Alberto sits down and asks for chicken with rice and a glass of wine. He is in -------.

    (A) a restaurant
    (B) a circus
    (C) a bank
    (D) a shoe store

If you caught any of the food words in this sentence you would guess (A). None of the others is even in the ballpark.

20. ------- when have you (pl.) studied Spanish history?

    (A) Until
    (B) During
    (C) Since
    (D) In

This is another preposition question, and once again meaning is your savior. The only choice that really works in terms of meaning is **desde**. **Durante cuándo** is redundant (you would just say **cuándo**), and **hasta cuándo** suggests that the speaker already knew you were studying Spanish history. However, the sentence suggests that he didn't.

21. In April, the flowers grow quickly because it -------
    frequently.

    (A) last
    (B) cries
    (C) rains
    (D) arrives

The trick here is that the answers are so similar in sound. What would make flowers grow quickly? "Rain", so (C) is the best answer. "April" might have given you a hint (you know, April showers . . .).

22. My uncle knows how to cook black beans pretty
    -------.

    (A) well
    (B) good (singular)
    (C) good (plural)
    (D) baths

Just thought we'd sneak an adjective vs. adverb question in for fun. **Bueno** (good) is an adjective, and since you are describing an action (*how* the black beans are made) an adverb is used. **Baños** is thrown in there to see if you're awake. It sort of sounds and looks like **buenos**.

23. The concert that we saw last night was excellent.
    That ------- really knows how to play.

    (A) game
    (B) novel
    (C) food
    (D) orchestra

The word "concert" points to (D), which is the correct choice.

24. I'm afraid that the storm ------- during the wedding
    that we're going to have on the patio.

    (A) will arrive (pres. subj.)
    (B) arrives
    (C) would arrive
    (D) arrived

Expressions of fear are dead giveaways that you need to use the subjunctive. Then all you have to do is check the tense of the expression to tell you which subjunctive to use. **Tengo miedo** is in the present, so this time it's present subjunctive.

25. Carlos is an annoying kid who is always in some
kind of trouble. It's no miracle that everyone -------
him.

   (A) likes
   (B) rejects
   (C) helps
   (D) knows

There is some tough vocabulary here. Fortunately, there are lots of different clues that tell you that Carlos isn't a particularly likable fellow, and that makes (B) the best answer.

26. I drove for two hours to find that medicine—if you
don't take ------- I'll kill you!

   (A) it (masculine)
   (B) (to) him
   (C) them (feminine)
   (D) it (feminine)

The pronoun in this question is replacing **medicina**, which is singular and feminine. Singular eliminates (C), and feminine gets rid of (A). **Le** is an indirect object pronoun, but **medicina** is the direct object. (D) is correct.

27. After two years of research, the doctor finally -------
the cause of the disease.

   (A) discovered
   (B) directed
   (C) opened
   (D) looked for

Choices (B) and (C) don't make much sense here. Choice (D) would only make sense if the doctor hadn't yet begun his research. Choice (A) is correct.

28. We've never danced the samba, but sure ------- how
to dance the lambada!

   (A) we know
   (B) I know (subjunctive)
   (C) they will know
   (D) we know

Knowing how to do a type of dance falls under the category of facts (as opposed to people), so **saber** is the correct verb. (C) is not correct because there is no reason given in the sentence to change either the subject or to change the verb to the future tense.

29. They say that José Martí, the famous Cuban author,
began to write ------- when he was only six years old.

   (A) pencils
   (B) alphabets
   (C) languages
   (D) poems

What does an author write? Well, lots of things, but out of these choices only (D) is reasonable.

PART B

Emma dejó caer el papel. Su primera <u>impresión</u> fue
de malestar en el vientre y en las rodillas; luego, de ciega
culpa, de irrealidad, de frío, de <u>temor</u>; luego, quiso ya
<u>estar</u> en el día siguiente. Acto seguido comprendió que
ese deseo era inútil porque <u>la</u> muerte de su padre era
lo único que <u>había sucedido</u> en el mundo, y <u>seguiría</u>
sucediendo sin fin. Recogió el papel y se fue a su cuarto.
Furtivamente lo <u>guardó</u> en un cajón, como si de algún
modo ya <u>supiera</u> los hechos ulteriores.

Emma dropped the paper. Her first *impression* was of uneasiness in her belly and in her knees; then of blind guilt, of irreality, of coldness, of *fear*; then she wished *to be* already in the next day. Immediately afterwards she understood that that wish was futile because *the* death of her father was the only thing that *had happened* in the world, and it would go on happening endlessly. She picked up the paper and went to her room. Furtively, *she saved it* in a drawer, as if somehow she *already knew* the subsequent facts.

30. (A) time
    (B) sight
    (C) place
    (D) impression

In this sentence, Emma's initial reaction to a letter is being described. The word that makes sense in the blank has to be something along the lines of "reaction." Of the choices offered, only **impresión** is even remotely similar to "reaction."

31. (A) youth
    (B) fear
    (C) joy
    (D) hunger

At this point in the paragraph, you know from the rest of Emma's reactions that she's not feeling so well, and the blank should be filled with a word that's consistent with her bad reactions. The only really negative choice is **temor**. If you weren't sure whether she was feeling good or bad, you should have skipped this and read on—later we find out that her father has died, which tells you for sure how she's feeling.

32. **(A) to be (estar)**
    (B) to be (ser)
    (C) will be
    (D) to go

So we know Emma isn't happy. It makes sense that she'd want <u>to be</u> in the next day. That eliminates (C) and (D), but does this situation call for **estar** or **ser**? Being in the next day is a location in time, so **estar** is correct. Another approach to this question is to use the preposition that follows the blank (**en**). **Ir en** means to go via (as in **ir en avión**...), which makes no sense at all in this blank. Also, **quiso** (wanted to) implies the past, and so that tells you that **estaré** is wrong because it's the future tense.

33. (A) it
    (B) the (masc., sing.)
    (C) the (fem., sing.)
    (D) the (fem., pl.)

Muerte is a singular feminine noun, so the proper article is **la**.

34. (A) entered
    (B) grew
    (C) had finished
    (D) had happened

It doesn't make sense that the death of her father would enter or grow (cross out (A) and (B)). **Había terminado** is possible, but if you read on you find out that in fact Emma feels that it will go on affecting her. So the best answer is (D).

35. **(A) would continue**
    (B) would stop
    (C) would change
    (D) would feel

This is sort of a continuation of the last question. The expression **sin fin** (without end) is a big clue here, because it tells you that Emma's going to be unhappy for a long time. The fact that her grief is ongoing, without end, really only leaves one possible answer, and that's **seguiría**.

36. (A) took out
    (B) saved
    (C) found
    (D) took away

In this sentence, Emma does something with her letter. Since we know she already has it and has read it, (A) and (C) wouldn't make sense. **Quitó** is just strange, so that leaves us with (B).

37. (A) knows
    (B) knew
    (C) knew (imp. subj.)
    (D) began

The saving grace on this question is the **como si** that comes just before the blank, which tells you to use the imperfect subjunctive, since it is a hypothetical event. Luckily, only one choice is in the imperfect subjunctive, because this would be a very tough question to do based on meaning alone.

Después <u>de</u> haber mandado dos expediciones a

explorar la costa de México, el gobernador de Cuba

<u>organizó</u> otra expedición bajo el mando de Hernán Cortés

en 1519. En las tres expediciones <u>tomó</u> parte un soldado

que se <u>llamaba</u> Bernal Díaz del Castillo. <u>Este</u> soldado,

cuando ya era casi un viejo y <u>vivía</u> retirado en Guatemala,

<u>escribió</u> sus recuerdos de las guerras mexicanas, que

forman la mejor narración <u>sobre</u> la conquista de México

y que se titula "Historia verdadera de la conquista de la

Nueva España."

    La expedición de Cortés constaba de once navíos

que <u>llevaban</u> poco más de seiscientos hombres y dieciséis

<u>caballos</u>. Cuando Cortés estaba listo <u>para</u> salir, el

gobernador trató de quitarle el mando, pero él decidió

hacerse a la mar.

After having led two expeditions to explore the coast of Mexico, the governor of Cuba *organized* another expedition under the command of Hernán Díaz del Castillo in 1519. A soldier whose *name was* Bernal Díaz del Castillo *took* part in the three expeditions. *This* soldier, when he was almost an old man and *lived* retired in Guatemala, *wrote* his memoirs of the Mexican wars, which form the best narrative *about* the conquest of Mexico and are titled "The True History of the Conquest of New Spain."

Cortés's expedition consisted of eleven ships that *carried* little more than six hundred men and sixteen *horses*. When Cortés was ready to leave, the governor tried to take command from him, but he decided to set out to sea.

38. (A) that
    (B) of
    (C) to
    (D) for

The preposition that follows **después** to mean "after" is **de**. It's on your list of prepositions.

39. (A) put an end to
    (B) rehearsed
    (C) asked
    (D) organized

The only answers that make any kind of sense in the blank are (A) and (D). How do we know whether the governor organized or put an end to the next expedition? We know a third one happened because in the very next sentence it talks about three expeditions. By skipping a question and reading on you can sometimes find a clue that helps answer an earlier question.

40. (A) made
    (B) gave
    (C) left
    (D) took

Although a couple of the answers are a bit awkward in the blank (namely (A) and (C)), it really helps on this question if you know that the expression **tomar parte** means "to take part." If you didn't know this expression, you should've eliminated (A) and (C) and guessed.

41. (A) was named (preterite)
    (B) is named
    (C) was named (imperfect)
    (D) had been named

Here, what you want to say is "was named." We know it's going to be some kind of past tense, but which past tense is appropriate? Well, a person's name goes on for a period of time, so it's not the regular past, which cancels (A). (D) makes no sense, because it implies that Castillo's name changed at some point in the past. That leaves the imperfect, which is choice (C).

42. **(A) This (masc.)**
    (B) That (fem.)
    (C) A (masc.)
    (D) The (fem.)

Soldado is masculine, so (B) and (D) are immediately out. The sentence goes on to discuss the soldier in question, so what you want to say is "this soldier."

43. (A) stopped
    (B) thought
    (C) heard
    (D) lived

Look at the adjective that follows the blank (**retirado**). Even if you've never seen this word before, you can tell what it means because it's just like the English equivalent. Does a person *stop* retired, *think* retired, or *hear* retired? None of those makes sense, so that leaves only (D).

44. **(A) wrote**
    (B) ran
    (C) lost
    (D) asked for

The blank in this case precedes **recuerdos**, which can mean memories. However, in this case it means memoirs, which is a hint that something having to do with writing (like **escribió**) would be the correct answer. If you missed **recuerdos**, the word **título** is mentioned later on, followed by a title with quotes. Look around for clues; don't just stick to the immediate area where the blank is.

45. (A) on top of
    (B) next to
    (C) on; about
    (D) instead of

The meaning you want for this blank is roughly "about," because you're providing a preposition that describes the relationship between the memoirs and their subject (memoirs are *about* a subject). **Encima de** means "on," like "on top of" or "above," not "about." **En vez de** and **junto a** don't mean anything close to "about."

46. (A) carried
     (B) carried (pl.)
     (C) carried (pl. imperfect)
     (D) carry

The verb **(llevar)** in this blank refers back to the plural subject **navíos**, so you know the answer must be plural, which leaves (B), (C), and (D). If you back up just a bit earlier in the sentence, you notice that we're in the imperfect tense (**constaba** tells you). Even if you only knew it was some type of past tense you could eliminate (D) (**llevan** is present tense) and guess.

47. (A) cars
     (B) airplanes
     (C) horses
     (D) gloves

The big hint on this question is that the passage deals with events that happened in the late sixteenth century, before the invention of the airplane and the automobile. "Gloves" could work, but "horses" (a means of transportation) is a much more likely answer.

48. (A) for
     (B) to
     (C) in
     (D) of

This question asks for the preposition that precedes **salir**. Although (C) and (D) make no sense, that still leaves you with the decision between **para** and **por**. In this case, the destination of his being ready (his purpose) is to leave, so **para** is correct.

> Pero hoy, esta mañana fría, en que tenemos más prisa que nunca, la niña y yo <u>pasamos</u> de largo delante de la fila tentadora de autos parados. Por <u>primera</u> vez en la vida vamos al colegio... Al colegio, le digo, no <u>se puede</u> ir en taxi. Hay que correr un poco por las calles, hay que tomar el metro, hay que <u>caminar</u> luego, en un sitio determinado, a un autobús... Es que yo he escogido un colegio muy <u>lejano</u> para mi niña, ésa es la verdad; un colegio que <u>me gusta</u> mucho, pero está muy lejos.... Sin embargo, yo no estoy impaciente hoy, ni <u>cansada</u>, y la niña lo sabe. Es ella ahora la que inicia una caricia tímida con su manita <u>dentro de</u> la mía; y por primera vez me doy cuenta de que su mano de cuatro años es <u>igual a</u> mi mano grande: tan decidida, tan suave, tan nerviosa como la mía.

But today, on this cold morning, in which we're in a bigger hurry than ever, the girl and I *pass by* the tempting line of stopped cars. For *the first* time in our lives we're going to school... To school, I tell her, *you cannot* go by taxi. You have to run through the streets a bit, take the subway, then *walk* in a specific place to a bus.... It's that I've chosen a school that's very *far* for my daughter, that is the truth; a school that *I like* very much, but is very far away. However, I'm not impatient today, nor *tired*, and the girl knows it. It is now she who initiates a timid caress with her little hand *inside* mine; and for the first time I realize that her four-year-old hand is *the same as* my adult one: just as resolute, just as soft, and just as nervous as mine.

49. **(A) we passed**
    (B) we entered
    (C) we gave
    (D) we paid

The preposition **delante de** (in front of) that comes shortly after the blank is the main clue on this question. The only verb that makes sense before this expression is (A).

50. (A) none
    (B) first
    (C) always
    (D) habit

The word **vez** (time, occasion) immediately follows the blank, and the only choice that forms an expression in conjunction with **vez** is (B).

51. (A) tricks herself
    (B) we know
    (C) one can
    (D) have left over

The sentence is about getting to school by taxi. Earlier in the passage it says that they passed by a row of taxis. But that only gets rid of (A) and (D) because we don't know why they passed by the taxis. If you think about (B) carefully though, it doesn't make sense. *They* wouldn't have to know how to get to school in a taxi, the *taxi driver* would.

52. (A) to sleep
    (B) to touch
    (C) to play
    (D) to walk

You wouldn't "sleep," "touch," or "play" in order to get to a bus stop. Walking, on the other hand, seems likely.

53. (A) closed
    (B) far away
    (C) dark
    (D) difficult

This blank describes the type of school that the mother chose for her daughter. Common sense eliminates (A) and (C). If you're stuck at this point, you just need to look forward a bit to find the clue that singles out (B) as the best answer: **está muy lejos.**

54. **(A) I like**
    (B) I hate
    (C) I don't know
    (D) we doubt

The blank is followed by the expression **pero está muy lejos**. The **pero** tells you that a positive quality about the school came immediately before the expression (the word **pero** indicates a contrast, as in "strict *but* fair"). This gets rid of (B) and (D), and (C) makes no sense because the mother in the passage chose this school for her daughter, whom she seems to love very much. Would she send her daughter to a school she didn't know? Probably not.

55. (A) old
    (B) tall
    (C) tired
    (D) fresh

The verb **estar** is used in this sentence, and that eliminates **vieja** because **vieja** would be used with **ser** (ella *es* vieja). The same is true for **alta** (ella *es* alta). **Fresca** is a word you more likely use for fruit or vegetables.

56. **(A) inside**
    (B) outside
    (C) close to
    (D) without

Here the daughter is making an affectionate gesture **(caricia)** toward her mom by putting her hand somewhere in relation to her mom's hand. Choices (B) and (D) suggest just the opposite, as if she were making a negative gesture. Answer (C) is fine, but really doesn't make a lot of sense if you really think about it: You wouldn't put your hand *close to* someone else's to show affection, you'd put your hand *in* someone else's.

57. (A) different from
    (B) equal to, the same as
    (C) close to
    (D) on top of

The giveaway for this question follows the blank: **tan**. **Tan** by itself means "so," but the expression **tan...como** means "equal to."

PART C

Al pasar ante una granja, un perro mordió a mi amigo. Entramos a ver al granjero y le preguntamos si era suyo el perro. El granjero, para evitarse complicaciones, dijo que no era suyo.

—Entonces—dijo mi amigo—présteme una hoz para cortarle la cabeza, pues debo llevarla al Instituto para que la analicen.

En aquel momento apareció la hija del granjero y le pidió a su padre que no permitiera que le cortáramos la cabeza al perro.

—Si es suyo el perro—dijo mi amigo—enséñeme el certificado de vacunación antirrábica.

El hombre entró en la granja, y tardó largo rato en salir. Mientras tanto, el perro se acercó y mi amigo dijo:

—No me gusta el aspecto de este animal.

En efecto, babeaba y los ojos parecían arderle en las órbitas. Incluso andaba dificultosamente.

—Hace unos días—dijo la joven—le atropelló una bicicleta.

El granjero nos dijo que no encontraba el certificado de vacunación.

—Debo haberlo perdido.

—La vida de un hombre puede estar en juego—intervine yo. Díganos, con toda sinceridad, si el perro está vacunado o no.

El hombre bajó la cabeza y murmuró:

—Está sano.

Upon passing in front of a farm, a dog bit my friend. We went in to see the farmer and asked him if the dog were his. The farmer, in order to avoid trouble, said it was not his.

"Then," said my friend, "lend me a scythe to cut off his head, since I should take it to the Institute so they can analyze it."

At that moment the farmer's daughter appeared and asked her father not to let us cut off the dog's head.

"If the dog is yours," said my friend, "show me the certificate of rabies vaccination."

The man went into the farmhouse, and took a long time to come back out. Meanwhile, the dog approached, and my friend said:

"I don't like the way this animal looks."

Essentially, he foamed at the mouth and his eyes seemed to burn in their sockets. He also walked with difficulty.

"A few days ago," said the girl, "a bicycle hit him."

The farmer told us that he didn't find the certificate of vaccination.

"I must have lost it."

"The life of a man may be at stake," I interjected. "Tell us, in all honesty, if the dog is vaccinated or not."

The man bowed his head and murmured:

"He's healthy."

58. What happened to the men when they passed by the farm?

   (A) **a dog bit one of them**
   (B) a farmer asked them for directions
   (C) they avoided complications
   (D) they lost their dog

The answer to this question is in the first sentence of the passage. Normally the progression of the questions follows the progression of the passage. The earlier a question is, the earlier in the passage you'll find its answer.

59. Why did the farmer tell them that the dog wasn't his?

   (A) he didn't know whose dog it was
   (B) he didn't know the men who came to the door
   (C) **he didn't want to take blame for what the dog had done**
   (D) he didn't like dogs

In the passage (third line) it says that the farmer wanted to **evitarse complicaciones** (avoid trouble). The answer closest to that in meaning is (C). Some of the other answers are reasonable, but they aren't in the passage.

60. What did the farmer's daughter ask of him?

   (A) that he allow her to buy candies
   (B) that he take the dog to the doctor
   (C) that he give food to the dog
   (D) **that he not let the men hurt the dog**

The guide word for this question is **hija.** The first place where **hija** appears (and the source of the answer) is toward the beginning.

61. What did the men ask the farmer for?

   (A) a glass of water
   (B) **the certificate of rabies vaccination**
   (C) a telephone to call the police
   (D) proof that he was really a farmer

The certificate of rabies vaccination, and whether the farmer has it, is the focus of most of the passage, so (B) is the answer.

62. How did the farmer's dog seem?

   (A) healthy and in good humor
   (B) **sick, as if it had rabies**
   (C) youthful and full of energy
   (D) serious and thoughtful

Most of the passage is concerned with vaccinations (**vacunaciones**) and whether or not to cut off the dog's head and have it inspected. You probably wouldn't do this to a happy, healthy dog (unless you're some kind of sick weirdo), so you can eliminate (A) and (C) immediately. You probably wouldn't decapitate a dog for being **serio y pensativo** either, so (D) is out. That leaves you with (B). Pretty simple.

63. What reason did the girl give for the way the dog behaved?

(A) it had an accident with a bicycle
(B) it just had its rabies shot
(C) it's a very ferocious dog
(D) it was very hungry

Once again, this question deals with the daughter, who is referred to as **la joven** as well as **hija** and **niña** in different parts of the passage.

64. Finally, what does the farmer tell the men?

(A) to go to a hospital
(B) to adopt a dog
(C) that they should leave the farm right now
(D) that the dog has no disease

En fin is a pretty strong hint that the answer's toward the end. The correct choice is (D).

> En nuestra oficina regía el mismo presupuesto desde
> el año mil novecientos veintitantos, o sea desde una época
> en que la mayoría de nosotros estábamos luchando con
> la geografía y con los quebrados. Sin embargo, el Jefe se
> acordaba del acontecimiento y a veces, cuando el trabajo
> disminuía, se sentaba familiarmente sobre uno de nuestros
> escritorios, y así, con las piernas colgantes que mostraban
> después del pantalón unos inmaculados calcetines
> blancos, nos relataba con la misma emoción de antes y
> las quinientas noventa y ocho palabras de costumbre,
> el lejano y magnífico día en que su Jefe—él era entonces
> Oficial Primero—le había palmeado el hombro y le había
> dicho: "Muchacho, tenemos presupuesto nuevo", con la
> sonrisa amplia y satisfecha del que ya ha calculado cuántas
> camisas podrá comprar con el aumento.

In our office, the same budget was in force since the 1920s, that is, since a time in which the majority of us were struggling with geography and fractions. The Boss, however, remembered the event, and at times, when the work diminished, he would sit down familiarly on one of our desks, and there, with his legs dangling, and immaculate white socks showing below his trousers, he would tell us, with all his old feeling and with his usual five hundred and ninety-eight words, of that distant and splendid day when his Boss—he was Head Clerk then—had patted him on the shoulder and had said, "My boy, we have a new budget," with the broad and satisfied smile of a man who has already worked out how many new shirts he will be able to buy with the increase.

65. For more or less how much time have they had the same budget?

(A) for many decades
(B) for many centuries
(C) for a few weeks
(D) since yesterday

There are a few answers (namely B, C, and D) that are pretty silly in the context of the story, but this is more apparent as you read further into the passage. If you didn't get **novecientos veintitantos**, then you should have read on. There are lots of clues later on that give you the time frame of the budget.

66. The Boss told his story when

  (A) he was sad
  (B) he had drunk too much beer
  (C) the work was less than usual
  (D) they had a party

Disminuía means decreased or diminished. **Jefe** is one guide word on this question, and **cuento** is sort of another, although **acontecimiento** is the actual word in the passage.

67. The story of the new budget that the Boss told

  (A) had white socks
  (B) was always different
  (C) was interesting
  (D) was always the same

Palabras de costumbre (usual words) is the key to this one.

68. What was the boss's reaction when his Boss told him about the new budget?

  (A) he left the company
  (B) he became very happy
  (C) he gave his boss a hug
  (D) he bought new shirts

Answer (D) is a pretty nasty trap, but if you read carefully you could have avoided it.

> Para los arqueólogos y los historiadores, la civilización maya es, sin duda ninguna, la que alcanzó un mayor nivel de desarrollo entre todas las civilizaciones que existían antes de la llegada de Colón. Aunque todavía hay muchos secretos que no se han descifrado con relación a los mayas, parece que esta civilización empezó varios siglos antes del nacimiento de Cristo. Sin embargo se sabe que los mayas abandonaron los grandes centros ceremoniales en el siglo X de nuestra era.
>
> Los primeros templos que construyeron son de forma de pirámide de cuatro lados con una gran escalinata. Sobre la pirámide hay un edificio de un piso normalmente, y en algunos casos de dos, y en ellos podemos ver relieves de arcilla y esculturas de madera y piedra caliza. Las figuras son siempre de perfil y en ellas se puede apreciar los adornos y joyas que usaban. En la clasificación que se ha hecho de las épocas de esta civilización, se llama preclásica a la época primera, que se desarrolla en Guatemala y Honduras, y que según los arqueólogos duró hasta el fin del siglo III de nuestra era.

For archaeologists and historians, the Mayan civilization is, without a doubt, the one that reached the highest level of development among all the civilizations that existed before the arrival of Columbus. Although there are still many secrets that have not been deciphered with regard to the Mayas, it seems that this civilization began many centuries before the birth of Christ. However, it's known that the Mayas abandoned their large ceremonial centers in the tenth century of our era.

The first temples they built were pyramid-shaped, with four sides and a huge outside stairway. On top of the pyramid there is an edifice that is normally one story, and in some cases two, and in them we can see clay reliefs and statues made of wood and limestone. The figures are always in profile, and in them one can appreciate the adornments and jewels that they used. In the classification that has been made of the epochs of this civilization, the first, which developed in Guatemala and Honduras, is called the pre-classic era and, according to archaeologists, it lasted until the end of the third century of our era.

69. What do the archaeologists and historians think of the Mayan civilization?

   (A) that it was a very advanced civilization
   (B) that the Mayas wrote wonderful books
   (C) that they knew Columbus
   (D) that they had many secrets

Arqueólogos and **historiadores** are the guide words here.

70. When did the Mayan civilization begin?

   (A) in the tenth century of our era
   (B) immediately before Columbus's arrival
   (C) many centuries before Christ's birth
   (D) many centuries after Christ's birth

It's technically not a guide word, but **cuando** tells you that you want to look for a date or year.

71. How did the first Mayan temples seem?

   (A) they were very short buildings
   (B) they were made of wood and limestone
   (C) they were pyramids of four faces
   (D) they were ordinary houses, like the ones we have today

Templos is your guide for this question.

72. What can be said about the sculptures that the Mayas made?

   (A) they had large outside staircases
   (B) they give information about the jewels and adornments that they used
   (C) it costs a lot to buy them
   (D) one can find them in famous museums

Esculturas tells you where to look, but you've still got to read with care.

73. Where did the pre-classic era begin and develop?

   (A) in Nicaragua
   (B) in Mexico
   (C) in the pre-classic era
   (D) in Honduras and Guatemala

Preclásica only appears at the end of the passage, which is where the answer lies.

74. The passage deals with

  (A) Mayan civilization and architecture
  (B) Christ's influence on Mayan civilization
  (C) the difference between our civilization and
      Mayan civilization
  (D) the adornments and jewels that the Mayas used

This one's a little tricky. The passage does mention Christ (**Cristo**), whose name appears in (B), and adornments and jewels (**adornos y joyas**), which appear in answer choice (D), but it also deals with other stuff. (B) and (D) are too specific. Omit them. The passage doesn't specifically compare Mayan culture to any other culture, including ours, so (C) is out. That leaves (A), a nice, general, correct answer.

En 1992 se cumplieron cinco siglos ya del encuentro de Europa con América. Fue poco después de la medianoche del 11 al 12 de octubre de 1492, cuando Rodrigo de Triana, un tripulante de la carabela "La Niña", la cual se había adelantado a "La Santa María", donde iba Colón, dio el grito de "¡Tierra! ¡Tierra!" El lugar estaba muy cercano a la Florida, era una pequeña isla llamada Guanahaní a la que Colón llamó San Salvador y que pertenece al archipiélago de las Lucayas o Bahamas.

Lo que Colón encontró y describe en sus cartas a los Reyes Católicos fue mucha pobreza y gente que iba desnuda, como su madre los parió, todos jóvenes, con hermosos cuerpos, cabellos gruesos como los de los caballos y cortos, que les caían por encima de las cejas y otros largos por detrás.

Pocos días después, descubrió la costa de Cuba, que llamó Juana, por la hija de los reyes. Por entonces, Martín Alonso Pinzón, que mandaba "La Pinta", se separó de la expedición, lo cual consideró Colón como una deserción, aunque lo disimuló por mantener la unidad de la expedición. Al cabo de unos días llegó a Haití, que llamó la Hispaniola, pero debido a los muchos bajos y arrecifes que había, "La Santa María" encalló.

In 1992, five centuries were completed since the meeting of Europe and America. It was shortly after midnight between the 11th and 12th of October in 1492 when Rodrigo de Triana, a crew member of the ship "La Niña," which had gone ahead of "The Santa María," where Columbus went, let out the shout of "Land! Land!" The place was very close to Florida, a small island named Guanaháni which Columbus called San Salvador and which belongs to the archipelago of the Lucayas, or Bahamas.

What Columbus found and describes in his letters to the Catholic king and queen was much poverty and people who went about naked, as their mothers bore them, all young, with beautiful bodies, thick heads of hair like horse's which fell over their eyebrows and which others wore long in back.

A few days later, he discovered the coast of Cuba, which he called Juana, after the daughter of the king and queen. At that point, Martín Alonso Pinzón, who captained "The Pinta," pulled away from the expedition, which Columbus considered an act of desertion, although he overlooked it to maintain the unity of the expedition. At the end of a few days he reached Haiti, which he called Hispaniola, but because of the many sandbanks and reefs that were there, "The Santa María" ran aground.

75. Who was the first to see land in the expedition?

   (A) a sailor named Rodrigo de Triana
   (B) Columbus
   (C) *The Niña*
   (D) Guanahaní, Columbus's best friend

You can knock off (C) without looking back at the passage. Once you look back, the answer is in the sentence containing **tierra**.

76. What were the people who Columbus found like?

   (A) very poor, but also beautiful
   (B) violent and agressive
   (C) smarter than the sailors
   (D) very scared and confused

This question doesn't really have guide words, but luckily there is an entire paragraph about this topic, so it shouldn't have been too tough to locate the source of the question.

77. What did Columbus discover a few days after he discovered San Salvador?

   (A) the archipelago of the Bahamas
   (B) the island that today is called Cuba
   (C) Haiti
   (D) thick hair

This is a tricky question, because it's easy to think that **San Salvador** is the guide, when actually **pocos días después** is your clue on this one. If you have trouble locating the source of a question, just skip it and come back to it later.

78. What was Columbus's reaction when Martín Alonso Pinzón separated from the expedition?

   (A) he became furious
   (B) he started to cry
   (C) he gave the impression that he didn't know what had happened
   (D) he sent another ship after him

The name Martín Alonso Pinzón is the guide on this one, and it only appears once.

79. How did the *Santa María* end up?

   (A) it returned to Spain
   (B) it was lost and they have never found it
   (C) it sank
   (D) it ran aground as a result of reefs and shallows

The name of the ship is the big clue here. The location of the question tells you to look toward the end of the passage.

Si no fuera por el gusto exigente de los bebedores de café de Arabia Saudita, el pueblo guatemalteco de Cobán, al otro lado del mundo, estaría en problemas.

Cobán, capital de la región montañosa de Alta Verapaz, en Guatemala, es la fuente de la mayor parte del cardamomo que consume el mundo árabe: una especia dulce, picante y sumamente aromática que se emplea en la cocina de la India. De hecho, el café de cardamomo, conocido en el mundo árabe como *kahwe hal*, es considerado un símbolo de hospitalidad en todo el Cercano Oriente.

En Cobán, famoso por su iglesia católica del siglo XVI y las ruinas mayas que se encuentran en los alrededores, prácticamente nadie habla árabe y ninguno de sus 125.000 habitantes pone cardamomo en el café. Sin embargo, todos conocen perfectamente la conexión que existe entre la especia y el mundo árabe. "El cardamomo es la base de nuestra economía, y Guatemala es el principal exportador del mundo."

If it weren't for the demanding taste of the coffee drinkers of Saudi Arabia, the Guatemalan town of Cobán, on the other side of the world, would be in big trouble.

Cobán, capital of the mountainous region of Alta Verapaz, in Guatemala, is the source of the majority of cardamom that the Arab world consumes: a sweet spice, pungent and extremely aromatic that is used in Indian cooking. As a matter of fact, coffee with cardamom, known in the Arab world as *kahwe hal*, is considered a symbol of hospitality in all of the Near East.

In Cobán, famous for its 16th-century Catholic church and the Mayan ruins that are found in its environs, practically no one speaks Arabic, and none of its 125,000 inhabitants puts cardamom in his/her coffee. However, they all know perfectly well the connection that exists between the spice and the Arab world. "Cardamom is the base of our economy, and Guatemala is the principal exporter in the world."

80. In which country in particular do they drink coffee with cardamom?

    (A) in Guatemala
    (B) in Saudi Arabia
    (C) in Alta Verapaz
    (D) in the Near East

A couple of answers (the ones that aren't countries) can be eliminated right away.

81. What is cardamom?

    (A) a rare type of coffee
    (B) a spice
    (C) an Indian style of cooking
    (D) a type of tree

Even if you'd never seen the word **especia**, POE works really well on this question.

82. How does cardamom taste?

(A) sharp, but also sweet
(B) a bit bitter
(C) it hardly has any flavor
(D) it tastes like Colombian coffee

The answer to this one is in the paragraph that describes the spice.

83. For what is the city of Cobán known?

(A) for cardamom
(B) for the best coffee in North America
**(C) for its ruins, and for its
16th-century church**
(D) for the Indian food

Choice (A) is an easy trap to fall for if you're lazy on this one and don't look back. For those who weren't lazy, the answer is right at the top of the final paragraph. Look back to the passage on the specific questions.

84. What is the connection between the
Arab world and Guatemala?

(A) in Guatemala everyone speaks Arabic
(B) in both places they love coffee with cardamom
**(C) Guatemala exports much spice to the
Arab world**
(D) there really is no connection between the
two places

Although the answer to this one is in the last paragraph (**conexión** is your guide), the relationship is mentioned earlier in the passage as well.

85. What would be a good title for the passage?

(A) "Cobán: The City in the Mountains"
(B) "The Economy of Guatemala"
(C) "The Coffees of the World"
**(D) "Cardamom: What Joins Guatemala with the
Arab World"**

Remember, the answer to a question like this must include the ideas of the whole passage. (B) is only a partially correct answer (it's not wrong, but it doesn't tell the whole story).

Practice Test 2

SPANISH SUBJECT TEST 2

Your responses to Spanish Subject Test 2 questions must be filled in on Test 2 of your answer sheet (at the back of the book). Marks on any other section will not be counted toward your Spanish Subject Test score.

When your supervisor gives the signal, turn the page and begin the Spanish Subject Test.

SPANISH SUBJECT TEST

PLEASE NOTE THAT YOUR ANSWER SHEET HAS FIVE ANSWER POSITIONS MARKED A, B, C, D, E, WHILE THE QUESTIONS THROUGHOUT THIS TEST CONTAIN ONLY FOUR CHOICES. BE SURE <u>NOT</u> TO MAKE ANY MARKS IN COLUMN E.

Part A

<u>Directions:</u> This part consists of a number of incomplete statements, each having four suggested completions. Select the most appropriate completion and fill in the corresponding oval on the answer sheet.

---

1. Hay siete días en una semana y cuatro semanas en -------.

    (A) un siglo
    (B) una estación
    (C) un mes
    (D) una década

2. Me gustaría realmente comprar un traje nuevo, pero ¡me encantan estos zapatos! ¿ ------- ?

    (A) Cómo son
    (B) Cuáles son
    (C) Cuándo cuestan
    (D) Cuántos cuestan

3. Mi abuela me tejía un suéter y ------- una revista a la vez.

    (A) leyera
    (B) leía
    (C) había leído
    (D) lee

4. Los pulmones están ------- del pecho.

    (A) debajo
    (B) arriba
    (C) en medio
    (D) dentro

5. Los empleados no han trabajado desde el miércoles pasado porque ------- un incendio ese día que destruyó el edificio donde trabajan.

    (A) hubo
    (B) haya
    (C) habría
    (D) hay

6. Aunque no teníamos mucho dinero, no había ------- problema con pagar nuestra cuenta.

    (A) algún
    (B) alguna
    (C) ninguna
    (D) ningún

7. Tú ------- a Francisco en el estadio durante el partido de fútbol el sábado pasado.

    (A) conociste
    (B) conoces
    (C) conozcas
    (D) conocerás

8. ¿ ------- dónde son los Gutiérrez? Me parece que son guatemaltecos, pero no sé con toda seguridad.

    (A) Para
    (B) A
    (C) De
    (D) En

9. La música cubana fue ------- muy bien por la orquesta del Hotel Playa de Oro.

    (A) oída
    (B) hecha
    (C) leída
    (D) tocada

GO ON TO THE NEXT PAGE

10. Después de que yo los esperé una hora y media,
------- llegaron mis hermanos a visitarme.

   (A) por casualidad
   (B) por fin
   (C) por supuesto
   (D) por favor

11. Es ridículo que las naciones del mundo no
------- vivir en paz.

   (A) podían
   (B) puedan
   (C) pudieron
   (D) pueden

12. Me alegro que Ud. esté en casa, Don Alejandro,
quería ------- un favor.

   (A) sacarte
   (B) pedirlo
   (C) pedirle
   (D) prestarle

13. Uds. vivirían en una mansión gigante y espléndida si
------- millonarios.

   (A) son
   (B) habrían sido
   (C) sean
   (D) fueran

14. ------- tú no entiendes es que odio las alcachofas.

   (A) Que
   (B) Cual
   (C) Lo que
   (D) Como

15. Después de nadar un poco, Marta se secó porque
estaba muy -------.

   (A) mojada
   (B) molesta
   (C) enferma
   (D) lista

16. Nuestro primo es famoso porque ------- el papel de
Don Quijote en una obra de teatro hace muchos años.

   (A) tocó
   (B) puso
   (C) jugó
   (D) hizo

17. Yo tengo diez y siete años, pero mi hermana
------- sólo tiene quince años.

   (A) mayor
   (B) mejor
   (C) menor
   (D) peor

18. Cuando vayamos de compras el lunes que viene
------- a las tiendas más exclusivas.

   (A) vayamos
   (B) iremos
   (C) fuimos
   (D) vamos

19. Ricardo habla alemán y ruso muy -------.

   (A) malos
   (B) malas
   (C) mal
   (D) maldad

20. Uds. están furiosos que nosotros no ------- nada de la
cultura puertorriqueña.

   (A) sabemos
   (B) supimos
   (C) hemos sabido
   (D) sepamos

21. Allí está el paraguas de Alicia, pero ¿dónde está
------- ?

   (A) el tuyo
   (B) tuyo
   (C) la tuya
   (D) tuya

22. Ramón compró un anillo para su amiga y ------- dio a
ella para su cumpleaños.

   (A) lo
   (B) le
   (C) se la
   (D) se lo

GO ON TO THE NEXT PAGE

23. Ya que has pasado tanto tiempo en el campo, ahora te ------- las montanas.

    (A) encantas
    (B) encantan
    (C) encanta
    (D) encantes

24. La prestigiosa familia contrató al pintor para pintar ------- de su matriarca, la Sra. Pedregal.

    (A) un retrato
    (B) un vaso
    (C) un césped
    (D) un recado

25. Aunque Lucía y Roberto no querían hacer su trabajo, lo hicieron -------.

    (A) de todos modos
    (B) a primera vista
    (C) al azar
    (D) por desgracia

26. Después de recibir una mala nota en su examen final, Manuel ------- muy enojado y se fue del cuarto.

    (A) se volvió
    (B) se hizo
    (C) se puso
    (D) llegó a ser

27. Las butacas mejores ------- en el fondo del teatro, porque se puede ver toda la pantalla desde allí.

    (A) son
    (B) están
    (C) hay
    (D) hayan

28. El papá de Joaquín es un abogado que se especializa en ------- de los impuestos.

    (A) la piedra
    (B) el ajo
    (C) el sótano
    (D) la ley

29. Desde que me mudé a la Argentina paso mucho tiempo pensando ------- mis amigos en Paraguay.

    (A) de
    (B) en
    (C) que
    (D) con

GO ON TO THE NEXT PAGE

SPANISH SUBJECT TEST–*Continued*

Part B

<u>Directions:</u> In each of the following passages, there are numbered blanks indicating that words or phrases have been omitted. For each numbered blank, four completions are provided. First read through the entire paragraph. Then, for each numbered blank, choose the completion that is most appropriate given the context of the entire paragraph and fill in the corresponding oval on the answer sheet.

La Sra. Jensen llegó el primer día a la clase diciendo que __(30)__ aprender español. Era obviamente una persona alerta y vivaz. Lo único que __(31)__ distinguía de los otros estudiantes era su __(32)__: en ese momento tenía sesenta y nueve años. Su historia es interesante. El esposo de la Sra. Jensen __(33)__ inesperadamente de un ataque cardíaco cuando ella tenía apenas treinta años, dejándola sola con cuatro hijos y ningún oficio para ganarse la vida. Sus padres habían muerto, los abuelos paternos de sus hijos tenían muy pocos recursos, y ella no tenía otros __(34)__ que la ayudaran. En efecto, la muerte de su esposo __(35)__ destruyó la vida. __(36)__ ver bien su situación, ella __(37)__ que tenía que volver a pensar todos sus planes y rehacer su vida sobre otras bases.

30. (A) querría
    (B) quiera
    (C) quiere
    (D) quería

31. (A) la
    (B) lo
    (C) los
    (D) le

32. (A) ropa
    (B) edad
    (C) comportamiento
    (D) mochila

33. (A) nació
    (B) murió
    (C) habló
    (D) oyó

34. (A) brazos
    (B) cuentos
    (C) mapas
    (D) parientes

35. (A) la
    (B) lo
    (C) le
    (D) se

36. (A) Al
    (B) Para
    (C) Antes de
    (D) A

37. (A) reconoce
    (B) reconozca
    (C) reconocerá
    (D) reconoció

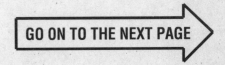

GO ON TO THE NEXT PAGE

—Cuando te sientas mal, mi hijita; le (38) consejos al retrato. El (39) dará. Puedes rezarle, ¿acaso no rezas a los santos?

Este (40) de proceder le pareció extraño a Alejandrina. Mi vida transcurría monótonamente, pues tengo un testigo constante que me prohibe la felicidad: mi dolencia. El doctor Edgardo es la única persona que lo (41) . Hasta el momento de conocerlo (42) ignorando que algo (43) mi organismo me carcomía. Ahora conozco todo lo que sufro: el doctor Edgardo me lo (44). Es mi naturaleza. Algunos (45) con ojos negros, otros con ojos azules. Parece imposible que siendo tan joven él (46) tan sabio; (47) , me he enterado de que no se precisa ser un anciano para serlo. Su piel lisa, sus ojos de niño, su cabellera rubia, ensortijada, son para (48) el emblema de la sabiduría.

38. (A) pidas
    (B) pedirás
    (C) pides
    (D) pediste

39. (A) me lo
    (B) me las
    (C) te los
    (D) te la

40. (A) guante
    (B) tópico
    (C) modo
    (D) relato

41. (A) sabe
    (B) anuncia
    (C) ignora
    (D) muestra

42. (A) viviera
    (B) viví
    (C) vivo
    (D) viva

43. (A) fuera de
    (B) al lado de
    (C) dentro de
    (D) alrededor de

44. (A) ha explicado
    (B) hubiera explicado
    (C) habré explicado
    (D) haya explicado

45. (A) salen
    (B) andan
    (C) mueren
    (D) nacen

46. (A) sería
    (B) fue
    (C) es
    (D) sea

47. (A) porque
    (B) sin embargo
    (C) además
    (D) entonces

48. (A) yo
    (B) mi
    (C) mí
    (D) mío

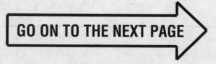
GO ON TO THE NEXT PAGE

Cortejar es pretender en matrimonio a una señorita. En la España del siglo XIX, y en particular en la clase media, existían ciertas costumbres muy (49) que se observaban durante el cortejo. Así, un joven y una joven eran presentados el uno al otro en un evento (50) , por ejemplo, en un baile o una fiesta. Si ellos se gustaban y querían verse otra vez, tenían que (51) una ocasión para un nuevo encuentro. Cuando se veían, a la salida de la misa, durante el intermedio de una obra de teatro, o en el paseo de la tarde, intercambiaban cartitas (52) . La joven le informaba al pretendiente (53) la hora en que (54) al balcón para verse o hablarse calladamente o cuándo iría al paseo, con quién estaría acompañada, dónde se sentaría y las demás señas necesarias. Una vez que la joven pareja decidía (55) , el joven hacía una cita con los padres de la novia y les pedía la mano de su hija en matrimonio. (56) ese momento, se les permitía a los novios verse más a menudo. Pero, por supuesto, la novia siempre era acompañada de una hermana mayor, una tía, una dueña, un hermano u otra persona mayor hasta el día de (57) .

49. (A) perturbadores
    (B) tradicionales
    (C) chocantes
    (D) tontas

50. (A) social
    (B) secreto
    (C) sombrío
    (D) inapropiado

51. (A) olvidar
    (B) mencionar
    (C) buscar
    (D) recordar

52. (A) amorosas
    (B) profesionales
    (C) antiguas
    (D) odiosas

53. (A) para
    (B) de
    (C) a
    (D) con

54. (A) salga
    (B) habían salido
    (C) saldría
    (D) saldrá

55. (A) casarse
    (B) despedirse
    (C) divorciarse
    (D) enfadarse

56. (A) Antes de
    (B) A partir de
    (C) Para
    (D) Con

57. (A) la fiesta
    (B) la boda
    (C) la muerte
    (D) el baile

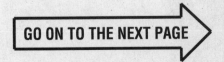
GO ON TO THE NEXT PAGE

Part C

Directions: Read the following texts carefully for comprehension. Each passage is followed by a number of questions or incomplete statements. Select the answer or completion that is best according to the text and fill in the corresponding oval on the answer sheet.

Pasaron días atroces, sin que llegara respuesta. Le envié una segunda carta y luego una tercera y una cuarta, diciendo siempre lo mismo, pero cada vez con mayor desolación. En la última, decidí relatarle todo lo que había pasado aquella noche que siguió a nuestra separación. No escatimé detalle ni bajeza, como tampoco dejé de confesarle la tentación de suicidio. Me dio vergüenza usar eso como arma, pero la usé. Debo agregar que mientras describía mis actos más bajos, y la desesperación de mi soledad en la noche, frente a su casa de la calle Posadas, sentía ternura para conmigo mismo y hasta lloré de compasión. Tenía muchas esperanzas de que María sintiese algo parecido al leer la carta y con esa esperanza me puse bastante alegre.

Cuando despaché la carta, certificada, estaba francamente optimista. A vuelta de correo llegó una carta de María, llena de ternura. Sentí que algo de nuestros primeros instantes de amor volvería a reproducirse…Quería que fuera a la estancia. Como un loco, preparé una valija, una caja de pinturas y corrí a la estación Constitución.

58. ¿Cómo se describiría el estado mental del narrador al principio de este pasaje?

(A) optimista
(B) contento
(C) impaciente
(D) triste

59. ¿A quién le está enviando el narrador sus cartas?

(A) al correo
(B) a la Srta. Posadas
(C) a su prima en la estación Constitución
(D) a su novia lejana

60. ¿Por qué está escribiendo el narrador estas cartas?

(A) quiere visitar a María en su casa
(B) quiere jactarse de las cosas malas que ha hecho
(C) quiere escribirle a María tantas veces como sea posible
(D) quiere explicarse para que María lo entienda mejor

61. ¿Cómo se ha sentido el narrador desde su confrontación con María?

(A) avergonzado
(B) tranquilo
(C) irritado
(D) estable

62. ¿Por qué está feliz el narrador cuando envía su carta?

(A) recibe una carta afectuosa de María
(B) piensa que la carta le va a inspirar el amor a María
(C) no tiene que escribir cartas nunca más
(D) sabe que María va a llorar de compasión

63. ¿Cuál sería la profesión del narrador?

(A) es pintor
(B) es banquero
(C) es soldado
(D) es abogado

GO ON TO THE NEXT PAGE

Los mayas eran oriundos de Guatemala. De Guatemala pasaron a la península de Yucatán en México, a Belice y Honduras. La cultura de los mayas era aún más avanzada que la de los aztecas, a quienes encontró Cortés cuando llegó a México. La arquitectura de los mayas era notable, como atestiguan las famosas ruinas de templos y pirámides en Palenque, Uxmal, Tikal y Copán. Se sitúa el apogeo de su cultura y civilización en el año 250 D.C. Poco antes del año 900 D.C. desaparecieron. Su desaparición ha sido un enigma. No se sabe precisamente por qué desaparecieron. Nuevos descubrimientos arqueológicos indican que existe la posibilidad de que los mayas quisieran lograr una gran expansión territorial y que las confrontaciones bélicas que acompañaban esa expansión fueran la causa más importante de la decadencia del Imperio Maya.

64. Belice y Honduras

    (A) son partes de la cultura azteca
    (B) son los sitios de los templos
        de los mayas
    (C) están cerca de la península de Yucatán
    (D) están en Guatemala

65. El Imperio Maya

    (A) no existió después del año 900 D.C.
    (B) fue una expansión territorial
    (C) fue destruido por Cortés cuando llegó
        a México
    (D) era mejor que el Imperio Azteca

66. El gran misterio de los mayas es

    (A) su apogeo
    (B) sus ruinas
    (C) su éxito
    (D) su desaparición

67. La belicosidad de los mayas se debe a

    (A) los nuevos descubrimientos arqueológicos
    (B) sus confrontaciones en su expansión territorial
    (C) la decadencia de su imperio
    (D) su deseo de ampliar la extensión de su imperio

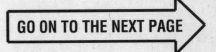

GO ON TO THE NEXT PAGE

Nos conviene pensar en los inmigrantes como miembros de tres grupos. El primer grupo consiste en los que vinieron aquí cuando eran adultos y ya hablaban su lengua materna. El segundo grupo consiste en los que nacieron aquí o vinieron aquí cuando eran niños; son hijos del primer grupo. El tercer grupo consiste en los que nacieron aquí, hijos del segundo grupo. El primer grupo suele aprender un inglés funcional. Es decir, aprenden a expresarse y a comprender bastante bien, pero casi nunca aprenden a hablar sin errores y sin acento. El segundo grupo aprende a hablar inglés perfectamente bien, sin ningún acento extranjero. Pero como hijos de inmigrantes este grupo retiene algo de su primera lengua y muchas veces son bilingües. El tercer grupo suele estar lingüísticamente asimilado, con poco conocimiento funcional de la lengua de sus abuelos. La asimilación de los hispanos se ha estudiado mucho, y se ha visto repetidas veces que la gran mayoría de los inmigrantes hispanos siguen exactamente el mismo patrón que todos los demás inmigrantes. Por lo tanto, la percepción de que los inmigrantes hispanos no quieren aprender inglés es totalmente falsa. Como en el caso de cualquier grupo de inmigrantes, casi todo depende del tiempo que lleve su generación en este país.

68. ¿Qué determina el grupo al cual pertenece el/la inmigrante?

(A) su deseo de aprender inglés
(B) el alcance de su conocimiento de inglés
(C) el país de donde vino originalmente
(D) el número de idiomas en que puede se comunicar

69. ¿Por qué no pierden sus acentos los miembros del primer grupo?

(A) su conocimiento de su lengua nativa es más fuerte
(B) no tienen deseo de aprender una lengua nueva
(C) no necesitan aprender inglés
(D) no se han asimilado bien a la cultura nueva

70. ¿Cuál es la característica principal del segundo grupo?

(A) aprendieron la lengua nueva de sus padres
(B) nacieron en este país
(C) tienen facilidad en dos idiomas
(D) han pasado muy poco tiempo en Estados Unidos

71. ¿Cuál es la gran similitud entre el primer y el tercer grupos?

(A) no están bien asimilados lingüísticamente en este país
(B) solamente pueden hablar un idioma sin error
(C) no creen que haya necesidad de aprender inglés
(D) son inmigrantes a este país

72. ¿Cuál es el patrón que siguen casi todos inmigrantes?

(A) sus oportunidades de aprender la lengua no son muchas
(B) se dividen en tres grupos que hablan sus propios idiomas
(C) tienen la misma percepción de que a ellos les falta el deseo de aprender inglés
(D) el alcance de su asimilación lingüística depende de cuánto tiempo han vivido aquí

73. ¿Cuál sería un buen título para este pasaje?

(A) "Generaciones de asimilación"
(B) "Dificultades con un idioma nuevo"
(C) "Inmigrantes que han aprendido inglés"
(D) "Percepciones erróneas de los inmigrantes"

GO ON TO THE NEXT PAGE

Los estudiantes se pusieron a reír. Primero me molestaron los modales del profesor—era mi segundo día en un país extranjero—pero ahora me daba cólera que me pusiera en ridículo. No dije nada.

—¿Tal vez, continuó, nos hará el honor de tocar "Souvenir de Spa"?

Se trataba de una composición superficialmente brillante, popular en la escuela belga. Contesté que sí, que la tocaría.

—Estoy seguro de que vamos a oírle algo asombroso a este joven que lo sabe todo. Pero, ¿y en qué va a tocar?

Más risa entre los estudiantes. Yo estaba tan furioso que estuve a punto de irme. Pero, recapacité. Quiera o no quiera, me dije, me va a escuchar. Le arrebaté el violoncelo al estudiante que estaba a mi lado y empecé a tocar. Se produjo un gran silencio en la sala. Cuando concluí no se oía un ruido. El profesor me observaba intensamente, tenía una rara expresión en la cara.

—¿Quiere venir a mi oficina?—dijo el profesor.

74. ¿Por qué reían los estudiantes?

(A) los modales del profesor eran muy chistosos
(B) la clase era muy divertida
(C) el maestro acabó de hacer burla del narrador
(D) no había otro ruido en la clase en ese momento

75. ¿Qué es "Souvenir de Spa"?

(A) es una obra de música bien conocida
(B) es una pieza maestra de literatura
(C) es una escultura magnífica
(D) es un poema clásico

76. ¿Cuál es la actitud del maestro hacia el narrador al principio del pasaje?

(A) respeto profundo
(B) apoyo humillado
(C) condescendencia entretenida
(D) desprecio abierto

77. ¿Por qué no sale el narrador en vez de tocar?

(A) es la primera oportunidad que ha tenido de tocar
(B) el profesor está en medio de una diatriba
(C) los otros estudiantes están riendo y divirtiéndose
(D) no ganaría el respeto de nadie si se fuera

78. ¿Qué le pasa al profesor después de la presentación del narrador?

(A) empieza el próximo tema
(B) cambia su opinión del narrador
(C) se expresa de una manera muy rara
(D) se ríe del narrador otra vez

79. ¿Cuál es la razón para el conflicto entre el profesor y el narrador?

(A) el narrador ha interrumpido su clase
(B) el narrador piensa que lo sabe todo
(C) el narrador es un estudiante de otro país
(D) el narrador no conoce "Souvenir de Spa"

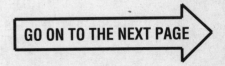
GO ON TO THE NEXT PAGE

Como haces falta, Basilio...Me gustaría tanto que estuvieras presente, con los ojos abiertos y que vieras lo que ha pasado con tu casa. Se está desmoronando, como si la hubieras levantado con ladrillos mal cocidos; se han quebrado las tejas y dejan entrar el sol y la lluvia por todas partes; a las paredes ya no les caben las cuarteaduras, y los hijos, ¡qué te puedo contar de nuestros hijos!

Manuel estuvo aquí, hace unos días, verdaderamente desesperado por las deudas. A él no le pudiste quitar los vicios. Y de ser el que más tenía, se ha quedado sin nada. Me contaron que hasta su mujer y sus hijos lo corrieron.

A Néstor hace mucho tiempo que no lo veo, te confieso que ya casi no veo nada. Pero creo que él anda por el Norte. Como tú no les enseñaste a trabajar, aquí no pudieron hacer nada, por eso se fueron a buscar entre los mendrugos de otra patria, el pan para sus hijos.

Allá también está José.

80. ¿Qué ha pasado durante la ausencia de Basilio?

(A) le han contado de sus hijos
(B) él ha cocido los ladrillos
(C) su casa ha empezado a caerse a pedazos
(D) se ha ido a otra patria

81. ¿Quién es Basilio?

(A) el esposo de la narradora
(B) el hijo de la narradora
(C) la narradora
(D) el hombre con las deudas

82. ¿Cuál es el problema de Manuel?

(A) no puede ver muy bien
(B) se ha quitado sus vicios
(C) su esposa tuvo un bebé
(D) le debe mucho dinero a la gente

83. ¿Dónde está Néstor?

(A) visitando a la narradora
(B) con los mendrugos
(C) en otro país
(D) cocinando pan para sus hijos

84. ¿Quién ha tenido éxito en el pasado y lo ha perdido?

(A) Basilio
(B) Manuel
(C) José
(D) Néstor

85. ¿Qué se podría asumir de José?

(A) a él no le gusta la narradora
(B) no tuvo nada en su propio país
(C) enseñó a Néstor a trabajar
(D) su mujer y sus hijos lo abandonaron

STOP

IF YOU FINISH BEFORE TIME IS CALLED, YOU MAY CHECK YOUR WORK ON THIS TEST ONLY.
DO NOT TURN TO ANY OTHER TEST IN THIS BOOK.

HOW TO SCORE THE PRINCETON REVIEW SPANISH SUBJECT TEST

When you take the real exam, the proctors take away your exam and your bubble sheet and send it to New Jersey where a computer looks at the pattern of filled-in ovals on your exam and gives you a score. We couldn't include even a small computer with this book, so we are providing this more primitive way of scoring your exam.

DETERMINING YOUR SCORE

STEP 1   Using the answers on the next page, determine how many questions you got right and how many you got wrong on the test. Remember, questions that you do not answer do not count as either right answers or wrong answers.

STEP 2   List the number of right answers here.

(A) _____

STEP 3   List the number of wrong answers here. Now divide that number by 3.

(B) _____ ÷ 3 _____ = (C) _____

STEP 4   Subtract the number of wrong answers divided by 3 (C) from the number of correct answers (A). Round this score to the nearest whole number. This is your raw score.

(A) – (C)= _____

STEP 5   To determine your real score, take the number from Step 4 above and look it up in the left column of the Score Conversion Table on page 163; the corresponding score on the right is your score on the exam.

ANSWERS TO SPANISH SUBJECT TEST 2

Question Number	Correct Answer	Right	Wrong	Question Number	Correct Answer	Right	Wrong	Question Number	Correct Answer	Right	Wrong
1	C	___	___	33	B	___	___	65	A	___	___
2	D	___	___	34	D	___	___	66	D	___	___
3	B	___	___	35	C	___	___	67	D	___	___
4	D	___	___	36	A	___	___	68	B	___	___
5	A	___	___	37	D	___	___	69	A	___	___
6	D	___	___	38	B	___	___	70	C	___	___
7	A	___	___	39	C	___	___	71	B	___	___
8	C	___	___	40	C	___	___	72	D	___	___
9	D	___	___	41	A	___	___	73	A	___	___
10	B	___	___	42	B	___	___	74	C	___	___
11	B	___	___	43	C	___	___	75	A	___	___
12	C	___	___	44	A	___	___	76	C	___	___
13	D	___	___	45	D	___	___	77	D	___	___
14	C	___	___	46	D	___	___	78	B	___	___
15	A	___	___	47	B	___	___	79	C	___	___
16	D	___	___	48	C	___	___	80	C	___	___
17	C	___	___	49	B	___	___	81	A	___	___
18	B	___	___	50	A	___	___	82	D	___	___
19	C	___	___	51	C	___	___	83	C	___	___
20	D	___	___	52	A	___	___	84	B	___	___
21	A	___	___	53	B	___	___	85	B	___	___
22	D	___	___	54	C	___	___				
23	B	___	___	55	A	___	___				
24	A	___	___	56	B	___	___				
25	A	___	___	57	B	___	___				
26	C	___	___	58	C	___	___				
27	B	___	___	59	D	___	___				
28	D	___	___	60	D	___	___				
29	B	___	___	61	A	___	___				
30	D	___	___	62	B	___	___				
31	A	___	___	63	A	___	___				
32	B	___	___	64	C	___	___				

THE PRINCETON REVIEW SPANISH SUBJECT TEST
SCORE CONVERSION TABLE

Raw Score	Scaled Score	Raw Score	Scaled Score	Raw Score	Scaled Score
85	800	47	590	9	360
84	800	46	580	8	360
83	800	45	570	7	350
82	800	44	570	6	350
81	790	43	560	5	340
80	790	42	550	4	340
79	780	41	550	3	330
78	780	40	540	2	320
77	770	39	530	1	320
76	770	38	530	0	310
75	760	37	520	−1	310
74	760	36	520	−2	300
73	750	35	510	−3	290
72	750	34	500	−4	290
71	740	33	500	−5	280
70	730	32	490	−6	270
69	730	31	490	−7	260
68	720	30	480	−8	260
37	720	29	470	−9	250
66	710	28	470	−10	240
65	700	27	460	−11	230
64	700	26	460	−12	220
63	690	25	450	−13	220
62	680	24	450	−14	220
61	680	23	440	−15	210
60	670	22	430	−16	210
59	670	21	430	−17	210
58	660	20	420	−18	200
57	650	19	420	−19	200
56	650	18	410	−20	200
55	640	17	410	−21	200
54	630	16	400	−22	200
53	630	15	400	−23	200
52	620	14	390	−24	200
51	620	13	390	−25	200
50	610	12	380	−26	200
49	600	11	380	−27	200
48	590	10	370	−28	200

Practice Test 2:
Answers and
Explanations

PART A

1. There are seven days in a week and four weeks in
-------.

   (A) a century
   (B) a season
   (C) a month
   (D) a decade

The key to this question is time, but all the answers are expressions for specific lengths of time. What to do? Vocabulary knowledge is important here to decide among the answers. We might use POE to eliminate (B) because it's a length of time that's a little more obscure than the rest of the answers, but the only logical answer is (C).

2. I really would like to buy a new suit, but I love these
shoes! -------?

   (A) How are they
   (B) Which are they
   (C) When much are they
   (D) How much are they

The implication here is that I want to buy the shoes instead of a suit. What is the most appropriate question that follows? Choice (A) sounds as if one is asking for a description of the shoes, but if I love them, I must be able to see them! Likewise, (B) makes no sense, unless the person is extremely forgetful, and (C) is just silly and grammatically incorrect. The correct answer, then, is (D).

3. My grandmother knitted/was knitting me a sweater
and ------- a magazine at the same time.

   (A) read/was reading (subjunctive)
   (B) read/was reading
   (C) had read
   (D) reads

The verb **tejía** places the action of the sentence in the past, so (D) (the present) does not correspond. Choice (C) (the pluperfect) places the act of reading the magazine before that of knitting the sweater, but the sentence says **a la vez**, so this is incorrect. Answers (A) and (B) are both in the past tense, but there is no cue for the use of the subjunctive in this sentence, so (A) is out. The correct answer is (B).

4. The lungs are ------- the chest.

   (A) under
   (B) above
   (C) in between
   (D) inside

This is a basic anatomy question as long as you know what the prepositions mean. Answer (D) is obviously correct.

5. The employees haven't worked since last
    Wednesday because ------- a fire on that day which
    destroyed the building where they work.

    (A) there was
    (B) there is (subj.)
    (C) there would be
    (D) there is

The fire occurred last Wednesday, which is in the past, so (B) and (D) are eliminated. The conditional tense in (C) does not apply here because the fire doesn't depend on anything (it already happened), so (A) is the correct answer.

6. Although we didn't have a lot of money, there was
    not ------- problem with paying our bill.

    (A) any (masculine, affirmative)
    (B) any (feminine, affirm.)
    (C) any (fem., negative)
    (D) any (masc., neg.)

Translation doesn't really help here, as you can see. Remember the double negative rule in Spanish—it's mandatory, so (A) and (B) are gone because they are affirmative words, which cannot be used in a negative sentence. The word "any" is an adjective in this sentence, and so must agree in number and gender with the word it modifies, **problema**, which in Spanish is singular and masculine (even though it ends in an **a**), so (C) is eliminated and the correct answer is (D).

7. You ------- Francisco in the stadium during the
    soccer game last Saturday.

    (A) met
    (B) know
    (C) know (subj.)
    (D) will know

El sábado pasado indicates that the action took place in the past, so (B), (C) (the present) and (D) (the future) are omitted. Choice (A) is correct.

8. ------- where are the Gutiérrezes? It seems to me that
    they are Guatemalan, but I don't know for sure.

    (A) For
    (B) To
    (C) From
    (D) In

The sentence is speaking of the nationality of the family—their country of origin. Answers (A) and (B) imply destination, or movement toward something instead of away from it. Because these choices would also require the use of **estar** to make any grammatical sense, they are wrong. Likewise, (D) suggests their current location, and also requires the use of **estar**, so it is incorrect as well. Choice (C) is correct.

9. The Cuban music was ------- very well by the
   orchestra of the Hotel Playa de Oro.

   (A) heard
   (B) made
   (C) read
   (D) played

An orchestra doesn't generally listen to its own or other people's music, so (A) makes no sense whatsoever. "To make music" would make sense in English, but is better represented in Spanish by the verb **componer**, "to compose," so (B) is eliminated. Does an orchestra read music? Sure, and one supposes that if it reads music well then it might be a pretty decent orchestra, but that's not the main function of an orchestra, so (C) is out. Only (D) is right on target.

10. After I waited an hour and a half for them, ------- my
    brothers arrived to visit me.

    (A) by chance
    (B) finally
    (C) of course
    (D) please

The sentence indicates that the reason I was waiting was that my brothers were supposed to come, so (A) is silly, unless their visit is an unbelievable coincidence. Choice (C) indicates that there was never any doubt they would, but I waited an hour and a half—surely I must have started second-guessing at some point. In the context of the sentence, (D) makes no sense. Only (B) puts an end to the waiting.

11. It is ridiculous that the nations of the world ------ not
    live in peace.

    (A) could
    (B) can (subj.)
    (C) could
    (D) can

The implication of (A) and (C) is that the nations of the world were unable to coexist only in the past (or perhaps that these nations don't even exist anymore), which is not the case, and so they are wrong. The present tense is used in (B) and (D), but remember that the subjunctive is used with impersonal expressions that characterize the opinion of the speaker. **Es ridículo** is obviously a personal opinion, not a general truth, so the subjunctive is needed and (B) is the answer.

12. I'm glad you (formal) are home, Don Alejandro, I
    wanted to ------- you a favor.

    (A) extract from you
    (B) ask it
    (C) ask you
    (D) lend you

This question hinges on a student's knowledge of the indirect pronoun to use in formal situations. Choice (B) is a trap for those who attempt to match the pronoun to the direct object **favor**, which, as it's used in this context, does not need one.

13. You (plural) would live in a gigantic and splendid
    mansion if ------- millionaires.

    (A) you (pl.) are
    (B) you (pl.) would have been
    (C) you (pl.) are (subj.)
    (D) you (pl.) were (subj.)

The use of the conditional tense in combination with the word **si** tells us that we are talking about something that is not currently true—it has the condition of first already being a millionaire attached. Placing the action in the present tense, then, would be incorrect, which eliminates (A) and (C). Choice (B) is simply not logical; it is awkward and grammatically incorrect. When you speak about something hypothetical in Spanish, the imperfect subjunctive is always used to indicate such situations, so (D) is correct.

14. ------- you don't understand is that I hate artichokes.

    (A) That
    (B) Which
    (C) What
    (D) As

Choice (B) makes absolutely no sense here, while (D) would make sense only if we eliminated the words **es que**. Choice (A) might seem to make sense if you translate **que** to mean "what," but this is only true when **que** has an accent mark, which indicates that it is being used as an interrogative (question) word. In this instance, **que** (no accent) is a conjunction (connecting word) that should join the two parts of the sentence together logically, which doesn't happen here. Choice (C) means literally "that which" or "the thing which," and this is correct in the context of the sentence.

15. After swimming a while Marta dried off because
    she was very -------.

    (A) wet
    (B) bothered
    (C) sick
    (D) ready

Choice (C) is a basic word of high school Spanish and makes no sense in the context of this sentence, so it's gone. Choice (B) is a pseudo-cognate that indicates that someone is doing something to someone else that he/she doesn't appreciate, which makes no sense. That leaves (A) and (D). She didn't dry off because she was ready to but because of the normal reason, she was wet. The correct answer is (A).

16. Our cousin is famous because ------- the role of Don
    Quijote in a play many years ago.

    (A) he played
    (B) he played
    (C) he played
    (D) he played

Translation doesn't help at all here, as all these verbs mean the same thing in English; however, they have a variety of meanings in Spanish. Choice (A) means "to play an instrument," while (B) means "to play a record or compact disc." Choice (C) is "to play a game," while (D) carries the appropriate meaning of "to play a role" and is correct.

17. I am seventeen years old but my ------- sister is only fifteen.

    (A) older
    (B) better
    (C) younger
    (D) worse

Many people confuse the meanings of (A) and (B) because they seem so similar in spelling, but (A) and (C), and (B) and (D) are actually pairs of opposites. Unless I regularly compare my sisters, (B) and (D) really don't make any sense here. Choice (A) defies logic, so (C) is the appropriate response.

18. When we go shopping next Monday ------- to the most exclusive stores.

    (A) we go/are going (subj.)
    (B) we will go
    (C) we went
    (D) we go/are going

The shopping trip will occur in the future, and going to the stores will obviously occur at that time. Choices (A) and (D) are in the present, and thus don't correspond to the future, but the English translation might confuse some people. They may understand "we are going" to mean "we are going to go," which makes sense, but is not a proper translation. Choice (C) is in the past and does not correspond to the future either. Choice (B) is the only answer that speaks of the future.

19. Ricardo speaks German and Russian very -------.

    (A) bad (masc., pl.)
    (B) bad (fem., pl.)
    (C) badly
    (D) evil

Choices (A) and (B) are incorrect because they modify the wrong part of the sentence—the languages. Choice (D) is way off. The correct answer is (C), which is an adverb, modifying how Ricardo speaks.

20. You (pl.) are furious that we don't ------- anything about the Puerto Rican culture.

    (A) know
    (B) knew
    (C) have known
    (D) know (subj.)

The verb **están** places the action in the present, thus eliminating (B). Remember that the subjunctive is used with expressions of emotion, and the word **furioso** is definitely an emotion, so the use of the indicative in (A) and (C) is incorrect. Choice (D) is correctly in the present tense and the subjunctive mood.

21. There is Alicia's umbrella but where is -------?

    (A) yours (masc. pl.)
    (B) yours (masc.)
    (C) yours (fem. pl.)
    (D) yours (fem.)

The word **tuyo** cannot be used by itself. It is a possessive adjective and must be used in conjunction with the noun that it modifies, thus (B) and (D) are incorrect. In the case of (A) and (C), the words **tuyo** and **tuya** modify **el** and **la** respectively, and are thus appropriate. Remembering that adjectives agree in number with the nouns they modify, and seeing from the sentence that **el paraguas** is a masculine noun, one sees that (A) is correct.

22. Ramón bought a ring for his friend and gave -------
    for her birthday.

    (A) it (masc.)
    (B) him/her
    (C) it (fem.) to her
    (D) it (masc.) to her

Choice (B) makes no sense in the context of the sentence. Choice (A) may seem correct, but it eliminates important information—gave it to whom? Choice (C) says that Ramón gave a feminine noun to his friend. Since there is no feminine noun in the sentence, (C) is wrong. Choice (D) is correct.

23. Since you have spent so much time in the country,
    the mountains now ------- you.

    (A) (you) enchant
    (B) (they) enchant
    (C) (he/she/it) enchants
    (D) (you) enchant (subj.)

Encantar is a verb like **gustar**, which confuses many. Generally, this sentence would read, "now you love the mountains," but one loses the thread of who/what the subject is and who/what the object is with this translation. *The mountains* is the subject of the sentence, and thus the verb must correspond to the third person singular conjugation, which is (B). Choice (A) is a common mistake, which comes from not understanding the way this verb type functions. Choice (C) is way off base, while (D) is out because there are no cues in the sentence that require the use of the subjunctive.

24. The prestigious family commissioned the painter to
    paint ------- of its matriarch, Mrs. Pedregal.

    (A) a portrait
    (B) a glass
    (C) a lawn
    (D) a message

Choice (B) is a relatively common vocabulary word in high school Spanish, while (C) is a little less common, but still within reach. Both can be eliminated readily. Choices (A) and (D) sound very similar, but the proper response is (A).

25. Although Lucía and Roberto did not want to do
    their homework, they did it -------.

    (A) anyway
    (B) at first sight
    (C) at random
    (D) unfortunately

This question relies on a knowledge of idioms. Choice (B) makes absolutely no sense in the context of this sentence. One would hope that (C) were simply not true, but is incorrect because the conjunction **aunque** doesn't lead logically to the second part of the sentence—**porque** would make more sense. While (D) may be the opinion of Lucía and Roberto, it doesn't make any sense, either. Choice (A) is the appropriate response.

26. After receiving a bad grade on his final exam,
    Manuel ------- very angry and left the room.

    (A) became
    (B) became
    (C) became
    (D) became

Again translating doesn't help at all here, as all the verbs mean the same thing in English, though very different things in Spanish. Choice (A) means not only that he became angry, but that he never was happy again—his anger is a permanent condition. Choices (B) and (D) are essentially interchangeable, as they mean "became" in the sense of moving to a new social position or status ("he became a doctor" or "he became a success"). Choice (C) indicates a temporary change in emotional condition, which is the intention of the sentence, and it is thus correct.

27. The best seats ------- at the back of the theater,
    because one can see the entire screen from there.

    (A) are
    (B) are
    (C) there is/are
    (D) they have (subj.)

This sentence locates the best seats, and so this question hinges around the sometimes confusing **ser** vs. **estar** issue. Choice (C) is not correct because **hay** is used only to indicate the general existence of something, not its specific location. Choice (D) makes no sense at all, first because it is an auxiliary (helping) verb, which requires another verb afterwards, second because there are no cues in the sentence that require the use of the subjunctive. The verb **ser** is used to describe permanent characteristics, and so (A) is incorrect. **Estar** is used to locate things, and is thus the answer.

28. Joaquín's father is an attorney who specializes in tax
    -------.

    (A) stone
    (B) garlic
    (C) basement
    (D) law

This is another vocabulary question, just to prove that, no matter how much you think you know, there is always something you might not know. Choice (D) is the only one that makes sense.

29. Since I moved to Argentina I spend a lot of time
    thinking ------- my friends in Paraguay.

    (A) of
    (B) about
    (C) that
    (D) with

Prepositions in Spanish can often change the meaning of a verb very subtly, as is the case in this sentence. Choice (D) is obviously wrong, and we can use the literal translation to get rid of it. Choice (C) is incorrect because the word **que** must introduce a new clause. Choices (A) and (B) can both be translated as "of," but the preposition **de** can only be used with the verb **pensar** in a question. Choice (B) gives the appropriate meaning of the verb.

PART B

La Sra. Jensen llegó el primer día a la clase diciendo que <u>quería</u> aprender español. Era obviamente una persona alerta y vivaz. Lo único que <u>la</u> distinguía de los otros estudiantes era su <u>edad</u>: en ese momento tenía sesenta y nueve años. Su historia es interesante. El esposo de la Sra. Jensen <u>murió</u> inesperadamente de un ataque cardíaco cuando ella tenía apenas treinta años, dejándola sola con cuatro hijos y ningún oficio para ganarse la vida. Sus padres habían muerto, los abuelos paternos de sus hijos tenían muy pocos recursos, y ella no tenía otros <u>parientes</u> que la ayudaran. En efecto, la muerte de su esposo <u>le</u> destruyó la vida. <u>Al</u> ver bien su situación, ella <u>reconoció</u> que tenía que volver a pensar todos sus planes y rehacer su vida sobre otras bases.

Mrs. Jensen arrived to class the first day saying that *she wanted* to learn Spanish. She was obviously an alert and lively person. The only thing that distinguished *her* from the other students was her *age*: at that moment she was seventy-nine years old. Her story is interesting. Mrs. Jensen's husband *died* unexpectedly of a heart attack when she was scarcely thirty, leaving her alone with four children and no job in order to earn a living. Her parents were dead, the children's paternal grandparents had very few resources, and she did not have other *relatives* to help her. In effect, the death of her husband destroyed life for *her*. *Upon* looking well at her situation, she *recognized* that she had to rethink all her plans and remake her life upon other foundations.

30. (A) would want
    (B) wants (subj.)
    (C) wants
    (D) wanted

The action of the first sentence is in the past, so the verb **querer** must correspond, thus eliminating (B) and (C). Choice (A) makes no sense in the context of the sentence, as the conditional is most often used in hypothetical situations or situations of conjecture. The class is happening—it is not hypothetical, so (A) is incorrect. Choice (D) is in the past and is the correct response.

31. **(A) her**
    (B) him
    (C) them (masc.)
    (D) (to) her/him

Distinguished what? Distinguished *her*—Mrs. Jensen receives the action of the verb. A direct object pronoun is needed here, thus eliminating (D), which is indirect. Choice (B) suggests that there is a man in this passage. Unless we're talking about the deceased Mr. Jensen being in the class, this is incorrect. Likewise, the only noun to which (C) might be referring is **los estudiantes**, which would not make sense in the context of the sentence. Choice (A) is correct.

32. (A) clothes
    (B) age
    (C) behavior
    (D) knapsack

The clue to the answer of this problem follows the colon: **en ese momento tenía sesenta y nueve años.** This is a pretty distinguishing characteristic, and (B) is the correct answer.

33. (A) was born
    (B) died
    (C) spoke
    (D) heard

Important words in this sentence are **ataque cardíaco** and **dejándola sola**. People are not born of a heart attack, so (A) is incorrect. Likewise, it hardly seems possible that Mr. Jensen unexpectedly spoke or heard of a heart attack and then left his family almost fifty years ago. Choice (B) is the only one that makes any sense here.

34. (A) arms
    (B) stories
    (C) maps
    (D) relatives

The sentence before says that Mrs. Jensen was with **ningún oficio para ganarse la vida**. What are some things, then, that could help Mrs. Jensen financially following the death of her husband? Certainly not (B) and probably not (A) or (C) (unless it's a treasure map and they'll dig for the gold...), and so we are left with (D), the only choice that could offer this type of help.

35. (A) her
    (B) him
    (C) (for) her/him
    (D) itself

Destroyed what? Destroyed life—life is the direct object, receiving the action of the verb directly. We are not, then, looking for a direct object pronoun, because the direct object is already in the sentence, thus (A) and (B) are incorrect. Is life destroying itself? That doesn't make much sense, so (D) is out, as well. Choice (C) is correct, as Mrs. Jensen is the person who receives the effect of the destroyed life—she is the indirect object of the sentence.

36. **(A) Upon**
    (B) In order to
    (C) Before
    (D) Let's

This question depends on a knowledge of idiomatic expressions. Choices (B) and (C) present situations that are backwards in their logic: to see (before seeing) her situation well, she has to rethink her life. It's the other way around, so both are out. **A ver** in Spanish means "Let's see," and does not fit in the sentence, so (D) is eliminated. Choice (A) presents a logical introduction to the situation in the sentence and is correct.

37. (A) recognizes
    (B) recognizes (subj.)
    (C) will recognize
    (D) recognized

The verb **tenía** tells us that we are in the past, so (A), (B), and (C) are all incorrect because they don't correspond to the proper tense. Choice (D) is the answer.

> —Cuando te sientas mal, mi hijita, le <u>pedirás</u> consejos al retrato. El <u>te los</u> dará. Puedes rezarle, ¿acaso no rezas a los santos?
>
> Este <u>modo</u> de proceder le pareció extraño a Alejandrina. Mi vida transcurria monótonamente, pues tengo un testigo constante que me prohibe la felicidad: mi dolencia. El doctor Edgardo es la única persona que lo <u>sabe</u>.
>
> Hasta el momento de conocerlo <u>viví</u> ignorando que algo dentro de mi organismo me carcomía. Ahora conozco todo lo que sufro: el doctor Edgardo me lo <u>ha explicado</u>. Es mi naturaleza. Algunos <u>nacen</u> con ojos negros, otros con ojos azules.
>
> Parece imposible que siendo tan joven él <u>sea</u> tan sabio; <u>sin embargo</u>, me he enterado de que no se precisa ser un anciano para serlo. Su piel lisa, sus ojos de niño, su cabellera rubia, ensortijada, son para <u>mí</u> el emblema de la sabiduría.

"When you feel bad, my little girl, *you will ask* the portrait for advice. It will give *it to you*. You can pray to it—perhaps you don't pray to the saints?"

This *way* of proceeding seemed strange to Alejandrina. My life was passing monotonously, as I have a constant witness which prohibits happiness for me: my ailment. Dr. Edgardo is the only person who *knows* it.

Until the time I recognized it *I lived* ignoring that something inside my organism was consuming me. Now I know all that I suffer: Dr. Edgardo *has explained* it to me. It is my nature. Some *are born* with dark eyes, others with blue eyes.

It seems impossible that, being so young, *he is* so wise; *however*, I have gotten to know that you don't need to be an old man to be wise. His smooth skin, his childlike eyes, his blond, curly head of hair are for *me* the emblem of wisdom.

38. (A) you ask for (subj.)
    (B) you will ask for
    (C) you ask for
    (D) you asked for

Cuando anticipates a time in the future when the narrator will feel bad (the use of the subjunctive tells us this, also), so the answer must also be in the future tense. Answer (D) is thus incorrect. You can use the present tense to speak of the near future, but it is already used in the subjunctive with **sientas** and would indicate the present if used again in a different part of the sentence, so (A) and (C) are out. Only (B) is in the appropriate future tense.

39. (A) it (masc.) to me
    (B) them (fem.) to me
    (C) them (masc.) to you
    (D) it (fem.) to you

Will give what? Will give advice. **Consejos**, the direct object, is replaced by the masculine plural pronoun **los**. This eliminates everything except (C), which is the answer.

40. (A) glove
    (B) topic
    (C) way
    (D) story

The word **este** refers to what immediately precedes it—the first paragraph, which involves someone telling the narrator to pray to the saints when she feels bad. Which word would describe this situation best? Answer (A) is obviously quite silly and can be eliminated. The answer must also be an adjective that is logical with the word **proceder**—"proceeding"—and thus (D) seems silly. Because the person speaking seems to be suggesting a method of reaction to illness, (C) is the most logical fit.

41. **(A) knows**
    (B) announces
    (C) ignores
    (D) shows

A doctor who announces patients' illnesses? Or ignores them? Answers (B) and (C) are eliminated for making no sense whatsoever. Answer (D) is a little strange—Dr. Edgardo is the only person who shows it. To whom? When? Where? Why? The most logical answer is (A).

42. (A) I lived (subj.)
    (B) I lived
    (C) I live
    (D) I live (subj.)

The narrator already knows that she is sick, so her life **ignorando** obviously took place in the past, before she knew, thus eliminating (C) and (D). There are no cues in the sentence that require the use of the subjunctive, so (B) is the correct answer.

43. (A) outside
    (B) next to
    (C) inside
    (D) around

Where is the illness that is consuming the narrator's body? Obviously inside, thus (C) is the correct answer. All the other choices are prepositions referring to the outside of the body, which is hard to imagine.

44. **(A) has explained**
    (B) had explained (subj.)
    (C) will have explained
    (D) has explained (subj.)

If the narrator now understands **todo lo que sufro**, then the doctor has already explained it to her. We need the past tense, which eliminates (C). There are no cues in the sentence that require the use of the subjunctive, thus eliminating (B) and (D), so (A) is the answer.

45. (A) leave
    (B) walk
    (C) die
    (D) are born

Dark eyes and blue eyes are a relatively permanent condition throughout one's life, so (A), (B), and (C) seem rather silly. Choice (D) establishes this permanent condition for life, and so is the answer.

46. (A) would be
    (B) was
    (C) is
    (D) is (subj.)

The verb **parece** places the action in the present tense, thus eliminating (A) and (B). The phrase **Parece imposible que** is an impersonal expression of opinion on the part of the speaker (not a statement of general fact), and thus requires the use of the subjunctive. Choice (D) is the proper response.

47. (A) because
    (B) however
    (C) furthermore
    (D) then

Look at what's happening on either side of the semicolon: it seems impossible to be so smart / you don't have to be old to be wise. Which conjunction most logically connects these two ideas? They seem not to be saying the same thing, which eliminates (A), (C), and (D). Choice (B) gives us the proper word to show the contradiction of the two parts of the sentence.

48. (A) I
    (B) my
    (C) me
    (D) mine

Para is a preposition, and nouns in prepositional phrases are the objects of those prepositions. Choice (A) is a subject pronoun, and can be eliminated. Choices (B) and (D) are gone because they are types of possessive pronouns. The proper response is (C).

Cortejar es pretender en matrimonio a una señorita. En la España del siglo XIX, y en particular en la clase media, existían ciertas costumbres muy <u>tradicionales</u> que se observaban durante el cortejo.

Así, un joven y una joven eran presentados el uno al otro en un evento <u>social</u>, por ejemplo, en un baile o una fiesta. Si ellos se gustaban y querían verse otra vez, tenían que <u>buscar</u> una ocasión para un nuevo encuentro. Cuando se veían, a la salida de la misa, durante el intermedio de una obra de teatro, o en el paseo de la tarde, intercambiaban cartitas <u>amorosas</u>. La joven le informaba al pretendiente <u>de</u> la hora en que <u>saldría</u> al balcón para verse o hablarse calladamente o cuándo iría al paseo, con quién estaría acompañada, dónde se sentaría y las demás señas necesarias.

Una vez que la joven pareja decidía <u>casarse</u>, el joven hacía una cita con los padres de la novia y les pedía la mano de su hija en matrimonio. <u>A partir de</u> ese momento, se les permitía a los novios verse más a menudo.

Pero, por supuesto, la novia siempre estaba
acompañada de una hermana mayor, una tía, una dueña,
un hermano u otra persona mayor hasta el día de
<u>la boda</u>.

Courtship is to "obtain" a woman for marriage. In the Spain of the nineteenth century and, in particular, in the middle class certain very *traditional* customs that one observed during the courtship existed.

Thus, a young man and a young woman were presented to each other at a *social* event, for example, at a dance or a party. If they liked each other and wanted to see each other again, they had to *look for* an occasion for a new encounter. When they saw each other, at departure from Mass, during the intermission of a play, or on an afternoon walk, they exchanged *love* letters.

The young woman informed the suitor *of* the time in which *she would go out* onto the balcony to see or talk to him quietly or when she would go for a walk, by whom she would be accompanied, where she would sit and other necessary signs.

Once the young couple decided *to be married*, the young man made an appointment with the young woman's parents and asked them for their daughter's hand in marriage. *From* that moment, they would allow the couple to see each other more often.

But, of course, the young woman was always accompanied by an older sister, an aunt, a chaperone, a brother or another older person until the day of *the wedding*.

49. (A) annoying
    (B) traditional
    (C) shocking
    (D) stupid

Customs are customs because of their tradition, so (B) is the answer. The other three terms would not normally be applied to customs.

50. **(A) social**
    (B) secret
    (C) somber
    (D) inappropriate

What kind of events are dances and parties? They involve being with other people, and thus are social, so (A) is the answer. Again, the other three terms are not normally associated with dances and parties.

51. (A) forget
    (B) mention
    (C) look for
    (D) remember

If the two people want to see each other again, they have to be reasonably active in setting up another meeting. Choices (B) and (D) are a little too passive, and (A) would certainly defeat their purpose. Answer (C) makes sense—they would try to find another time to meet.

52. (A) love
    (B) professional
    (C) ancient
    (D) hateful

What kinds of letters would two people who like each other a lot exchange? The answer is understandably (A).

53. (A) for
    (B) of
    (C) to
    (D) with

This is a question regarding the use of idiomatic expressions. Luckily, the expression in Spanish here is the same as that in English. You inform someone about or of something, and so (B) is the correct answer.

54. (A) leaves (subj.)
    (B) had left
    (C) would leave
    (D) will leave

The use of the verb **informaba** puts us in a tense that corresponds with the past, so (A) and (D) are eliminated. Look at the tense of the other verbs in this sentence: **iría, estaría, sentaría**. They are all in the conditional, as they are speaking of anticipated events, not events that have already happened. Choice (B) is the conditional perfect, which is only used to describe an event occurring in the past before another past event (and is thus not anticipated). Choice (C) corresponds to the other verbs in the sentence and speaks of anticipated events.

55. **(A) to be married**
    (B) to say good-bye
    (C) to be divorced
    (D) to become angry

The key phrase in this sentence is **les pedía la mano de su hija en matrimonio**. These people obviously like each other a lot. Answer (A) describes the next logical step in their relationship. The other three choices don't really describe what a couple in love would want to do.

56. (A) Before
    (B) From
    (C) For
    (D) With

Logic is important here. Would the young woman's parents allow the two to see each other more often before asking for her hand? Probably not, so (A) is out. Likewise, (C) is eliminated because it would not be for that moment only that they would allow it, especially since the sentence continues by suggesting various chaperones for their future dates. Choice (D) doesn't really make a whole lot of sense either, thus (B) is the proper answer—from that moment on.

57. (A) the party
    (B) the wedding
    (C) the death
    (D) the dance

We've been clobbered over the head with the words **matrimonio** and **amor** in this passage. What's the obvious conclusion we can draw? Choice (B) is correct.

PART C

Pasaron días atroces, sin que llegara respuesta. Le envié una segunda carta y luego una tercera y una cuarta, diciendo siempre lo mismo, pero cada vez con mayor desolación. En la última, decidí relatarle todo lo que había pasado aquella noche que siguió a nuestra separación. No escatimé detalle ni bajeza, como tampoco dejé de confesarle la tentación de suicidio. Me dio vergüenza usar eso como arma, pero la usé. Debo agregar que mientras describía mis actos más bajos, y la desesperación de mi soledad en la noche, frente a su casa de la calle Posadas, sentía ternura para conmigo mismo y hasta lloré de compasión. Tenía muchas esperanzas de que María sintiese algo parecido al leer la carta y con esa esperanza me puse bastante alegre.

Cuando despaché la carta, certificada, estaba francamente optimista.

A vuelta de correo llegó una carta de María, llena de ternura. Sentí que algo de nuestros primeros instantes de amor volvería a reproducirse...Quería que fuera a la estancia. Como un loco, preparé una valija, una caja de pinturas y corrí a la estación Constitución.

Awful days passed without a response arriving. I sent her a second letter and then a third and a fourth, always saying the same thing, but each time with greater distress. In the last one, I decided to relate to her all that had happened that night that followed our separation. I didn't skimp on detail or baseness, as I also didn't neglect to confess to her the temptation of suicide. I was ashamed to use that as a weapon, but I used it. I should add that, while I described my lowest acts and the desperation of my solitude on that night in front of her house on Posadas Street, I felt tenderness towards myself and I almost cried in pity. I had much hope that María would feel something similar upon reading the letter, and with that hope I became quite happy.

When I sent the letter, certified, I was clearly optimistic.

Once back from the post office, a letter from María arrived, full of tenderness. I felt that something of our first moments of love would start to happen again...I wished that I were at the hacienda. Like a fool, I prepared a suitcase, a box full of paints, and I ran to Constitution station.

58. How would one describe the mental state of the narrator at the beginning of this passage?

(A) optimistic
(B) content
(C) impatient
(D) sad

The guy has sent four letters to the same person and is complaining that he has not received a response yet. He is certainly not content with or optimistic about the situation, so (A) and (B) are gone. While he may be sad that María has not responded, one doesn't sense this emotion as much as his impatience (four letters?). Choice (C) is correct.

59. To whom is the narrator sending his letters?

    (A) to the post office
    (B) to Miss Posadas
    (C) to his cousin at Constitution station
    (D) to his estranged girlfriend

We know that María is receiving the letters, and that the narrator once had a relationship with her that he wants to recapture. He is sending the letters from, not to, the post office, so (A) is incorrect. Posadas is the name of María's street, so (B) is wrong, and there is no cousin mentioned in the passage, so (C) is incorrect as well. Choice (D) describes the narrator's relationship with María well.

60. Why is the narrator writing these letters?

    (A) he wants to visit María in her home
    (B) he wants to brag about the bad things he
         has done
    (C) he wants to write to María as many times
         as possible
    (D) he wants to explain himself so that María
         understands him better

The narrator does not want to visit María—he already did that when they separated, so (A) is out. He doesn't necessarily want to brag about his deeds as he wants to explain them to her, so (B) is not correct. While it may seem that the narrator is going for the world record in letter writing, this is not his intention in writing them, either. He wants María to understand him, so (D) is the correct response.

61. How has the narrator felt since his confrontation with María?

    (A) ashamed
    (B) calm
    (C) irritated
    (D) stable

In addition to seeming a little desperate, the narrator does not seem at all proud of his actions. Why else would he write four letters trying to explain himself and his actions to María? He is certainly not stable (he thought about suicide), nor calm (he's a nervous wreck waiting for her response), so (B) and (D) are eliminated. While he may be a little irritated that he hasn't received a response to his letters, the focus of the passage is on his motive for writing the letters, which is his shame, thus (A) is the answer.

62. Why is the narrator happy when he sends his letter?

    (A) he receives an affectionate letter from María
    (B) he thinks that the letter will inspire
         María's love
    (C) he doesn't have to write letters anymore
    (D) he knows that María is going to cry in pity

Choice (A) is incorrect because he receives the letter after he returns from the post office. Choice (D) is a misreading of the passage—it is the narrator who cried when he wrote the letter. Choice (C) is a little strange when it seems that the narrator didn't seem to mind writing four letters in order to get a response. The next to the last sentence says that he hoped that María would feel tenderness toward him upon reading the letter, and so (B) is the answer.

63. What might the narrator's profession be?

   (A) he is a painter
   (B) he is a banker
   (C) he is a soldier
   (D) he is a lawyer

There is no evidence in the passage to support (B) or (D). Choice (C) is a result of misunderstanding the use of the word **arma** in the middle of the first paragraph. The very last line of the passage says that the narrator prepared **una caja de pinturas** before he went to the station, so we might assume that he is a painter, which is choice (A).

Los mayas eran oriundos de Guatemala. De Guatemala pasaron a la península de Yucatán en México, a Belice y Honduras. La cultura de los mayas era aún más avanzada que la de los aztecas, a quienes encontró Cortés cuando llegó a México. La arquitectura de los mayas era notable, como atestiguan las famosas ruinas de templos y pirámides en Palenque, Uxmal, Tikal y Copán. Se sitúa el apogeo de su cultura y civilización en el año 250 D.C. Poco antes del año 900 D.C. desaparecieron. Su desaparición ha sido un enigma. No se sabe precisamente por qué desaparecieron. Nuevos descubrimientos arqueológicos indican que existe la posibilidad de que los mayas quisieran lograr una gran expansión territorial y que las confrontaciones bélicas que acompañaban esa expansión fueran la causa más importante de la decadencia del Imperio Maya.

The Mayas were natives of Guatemala. From Guatemala they moved to the Yucatán Peninsula in Mexico, to Belize and Honduras. The culture of the Mayas was even more advanced than that of the Aztecs, whom Cortés encountered when he arrived in Mexico. The architecture of the Mayas was notable, as the famous ruins of temples and pyramids in Palenque, Uxmal, Tikal, and Copán prove. The apex of their culture and civilization is situated in the year 250 A.D..

A little before 900 A.D. they disappeared. Their disappearance has been an enigma. One does not know precisely why they disappeared. New archeological discoveries indicate that the possibility exists that the Mayas wanted to achieve a great territorial expansion and that the warlike confrontations that accompanied that expansion were the most important cause of the decline of the Mayan Empire.

64. Belize and Honduras

   (A) are parts of the Aztec culture
   (B) are the sites of the Mayan temples
   (C) are near the Yucatán Peninsula
   (D) are in Guatemala

The passage does not focus on the Aztecs at all, therefore (A) is incorrect. The Mayas moved from Guatemala—they left, so Belize and Honduras cannot be in Guatemala, thus (D) is incorrect. The sites of the Mayan temples and pyramids are the four cities mentioned, not these two countries, so (B) is incorrect. That leaves (C) as the answer.

65. The Mayan Empire

 (A) didn't exist after 900 A.D.
 (B) was a territorial expansion
 (C) was destroyed by Cortés when he arrived in
    Mexico
 (D) was better than the Aztec Empire

The Empire was not a territorial expansion and was not destroyed by Cortés, so choices (B) and (C) are incorrect. Although the passage says that **La cultura de los mayas era aún más avanzada** than that of the Aztecs, it doesn't say that it was better, so (D) is incorrect. Choice (A) corresponds with the time of the disappearance of the Mayan civilization.

66. The great mystery of the Mayas is

 (A) their apex
 (B) their ruins
 (C) their success
 (D) **their disappearance**

Nearly the entire second half of the passage talks about the disappearance of the Mayas, and says that it has been **un enigma.** Choice (D) is correct.

67. The bellicosity of the Mayas is because of

 (A) the new archeological discoveries
 (B) their confrontations in their territorial expansion
 (C) the decline of their empire
 (D) **their desire to increase the extent of
    their empire**

The passage says that **las confrontaciones bélicas...acompañaban esa expansión**—that is, they became more aggressive in trying to expand their empire. Choice (D) summarizes this nicely.

Nos conviene pensar en los inmigrantes como
miembros de tres grupos. El primer grupo consiste en los
que vinieron aquí cuando eran adultos y ya hablaban su
lengua materna. El segundo grupo consiste en los que
nacieron aquí o vinieron.aquí cuando eran niños; son
hijos del primer grupo. El tercer grupo consiste en los que
nacieron aquí, hijos del segundo grupo.
 El primer grupo suele aprender un inglés funcional.
Es decir, aprenden a expresarse y a comprender bastante
bien, pero casi nunca aprenden a hablar sin errores y
sin acento. El segundo grupo aprende a hablar inglés
perfectamente bien, sin ningún acento extranjero. Pero
como hijos de inmigrantes este grupo retiene algo de su
primera lengua y muchas veces son bilingües. El tercer
grupo suele estar lingüísticamente asimilado, con poco
conocimiento funcional de la lengua de sus abuelos.
 La asimilación de los hispanos se ha estudiado mucho,
y se ha visto repetidas veces que la gran mayoría de los
inmigrantes hispanos sigue exactamente el mismo patron
que todos los demás inmigrantes. Por lo tanto, la percepción
de que los inmigrantes hispanos no quieren aprender inglés
es totalmente falsa. Como en el caso de cualquier grupo
de inmigrantes, casi todo depende del tiempo que lleve su
generación en este país.

It is fitting for us to think about immigrants as members of three groups. The first group consists of those who came here when they were adults and already spoke their mother language. The second group consists of those who were born here or who came here when they were children; they are children of the first group. The third group consists of those who were born here, children of the second group.

The first group usually learns a functional English. That is to say, they learn to express themselves and to understand well enough, but almost never learn to speak without errors or without accent. The second group learns to speak English perfectly well, without any foreign accent. But as children of immigrants this group retains something of its first language and often they are bilingual. The third group is usually linguistically assimilated, with little functional knowledge of their grandparents' language.

The assimilation of Hispanics has been much studied and it has been seen repeatedly that the great majority of Hispanic immigrants follows exactly the same pattern as all the rest of the immigrants.

Therefore, the perception that Hispanic immigrants don't want to learn English is totally false. As in the case of any group of immigrants, almost everything depends on the time that their generation has been in this country.

68. What determines the group to which an immigrant belongs?

   (A) his/her desire to learn English
   (B) the extent of his/her knowledge of English
   (C) the country from which he/she came originally
   (D) the number of languages in which he/she can communicate

The focus of this passage is on an immigrant's relative knowledge of English, as it is explained extensively in the second paragraph, so (B) is the correct answer.

69. Why don't the members of the first group lose their accents?

   (A) their knowledge of their native language is stronger
   (B) they don't have the desire to learn a new language
   (C) they don't need to learn English
   (D) they haven't assimilated well in the new culture

Choice (B) is a myth that this passage hopes to end, so it is incorrect. Choice (C) is negated by the phrase **suele aprender un inglés funcional**. If they don't need to, why bother? Choice (D) really has nothing to do with their accents, and so (A) is the correct answer. Remember: when they come to this country **ya hablaban su lengua materna**.

70. What is the principal characteristic of the second group?

   (A) they learned the new language from their parents
   (B) they were born in this country
   (C) they have facility in two languages
   (D) they have spent very little time in the United States

Choice (A) is silly, because their parents speak only **un inglés funcional**. Choice (B) is not necessarily correct: They could have come here at an early age. If they were born here or came here early, then (D) is also silly. Choice (C) is the correct answer—**son bilingües**.

71. What is the great similarity between the first and third groups?

    (A) they are not well assimilated linguistically in this country
    (B) they can only speak one language without error
    (C) they don't believe that there is a necessity to learn English
    (D) they are immigrants to this country

The third group was born in the United States, so (A), (C), and (D) are all illogical, thus (B) is the answer. The first group only speaks Spanish well; the third group only English.

72. What is the pattern that almost all immigrants follow?

    (A) their opportunities to learn the language are not many
    (B) they divide themselves into three groups that speak their own languages
    (C) they have the same perception that they lack a desire to learn English
    (D) the extent of their linguistic assimilation depends on how much time they have lived here

Again, (C) is a point the passage is trying to disprove, so it is incorrect. Choice (A) is not logical, given the fact that they have to learn **un inglés funcional** in order to survive in the country. Choice (B) is a misunderstanding—these are not physical groups that the immigrants, themselves, form. They are groups formed theoretically to allow us to understand how generations of immigrants differ. Choice (D) is the ultimate point of the passage, expressed in the final sentence.

73. What would be a good title for this passage?

    (A) "Generations of Assimilation"
    (B) "Difficulties with a New Language"
    (C) "Immigrants who Have Learned English"
    (D) "Erroneous Perceptions of Immigrants"

The main idea of the passage is that of linguistic assimilation, and thus (A) is the answer. The other choices are either too narrow in scope (B) and (D), or completely off the map (C).

> Los estudiantes se pusieron a reír. Primero me molestaron los modales del profesor—era mi segundo día en un país extranjero—pero ahora me daba cólera que me pusiera en ridículo. No dije nada.
> —¿Tal vez, continuó, nos hará el honor de tocar "Souvenir de Spa"?
> Se trataba de una composición superficialmente brillante, popular en la escuela belga. Contesté que sí, que la tocaría.

　　　　—Estoy seguro de que vamos a oírle algo asombroso
a este joven que lo sabe todo. Pero, ¿y en qué va a tocar?
　　　　Más risa entre los estudiantes. Yo estaba tan furioso
que estuve a punto de irme. Pero, recapacité. Quiera
o no quiera, me dije, me va a escuchar. Le arrebaté el
violoncelo al estudiante que estaba a mi lado y empecé
a tocar. Se produjo un gran silencio en la sala. Cuando
concluí no se oía un ruido. El profesor me observaba
intensamente, tenía una rara expresión en la cara.
　　　　—¿Quiere venir a mi oficina? —dijo el profesor.

The students started to laugh. First the professor's manner bothered me—it was my second day in a foreign country—but now it angered me that he ridiculed me. I said nothing.

"Perhaps," he continued, "you will do us the honor of playing 'Souvenir de Spa'?"

He was talking about a superficially brilliant composition, popular in the Belgian school. I answered yes, I would play it.

"I am sure that we are going to hear something amazing from this young man who knows it all. But, on what are you going to play?"

More laughter among the students. I was so furious that I was at the point of leaving. But I thought things over. Like it or not, I told myself, he is going to listen to me. I snatched the cello from the student that was at my side and began to play. A great silence came over the room. When I finished not a sound was heard. The professor was observing me intensely, he had a strange expression on his face.

"Do you want to come to my office?" he said.

74. Why were the students laughing?

(A) the manners of the professor were very funny
(B) the class was having fun
(C) the teacher had just made fun of the narrator
(D) there was no other sound in the class at
　　　that moment

At the end of the first paragraph, the narrator says **me daba cólera que me pusiera en ridículo**. There is no anger in (A) or (B), and (D) is sort of an inane reason to laugh, so (C) is the answer.

75. What is "Souvenir de Spa"?

(A) it is a well-known work of music
(B) it is a masterpiece of literature
(C) it is a magnificent sculpture
(D) it is a classic poem

The word **composición** may fool some people here into picking (B) or (D). When we see, however, the words **violoncelo** and **tocar**, we should realize that we are talking about music, and (A) is thus the answer.

76. What is the attitude of the teacher toward the
    narrator at the beginning of the passage?

    (A) profound respect
    (B) humbled support
    (C) amused condescension
    (D) open disdain

The passage begins with the teacher having just ridiculed the narrator, so (A) and (B) seem unlikely. Choice (D) is a little too extreme an answer here; the point is that the teacher is subtly questioning the ability of the narrator, not openly saying that he hates him. Choice (C) is the proper response.

77. Why doesn't the narrator leave instead of playing?

    (A) it is the first opportunity that he has had
        to play
    (B) the professor is in the middle of a tirade
    (C) the other students are laughing and
        having fun
    **(D) he would not earn the respect of anyone if
        he left**

Choice (B) is too extreme; the professor is not angry in the passage. Choice (C) seems correct, until we realize that the fun and games are at the narrator's expense! Choice (A) implies enthusiasm on the narrator's part, and he is anything but enthusiastic—**quiera o no quiera**, he says. Choice (D) shows the determination of the narrator to give everyone a reason to stop laughing.

78. What happens to the professor after the
    narrator's presentation?

    (A) he begins the next topic
    (B) he changes his opinion of the narrator
    (C) he expresses himself in a very strange way
    (D) he makes fun of the narrator again

The profound silence in the room leads us to believe that the narrator plays extremely well. The professor is intense, and the expression on his face has changed. Choice (C) is a misunderstanding of this last and is incorrect. Choices (A) and (D) simply don't happen. Choice (B) is the correct answer—the is sufficiently impressed now.

79. What is the reason for the conflict between the
    professor and the narrator?

    (A) the narrator has interrupted his class
    (B) the narrator thinks that he knows everything
    (C) the narrator is a student from another country
    (D) the narrator doesn't know "Souvenir de Spa"

Choice (D) is obviously wrong, because the narrator plays it. Answer (B) is the opinion of the professor, not necessarily the truth, and so it is incorrect. Choice (A) is incorrect in that the narrator is receiving unwanted attention from the professor. Answer (C) is correct in that the narrator himself states **era mi segundo día en un país extranjero**.

Como haces falta, Basilio...Me gustaría tanto que
estuvieras presente, con los ojos abiertos y que vieras
lo que ha pasado con tu casa. Se está desmoronando,
como si la hubieras levantado con ladrillos mal cocidos;
se han quebrado las tejas y dejan entrar el sol y la
lluvia por todas partes; a las paredes ya no les caben
las cuarteaduras, y los hijos, ¡qué te puedo contar de
nuestros hijos!

Manuel estuvo aquí, hace unos días, verdaderamente
desesperado por las deudas. A él no le pudiste quitar los
vicios. Y de ser el que más tenía, se ha quedado sin nada.
Me contaron que hasta su mujer y sus hijos lo corrieron.

A Néstor hace mucho tiempo que no lo veo, te
confieso que ya casi no veo nada. Pero creo que él anda
por el Norte. Como tú no les enseñaste a trabajar, aquí no
pudieron hacer nada, por eso se fueron a buscar entre los
mendrugos de otra patria, el pan para sus hijos.

Allá tambíen está José.

How you are missed, Basilio...I would like it so much if you were here, with your eyes open and that
you saw what has happened with your house. It is falling to pieces as if you had built it with badly baked
bricks; the tiles have broken and they let the sun and the rain enter everywhere; there's no more room for
cracks on the walls, and the children, what I can tell you about our children!

Manuel was here a few days ago, truly exasperated by his debts. You could not rid him of his vices.
And for being the one who had the most, he's ended up with nothing. They tell me that even his wife
and children chased him away.

I haven't seen Néstor for a long time; I confess that now I see almost nothing. But I think that he is
in the United States. Since you didn't teach them to work, here they couldn't do anything, so they left to
search for bread for their children among the crusts of stale bread of another country.

José is there too.

80. What has happened during Basilio's absence?

    (A) he has been told of his children
    (B) he has baked the bricks
    (C) his house has started to fall apart
    (D) he has gone to another country

The passage says that Basilio's house **Se está desmoronando**—it's falling apart, so (C) is the answer.
Choice (A) is incorrect because it is what the narrator is doing. We cannot assume either (B) or (D) because
there is not enough information to support these answers.

81. Who is Basilio?

    (A) the husband of the narrator
    (B) the son of the narrator
    (C) the narrator
    (D) the man with the debts

The narrator is talking to Basilio ((C) is out) and refers to **nuestros hijos** ((B) is out), thus (A) is logical.
The man referred to in (D) is Manuel, not Basilio.

82. What is Manuel's problem?

   (A) he can't see very well
   (B) he has gotten rid of his vices
   (C) his wife had a baby
   (D) he owes people a lot of money

Manuel is **desesperado por las deudas**, so (D) is the proper response. Choice (B) is incorrect because it is a misreading of the passage, which says just the opposite. Choice (A) is true of the narrator and (C) simply doesn't happen.

83. Where is Néstor?

   (A) visiting the narrator
   (B) with the stale crusts of bread
   (C) in another country
   (D) baking bread for his children

The passage says that **se fueron a...otra patria**, so (C) is the correct answer. The narrator complains that (A) has not happened, and (B) and (D) are silly answers.

84. Who has had success in the past and lost it?

   (A) Basilio
   (B) Manuel
   (C) José
   (D) Néstor

This is hidden within some tricky wording—**el que más tenía, se ha quedado sin nada**—thus (B) is correct. There is not enough information about Basilio to assume that he was successful, thus (A) is out, and José and Néstor have left because they couldn't find success in their own country, so (C) and (D) are incorrect as well.

85. What could we assume about José?

   (A) he doesn't like the narrator
   (B) he didn't have anything in his own country
   (C) he taught Néstor how to work
   (D) his wife and children abandoned him

The passage ends by telling us that José went north also, just like Néstor, but says nothing else. As such, (A), (C), and (D) are way too specific to be correct, and are thus out. This leaves (B) as the proper response—it offers a plausible reason for leaving home and going to the United States.

Practice Test 3

SPANISH SUBJECT TEST 3

Your responses to Spanish Subject Test 3 questions must be filled in on Test 3 of your answer sheet (at the back of the book). Marks on any other section will not be counted toward your Spanish Subject Test score.

When your supervisor gives the signal, turn the page and begin the Spanish Subject Test.

SPANISH SUBJECT TEST

Part A

<u>Directions:</u> This part consists of a number of incomplete statements, each having four suggested completions. Select the most appropriate completion and fill in the corresponding oval on the answer sheet.

---

1. Manuel no pudo comer _____ porque estaba demasiado caliente.

   (A) la naranja
   (B) las medias
   (C) la sopa
   (D) la acera

2. Mis amigos van de compras _____: cada lunes, jueves y sábado.

   (A) a menudo
   (B) de mala gana
   (C) diariamente
   (D) poco

3. Comeríamos mucho menos si no _____ comida en casa.

   (A) hay
   (B) haya
   (C) habría
   (D) hubiera

4. Cuando el fin de semana venga, _____ tiempo para hacer tus deberes en casa.

   (A) tienes
   (B) tenías
   (C) tendrías
   (D) tendrás

5. Como ella trabaja en Nueva York y Connecticut, tiene que pagar ------- en los dos estados.

   (A) ingresos
   (B) impuestos
   (C) deudas
   (D) luto

6. El equipo tuvo que cancelar el partido _____ la lluvia.

   (A) para
   (B) sin
   (C) a causa de
   (D) dentro de

7. Mi sofá es muy cómodo porque es viejo; _____ es nuevo y no muy cómodo.

   (A) el suyo
   (B) la suya
   (C) los suyos
   (D) las suyas

8. Mi mamá fue al dentista porque le dolían los dientes. El dentista necesitó sacarle _____.

   (A) las carteras
   (B) las muelas
   (C) los techos
   (D) los hombros

9. Rodrigo sabe esquiar muy bien, pero yo no. Él es mejor _____ yo.

   (A) que
   (B) como
   (C) para
   (D) de

10. A Susana no le gusta que casi todo el mundo _____ todo lo que pasa en su vida.

    (A) sabe
    (B) sepa
    (C) conoce
    (D) conozca

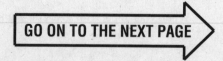

GO ON TO THE NEXT PAGE

11. Fue imposible sacar agua del pozo porque el pozo estaba completamente _____.

    (A) alto
    (B) fresco
    (C) anaranjado
    (D) seco

12. El policía va a dudar que le _____ la verdad si nos detiene.

    (A) digamos
    (B) decimos
    (C) diríamos
    (D) habremos dicho

13. La tienda está en _____ de la Calle Santo Tomás y la Avenida de Toros.

    (A) el pasillo
    (B) la esquina
    (C) la red
    (D) el rincón

14. Bárbara y Nicolás siempre quieren dar su ayuda. Cuando _____ la dan a sus compañeros de clase, ellos están muy alegres.

    (A) le
    (B) se
    (C) les
    (D) lo

15. ¿_____ cuántas horas trabaja tu esposa todos los días?

    (A) Por
    (B) Para
    (C) Antes de
    (D) Desde

16. Si Uds. no se acuestan más temprano estarán muy _____ mañana.

    (A) borrachas
    (B) cansadas
    (C) activas
    (D) heridas

17. ¡No me _____ cuenta de que él era tu tío hasta este momento!

    (A) he dado
    (B) había dado
    (C) habría dado
    (D) habré dado

18. Roberto perdió la voz anoche, entonces no podrá _____ hoy.

    (A) correr
    (B) respirar
    (C) cantar
    (D) barrer

19. ¿No puedes encontrar tu anillo? Creo que lo _____ en la cocina cerca del fregadero.

    (A) vi
    (B) fui
    (C) di
    (D) oí

20. Si tengo un paquete, compro estampillas, y entonces se lo envío a alguien, probablemente estoy en la oficina de _____.

    (A) correos
    (B) platos
    (C) educación
    (D) regalos

21. Cuando una película nos confunde, la _____ después para entenderla mejor.

    (A) discutes
    (B) discute
    (C) discutimos
    (D) discuten

22. El jefe me sigue como si _____ que yo hiciera algo malo.

    (A) esperó
    (B) esperara
    (C) espera
    (D) espere

GO ON TO THE NEXT PAGE

23. Cuando el profesor terminó su lección, borró _____ y se fue de la sala de clase.

    (A) la pizarra
    (B) la basura
    (C) el escritorio
    (D) a la alumna

24. ¿Necesitas tomates y lechuga en la ensalada? Te _____ traeré en seguida.

    (A) lo
    (B) la
    (C) los
    (D) las

25. ¿Le _____ a Ud. un poco extraño que ellos no llevaran zapatos en la nieve?

    (A) veía
    (B) miraba
    (C) buscaba
    (D) parecía

26. ¿ _____ quién estaban preparando un pavo grande y puré de papas?

    (A) De
    (B) Dónde
    (C) A
    (D) Para

27. Estas dos rosas huelen exactamente similares, entonces esta rosa es _____ ésa.

    (A) poco aromática a
    (B) menos aromática que
    (C) más aromática que
    (D) tan aromática como

28. Nadie _____ los tambores como Tito Puente.

    (A) jugaba
    (B) hacía
    (C) tocaba
    (D) ponía

29. Cuando la compañía _____ quién ganó el premio, estoy segura que seré yo.

    (A) anuncia
    (B) anuncie
    (C) anunció
    (D) nunciara

Part B

Directions: In each of the following passages, there are numbered blanks indicating that words or phrases have been omitted. For each numbered blank, four completions are provided. First read through the entire paragraph. Then, for each numbered blank, choose the completion that is most appropriate given the context of the entire paragraph and fill in the corresponding oval on the answer sheet.

En cada segundo vivimos un momento nuevo y único del universo, un momento que no existió (30) y no existirá otra vez. ¿Y qué (31) enseñamos a los niños en las escuelas? Enseñamos que dos más dos son cuatro y que París es la capital de Francia. ¿Cuándo enseñamos (32) ellos son? Deberíamos decirle a cada niño: ¿Sabes lo que eres? Eres una maravilla. Único. No (33) en todo el mundo otro niño exactamente como (34). Todos debemos trabajar para hacer que este mundo (35) digno de sus niños. (36) familia es una sola, cada uno de nosotros tiene un deber (37) sus hermanos. Todos somos hojas de un solo árbol y (38) árbol es la humanidad.

30. (A) nada
    (B) nunca
    (C) siempre
    (D) alguna vez

31. (A) los
    (B) lo
    (C) le
    (D) les

32. (A) que
    (B) cuando
    (C) lo que
    (D) donde

33. (A) hay
    (B) está
    (C) esté
    (D) es

34. (A) ti
    (B) tú
    (C) tuyo
    (D) suyo

35. (A) es
    (B) sea
    (C) era
    (D) fuera

36. (A) Nosotros
    (B) Nos
    (C) Nuestra
    (D) Ningún

37. (A) para
    (B) con
    (C) desde
    (D) sin

38. (A) ese
    (B) esa
    (C) eso
    (D) esto

GO ON TO THE NEXT PAGE ➡

Una mañana se levantó y fue a buscar al amigo, al otro lado de la valla. Pero el amigo no (39) , y, cuando volvió, le dijo la madre:

—El amigo se murió. Niño, no pienses más (40) él y busca otros para jugar.

El niño se sentó en el quicio de la puerta, con la cara (41) las manos y los codos en las rodillas.

"Él (42) ", pensó. Porque no podía ser que allí (43) las canicas, el camión y la pistola de hojalata, y el reloj que ya no andaba, y el amigo no viniera a buscarlos. Vino la noche, con (44) muy grande, y el niño no quería entrar a comer.

—Entra niño, que (45) el frío—dijo la madre. Pero, (46) entrar, el niño se levantó del quicio y se fue en busca del amigo. Pasó buscándole toda la noche. Cuando llegó el sol, el niño pensó: "Qué tontos y pequeños son (47) juguetes. Y ese reloj que no anda, (48) sirve para nada." (49) tiró al pozo, y volvió a la casa, con mucha hambre.

39. (A) había
    (B) era
    (C) iba
    (D) estaba

40. (A) de
    (B) en
    (C) que
    (D) sobre

41. (A) entre
    (B) arriba de
    (C) debajo de
    (D) sin

42. (A) volvió
    (B) vuelva
    (C) volviera
    (D) volverá

43. (A) estaban
    (B) estuvieron
    (C) estuvieran
    (D) están

44. (A) una estrella
    (B) un sol
    (C) una flor
    (D) un océano

45. (A) lleva
    (B) llega
    (C) llueve
    (D) llora

46. (A) además
    (B) al
    (C) a pesar de
    (D) en lugar de

47. (A) esas
    (B) esos
    (C) esa
    (D) eso

48. (A) no
    (B) nadie
    (C) nada
    (D) ninguno

49. (A) La
    (B) Lo
    (C) Le
    (D) Les

GO ON TO THE NEXT PAGE

SPANISH SUBJECT TEST–*Continued*

Hoy día, con la facilidad de la fotografía, tendemos a olvidarnos (50) la importancia que tenía la pintura en el pasado como modo de conservar (51) de momentos históricos. El enorme (52) *La rendición de Breda* fue pintado para conmemorar la victoria militar española de 1625 contra los holandeses. Velázquez (53) pintó diez años después del incidente y (54) que usar todo su ingenio para representar a personajes y un paisaje que nunca (55) . Pero, ¡qué sorpresa! No es típico de las pinturas militares, porque (56) la violencia, la guerra y el orgullo nacional para evocar, en cambio, (57) de tranquilidad y compasión humana.

50. (A) con
    (B) a
    (C) de
    (D) en

51. (A) la basura
    (B) los recuerdos
    (C) la música
    (D) las muertes

52. (A) cuadro
    (B) abrazo
    (C) español
    (D) acontecimiento

53. (A) le
    (B) la
    (C) lo
    (D) se

54. (A) tuvo
    (B) tuviera
    (C) tendría
    (D) habría tenido

55. (A) ve
    (B) verá
    (C) habrá visto
    (D) había visto

56. (A) muestra
    (B) delinea
    (C) evita
    (D) adopta

57. (A) unos hechos
    (B) una salida
    (C) un mes
    (D) un sentido

GO ON TO THE NEXT PAGE

Part C

Directions: Read the following texts carefully for comprehension. Each passage is followed by a number of questions or incomplete statements. Select the answer or completion that is best according to the text and fill in the corresponding oval on the answer sheet.

Se marchó y Luisa quedó sola. Absolutamente sola. Se sentó desfallecida. Las manos dejaron caer el cuchillo contra el suelo. Tenía frío, mucho frío. Por el ventanuco entraban gritos de los vencejos, el rumor del río entre las piedras. "Marcos, tú tienes la culpa...tú, porque Amadeo..." De pronto, tuvo miedo. Un miedo extraño, que hacía temblar sus manos. "Amadeo me quería. Sí: él me quería." ¿Cómo iba a dudarlo? Amadeo era brusco, desprovisto de ternura, callado, taciturno. Amadeo—a medias palabras ella lo entendió—tuvo una infancia dura, una juventud amarga. Amadeo era pobre y ganaba su vida—la de él, la de ella y la de los hijos que hubieran podido tener—en un trabajo ingrato que destruía su salud. Y ella: ¿tuvo ternura para él? ¿Comprensión? ¿Cariño? De pronto, vio algo. Vio su silla, su ropa allí, sucia, a punto de lavar. Sus botas, en el rincón, aún llenas de barro. Algo le subió, como un grito. "Sí, me quería... acaso ¿será capaz de matarse?"

58. ¿Qué siempre ha dudado la narradora?

(A) que Amadeo tuviera sentimientos por ella
(B) que Marcos tuviera la culpa por
    sus problemas
(C) que Amadeo y ella pudieran tener hijos
(D) que Amadeo y ella fueran a ser ricos

59. ¿Qué tipo de persona es Amadeo?

(A) es muy amable y extrovertido
(B) es profundamente cruel y violento
(C) es apasionado y sensible
(D) es bastante tranquilo y no muy
    bien refinado

60. Según el pasaje, ¿por qué es la personalidad de Amadeo tal como es?

(A) la narradora no lo amaba
(B) siempre peleaba con Marcos
(C) tuvo una vida muy difícil
(D) tiene problemas de salud

61. ¿Adónde piensa la narradora que Amadeo fue?

(A) al río para pescar
(B) a su trabajo para ganar dinero
(C) afuera de la casa para suicidarse
(D) al cuarto de sus hijos

62. ¿Cuál es el punto central de este pasaje?

(A) la narradora no ha sabido que Amadeo la ama
    hasta este momento
(B) Marcos es la causa de los problemas entre
    Amadeo y la narradora
(C) la vida de Amadeo y la narradora es
    increíblemente próspera
(D) Amadeo y Marcos se odian

GO ON TO THE NEXT PAGE

Muchos científicos advierten con alarma que la Tierra está calentándose. Explican que esto podría significar un gran peligro debido al efecto invernadero. Un invernadero es un edificio donde se cultivan plantas usando el techo de vidrio (cristal) que permite la entrada de los rayos del sol, pero no deja que salga todo el calor reflejado. Según esta comparación, la atmósfera de nuestro planeta funciona como el techo de vidrio.

En realidad, el efecto invernadero, en proporciones moderadas, es positivo y aun necesario. Si no tuviera esta función nuestra atmósfera, la Tierra sufriría los radicales cambios de temperatura que ocurren en la luna, con un frío espantoso de noche y un calor insoportable de día. Mirándolo así, debemos darle gracias al efecto invernadero. Sin embargo, algunos expertos temen que la acumulación del bióxido de carbono, del metano y de otros gases producidos por las actividades humanas, aumente la eficiencia de nuestro "techo de vidrio" a tal punto que atrape demasiado calor.

Muchos factores, como los terremotos y las erupciones de volcanes, influyen momentáneamente en el clima, pero el gradual calentamiento de la Tierra parece casi inevitable. De acuerdo con sus cálculos, los científicos afirman que desde el año 1850 el aumento de la temperatura global ha sido de uno a cinco grados centígrados y que, hacia el año 2030, podría llegar a aumentar entre 1,5 a 4,5 grados más. Junto con esta subida, se pronostican consecuencias drásticas en las economías de muchas regiones debido a fluctuaciones en la producción agrícola, pérdida o ganancia en el negocio del turismo, y otros cambios.

63. ¿Cuál es la función de un efecto invernadero?

(A) aumentar la temperatura de la Tierra
(B) tener efectos positivos en la atmósfera del planeta
(C) dejar que el sol entre, pero que el calor no salga
(D) producir gases para el beneficio de la atmósfera

64. ¿Cuál es un resultado positivo del efecto invernadero?

(A) la temperatura de la Tierra no varía demasiado.
(B) el frío es espantoso y el calor insoportable
(C) atrapa el calor del sol para calentar el planeta
(D) la producción agrícola fluctúa

65. ¿Por qué piensan algunos expertos que la atmósfera es un "techo de vidrio"?

(A) nos deja ver las estrellas
(B) encierra el planeta de manera efectiva
(C) la temperatura fluctúa mucho
(D) causa problemas económicos

66. ¿Cuál es el gran temor de algunos científicos?

(A) que la situación empeore
(B) que los gases producidos por la actividad humana desaparezcan
(C) que no se pueda ver el universo fuera del "techo de vidrio"
(D) que la temperatura baje drásticamente antes del año 2030

67. ¿Cuál podría ser el aumento total de la temperatura de la Tierra hacia el año 2030?

(A) entre 1 y 5 grados centígrados
(B) entre 1,5 y 4,5 grados centígrados
(C) entre 2,5 y 9,5 grados centígrados
(D) entre 5 y 15 grados centígrados

68. ¿Por qué la economía sufriría si el efecto invernadero continuara en el futuro?

(A) los terremotos y los volcanes destuirían mucho del planeta
(B) la cantidad de comida cultivada en la tierra podría bajar mucho
(C) los científicos necesitarían más dinero para investigar más este fenómeno
(D) necesitaríamos más industrias que no dependan tanto del tiempo

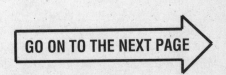

GO ON TO THE NEXT PAGE

El gobierno de los incas sera muy centralizado y autoritario. Estaba situado en la capital, Cuzco, que en su idioma, el quechua, quería decir *ombligo del mundo*. Todo se administraba desde allí. La propiedad no era privada. Cada parcela de tierra era cultivada por un *ayllu*, un grupo de familias que compartían el trabajo y los animales domésticos (llamas, alpacas y vicuñas). Al final del año, un tercio de los cultivos le correspondía al *ayllu*, un tercio a los sacerdotes y un tercio al Estado. El Estado usaba su parte para ayudar a las personas viejas o enfermas y para mantener a los artesanos y soldados. También guardaba una parte para dársela al pueblo en tiempos de escasez o emergencia. Por eso había una gran seguridad. Todo el mundo tenía dónde vivir y casi no había hambre. Pero, por supuesto, la gente tenía que pagar un impuesto, aunque no en moneda, ya que el dinero no existía en aquella sociedad, sino en trabajo. Cada hombre tomaba su turno en la *mita*, el servicio del estado, luchando como soldado en las guerras o trabajando en las minas, o en la construcción de obras públicas. Se ha calculado que el gobierno de los incas disponía anualmente de más de mil millones de horas de mano de obra.

69. ¿Qué era *el ombligo del mundo*?

(A) quechua
(B) la capital
(C) la propiedad
(D) los incas

70. ¿De quién era la propiedad y sus productos en la sociedad inca?

(A) la Iglesia
(B) el Estado
(C) los individuos
(D) una combinación de estos tres grupos

71. ¿Qué era un *ayllu*?

(A) el nombre de un tercio de los cultivos
(B) el nombre de cada parcela de tierra
(C) el nombre de un grupo de familias unidas por su trabajo
(D) un animal domesticado de los incas

72. ¿Qué pasaba en tiempos de emergencia?

(A) los sacerdotes ayudaban a la gente
(B) el estado le daba parte de los cultivos al pueblo para ayudarlo
(C) los soldados peleaban por la seguridad del pueblo
(D) los cultivos eran distribuidos entre la gente del pueblo

73. ¿Qué tipo de sociedad era la sociedad inca?

(A) una sociedad que le daba mucha protección y beneficios a su gente
(B) una sociedad muy avanzada en términos de su tecnología
(C) una sociedad en que cada persona cultivaba su propia parcela de tierra
(D) una sociedad bélica que siempre estaba en guerra

74. ¿Qué era una *mita*?

(A) el nombre de un soldado inca
(B) el nombre de las minas públicas donde los incas trabajaban
(C) el nombre del servicio que cada inca hacía por su sociedad
(D) el nombre del dinero de los incas

GO ON TO THE NEXT PAGE

Producto de enorme importancia cultural y comercial en el mundo, el café tiene una historia pintoresca y de origen incierto. Según una conocida leyenda, fue en Etiopía, por el año 850, que un pastor observó que su rebaño se agitaba tras ingerir los frutos de un arbusto misterioso, el cafeto. Él mismo probó los frutos, y le gustó tanto la sensación, que compartió los frutos con otros en su poblado.

Varios siglos más adelante, el café llegó a Venecia por medio de los turcos. Desde esta ciudad italiana, el café pasó al resto de Europa, llegando primero a París y, pocos años después, a Londres. En el año 1723 Gabriel de Clieu llevó un cafeto al Caribe, y así llegó esta deliciosa bebida a las Américas. Hoy en día, el café es la bebida más popular del mundo.

Los expertos dicen que hay cuatro factores clave en la producción del café: el clima, es decir, la proporción de sol y lluvia; la altura (cuanto mayor sea, mejor es la calidad); el terreno (el suelo volcánico es el más rico en nutrientes); y el cuidado durante la cosecha. Cada árbol tarda entre tres y cuatro años antes de dar fruto, pero una vez maduro, el árbol permanece activo y productivo durante muchas décadas.

Así, lo que conocemos como el café tuvo que pasar por una interesante historia antes de llegar a la taza que nos tomamos.

75. ¿Dónde tiene el café su origen, supuestamente?

   (A) en el Caribe
   (B) en Etiopía
   (C) en Turquía
   (D) en Venecia

76. ¿Quién descubrió el café?

   (A) Unos animales salvajes en el desierto
   (B) Agricultores musulmanes
   (C) Un pastor que observó cómo sus cabras se agitaban
   (D) Unos pintores inciertos

77. La popularidad del café se debe a

   (A) la facilidad con la que se cultiva
   (B) los efectos estimulantes que produce
   (C) su sabor a chocolate
   (D) su económico precio

78. Se podría deducir que el mejor sitio para cultivar el café sería

   (A) la playa
   (B) el desierto
   (C) una gran ciudad
   (D) las montañas

79. El árbol de café

   (A) tiene una vida corta
   (B) produce una libra de semillas desde el primer año
   (C) puede ser productivo durante más de diez años
   (D) tarda varias décadas en dar fruto

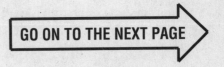

GO ON TO THE NEXT PAGE

Nos gustaba la casa porque, aparte de espaciosa y antigua, guardaba los recuerdos de nuestros bisabuelos, el abuelo paterno, nuestros padres y toda la infancia.

Nos habituamos Irene y yo a vivir solos en ella, lo que era una locura, pues en esa casa podían vivir ocho personas sin estorbarse. Hacíamos la limpieza por la mañana, levantándonos a las siete, y a eso de las once yo le dejaba a Irene las últimas habitaciones por repasar y me iba a la cocina. Almorzábamos a mediodía, siempre puntuales; ya no quedaba nada por hacer fuera de unos pocos platos sucios. Nos resultaba grato almorzar pensando en la casa profunda y silenciosa. A veces llegamos a creer que era ella la que no nos dejó casarnos. Irene rechazó dos pretendientes sin mayor motivo, a mí se me murió María Esther antes que llegáramos a comprometernos. Entramos en los cuarenta años con la inexpresada idea de que el nuestro, simple y silencioso matrimonio de hermanos, era necesaria clausura de la genealogía asentada por los bisabuelos en nuestra casa.

Pero es de la casa que me interesa hablar, de la casa y de Irene, porque yo no tengo importancia. Me pregunto qué hubiera hecho Irene sin el tejido. No necesitábamos ganarnos la vida, todos los meses llegaba la plata de los campos y el dinero aumentaba. Pero a Irene solamente le entretenía el tejido, mostraba una destreza maravillosa y a mí se me iban las horas viéndole las manos. Era hermoso.

80. ¿Cómo es la vida del narrador e Irene?

(A) es excitante y llena de aventura
(B) es repetitiva y bastante pasiva
(C) es triste y muy deprimente
(D) no es muy próspera

81. ¿Cómo es la casa del narrador e Irene?

(A) es pequeña y básicamente cómoda
(B) está mal construida
(C) está muy sucia
(D) es enorme y está bastante vacía

82. ¿Por qué rechazó Irene a sus dos novios?

(A) no hay una razón aparente
(B) al narrador no le gustaban
(C) ellos no querían vivir en la casa
(D) los padres de Irene los rechazaron también

83. ¿Quién es María Esther?

(A) otra hermana del narrador
(B) la madre del narrador
(C) la novia muerta del narrador
(D) la esposa del narrador

84. ¿Cuál es el estado financiero del narrador e Irene?

(A) son muy pobres porque no trabajan
(B) tienen una vida difícil, pero tienen pocos problemas financieros
(C) no se puede determinar su estado financiero en el pasaje
(D) ellos son muy ricos con el dinero de su propiedad

85. ¿Cómo pasa el narrador su tiempo?

(A) sale con María Esther
(B) investiga la genealogía de su familia
(C) teje
(D) mira a Irene hacer su propio trabajo

STOP
IF YOU FINISH BEFORE TIME IS CALLED, YOU MAY CHECK YOUR WORK ON THIS TEST ONLY.
DO NOT TURN TO ANY OTHER TEST IN THIS BOOK.

HOW TO SCORE THE PRINCETON REVIEW SPANISH SUBJECT TEST

When you take the real exam, the proctors take away your exam and your bubble sheet and send it to New Jersey where a computer looks at the pattern of filled-in ovals on your exam and gives you a score. We couldn't include even a small computer with this book, so we are providing this more primitive way of scoring your exam.

DETERMINING YOUR SCORE

STEP 1   Using the answers on the next page, determine how many questions you got right and how many you got wrong on the test. Remember, questions that you do not answer do not count as either right answers or wrong answers.

STEP 2   List the number of right answers here.

(A) _____

STEP 3   List the number of wrong answers here. Now divide that number by 3.

(B) _____ ÷ 3 _____ = (C) _____

STEP 4   Subtract the number of wrong answers divided by 3 (C) from the number of correct answers (A). Round this score to the nearest whole number. This is your raw score.

(A) – (C) _____

STEP 5   To determine your real score, take the number from Step 4 above and look it up in the left column of the Score Conversion Table on page 207; the corresponding score on the right is your score on the exam.

ANSWERS TO SPANISH SUBJECT TEST 3

Question Number	Correct Answer	Right	Wrong	Question Number	Correct Answer	Right	Wrong	Question Number	Correct Answer	Right	Wrong
1	C	_____	_____	33	A	_____	_____	65	B	_____	_____
2	A	_____	_____	34	B	_____	_____	66	A	_____	_____
3	D	_____	_____	35	B	_____	_____	67	C	_____	_____
4	D	_____	_____	36	C	_____	_____	68	B	_____	_____
5	B	_____	_____	37	B	_____	_____	69	B	_____	_____
6	C	_____	_____	38	A	_____	_____	70	D	_____	_____
7	A	_____	_____	39	D	_____	_____	71	C	_____	_____
8	B	_____	_____	40	B	_____	_____	72	B	_____	_____
9	A	_____	_____	41	A	_____	_____	73	A	_____	_____
10	B	_____	_____	42	D	_____	_____	74	C	_____	_____
11	D	_____	_____	43	C	_____	_____	75	B	_____	_____
12	A	_____	_____	44	A	_____	_____	76	C	_____	_____
13	B	_____	_____	45	B	_____	_____	77	B	_____	_____
14	B	_____	_____	46	D	_____	_____	78	D	_____	_____
15	A	_____	_____	47	B	_____	_____	79	C	_____	_____
16	B	_____	_____	48	A	_____	_____	80	B	_____	_____
17	B	_____	_____	49	B	_____	_____	81	D	_____	_____
18	C	_____	_____	50	C	_____	_____	82	A	_____	_____
19	A	_____	_____	51	B	_____	_____	83	C	_____	_____
20	A	_____	_____	52	A	_____	_____	84	D	_____	_____
21	C	_____	_____	53	C	_____	_____	85	D	_____	_____
22	B	_____	_____	54	A	_____	_____				
23	A	_____	_____	55	D	_____	_____				
24	C	_____	_____	56	C	_____	_____				
25	D	_____	_____	57	D	_____	_____				
26	D	_____	_____	58	A	_____	_____				
27	D	_____	_____	59	D	_____	_____				
28	C	_____	_____	60	C	_____	_____				
29	B	_____	_____	61	C	_____	_____				
30	B	_____	_____	62	A	_____	_____				
31	D	_____	_____	63	C	_____	_____				
32	C	_____	_____	64	A	_____	_____				

THE PRINCETON REVIEW SPANISH SUBJECT TEST
SCORE CONVERSION TABLE

Raw Score	Scaled Score	Raw Score	Scaled Score	Raw Score	Scaled Score
85	800	47	590	9	360
84	800	46	580	8	360
83	800	45	570	7	350
82	800	44	570	6	350
81	790	43	560	5	340
80	790	42	550	4	340
79	780	41	550	3	330
78	780	40	540	2	320
77	770	39	530	1	320
76	770	38	530	0	310
75	760	37	520	−1	310
74	760	36	520	−2	300
73	750	35	510	−3	290
72	750	34	500	−4	290
71	740	33	500	−5	280
70	730	32	490	−6	270
69	730	31	490	−7	260
68	720	30	480	−8	260
37	720	29	470	−9	250
66	710	28	470	−10	240
65	700	27	460	−11	230
64	700	26	460	−12	220
63	690	25	450	−13	220
62	680	24	450	−14	220
61	680	23	440	−15	210
60	670	22	430	−16	210
59	670	21	430	−17	210
58	660	20	420	−18	200
57	650	19	420	−19	200
56	650	18	410	−20	200
55	640	17	410	−21	200
54	630	16	400	−22	200
53	630	15	400	−23	200
52	620	14	390	−24	200
51	620	13	390	−25	200
50	610	12	380	−26	200
49	600	11	380	−27	200
48	590	10	370	−28	200

13

Practice Test 3:
Answers and
Explanations

PART A

1. Manuel couldn't eat _____ because it was too hot.

   (A) the orange
   (B) the stockings
   (C) the soup
   (D) the sidewalk

Generally, we don't eat articles of clothing or parts of the street, so (B) and (D) are wrong. Oranges are not usually heated, so (C) is the correct answer.

2. My friends go shopping _____: every Monday, Thursday, and Saturday.

   (A) often
   (B) reluctantly
   (C) daily
   (D) little

If my friends go shopping three days per week, we can hardly say that that's reluctantly or little, so (B) and (D) are wrong. Answer (C) cannot be right because there are four days on which they don't go shopping, so the correct answer is (A).

3. We would eat much less if _____ no food at home.

   (A) there is
   (B) there is (subj.)
   (C) there would be
   (D) there were (subj.)

This sentence describes a situation that does not currently exist, so the present tense cannot be right—eliminate (A) and (B). The imperfect subjunctive is needed with the conditional to describe hypothetical events, so (D) is the correct answer.

4. When the weekend comes, _____ time to do your chores at home.

   (A) you have
   (B) you had
   (C) you would have
   (D) you will have

The weekend is an anticipated event in the *future*, so (D) is the only answer that makes sense.

5. Since she works in New York and Connecticut, she has to pay ------- in both states.

   (A) income
   (B) taxes
   (C) debts
   (D) mourning

This is a difficult question based on a student's knowledge of difficult vocabulary. While debts are certainly paid, **trabaja** is a clue that **impuestos** are what is at issue, so the correct answer is (B).

6. The team had to cancel the game _____ the rain.

   (A) for
   (B) without
   (C) because of
   (D) inside of

Why would a team cancel a game when it isn't raining? (B) is obviously wrong. (D) and (A) don't make a tremendous amount of sense, while (C) is quite logical.

7. My sofa is very comfortable because it is old;
   _____ is new and not very comfortable.

   (A) his/hers (masc., sing.)
   (B) his/hers (fem., sing.)
   (C) his/hers (masc., pl.)
   (D) his/hers (fem., pl.)

Translating is not a big help here, since all the choices mean the same thing in English. Remember that stressed possessive adjectives agree in number and gender with the word they are modifying. In this case, they must agree with **sofá**, which is masculine and singular, so (A) is the answer.

8. My mother went to the dentist because her teeth hurt her. The dentist needed to take out _____.

   (A) her wallets
   (B) her molars
   (C) her ceilings
   (D) her shoulders

This is a vocabulary question. **Dentista** and **dientes** are big clues that we need a type of tooth, so (B) is correct.

9. Rodrigo knows how to ski very well, but I don't.
   He is better _____ I.

   (A) than
   (B) as
   (C) for
   (D) from

This is an idiomatic expression. (C) and (D) are wrong because they are prepositions and would require the prepositional pronoun **mí** at the end of the sentence. **Mejor que** is the proper expression.

10. Susana doesn't like that almost everyone _____ everything that's happening in her life.

    (A) knows
    (B) knows (subj.)
    (C) knows
    (D) knows (subj.)

Our first hurdle here is the **saber/conocer** thing: Does everyone know a fact, or is everyone familiar with a person, place, or thing? **Todo lo que pasa en su vida** would be a series of *facts*, and we would thus use **saber**, which eliminates (C) and (D). Now, do we use the subjunctive or not? **No le gusta** is an expression of emotion, which always requires the subjunctive, so (B) is correct.

11. It was impossible to take water from the well because the well was completely _____.

    (A) tall
    (B) fresh
    (C) orange
    (D) dry

Even if you don't know what the word **pozo** means, the sentence has something to do with **agua**, so you should be looking for a word in the answer choices that relates to water. (A) and (C) do not work. (B) is possible, and is a good second choice if you're unsure of the vocabulary, but it doesn't make as much sense as choice (D).

12. The policeman is not going to believe that we _____ him the truth if he detains us.

    (A) are telling (subj.)
    (B) are telling
    (C) would tell
    (D) will have told

The action of the sentence will occur in the *future*, and so (C)—which is used in the past or in hypothetical situations in the present—cannot be correct. The real key to this sentence is the expression **va a dudar**, which is an expression of doubt, which always requires the subjunctive. (A) is the only choice in the subjunctive.

13. The store is on _____ of Santo Tomás Street and the Avenue of Bulls.

    (A) the hallway
    (B) the corner
    (C) the net
    (D) the corner

If we are out on the street, then (A) can't be correct. Likewise, because we're not playing sports, (C) is not right. The answer here is tricky because it relies on a knowledge of the difference between a corner found *outside* a building (where two streets intersect), which is an **esquina**, and a corner found *inside* a building (where two walls intersect), which is a **rincón**.

14. Bárbara and Nicolás always want to give help. When they give it _____ (their classmates), they are very happy.

    (A) to him/her
    (B) to them
    (C) to them
    (D) it (masc., sing.)

What do they give? *Help*—direct object. Who gets the help? Their *classmates*—indirect object. (D) is eliminated because it is not an indirect object pronoun. **A sus compañeros de clase** is the clarification of the identity of the indirect object, so we know that we need a plural pronoun, which eliminates (A). Remember that we cannot use **le** or **les** before a direct object pronoun that begins with "l," like **la**. It changes to **se** in these cases, and so (B) is correct.

15. _____ how many hours does your wife work every day?

    (A) For
    (B) For
    (C) Before
    (D) Since

Choices (C) and (D) are not really logical in this context, which brings us to the dreaded **por** vs. **para** dilemma once again. Remember that **para** is used with destinations in time, which this sentence doesn't seem to be describing, while **por** is used with durations of time, which is the correct meaning here.

16. If you (pl.) don't go to bed earlier you will be very _____ tomorrow.

    (A) drunk
    (B) tired
    (C) active
    (D) injured

Vocabulary is important in this question as well. Not going to bed earlier means less sleep, which means less energy, which eliminates (C). Since no liquor or accidents are mentioned, eliminating (A) and (D), (B) is the only logical choice.

17. I _____ that he was your uncle until this moment!

    (A) have not realized
    (B) had not realized
    (C) would not have realized
    (D) will not have realized

When did this lack of realization take place? In the *past*, which eliminates (D). *When* in the past, though? Before or after this moment of realization that has just passed? *Before*. The tense that places past events before other past events is the pluperfect, which is choice (B).

18. Roberto lost his voice last night, so he won't be able to _____.

    (A) run
    (B) breathe
    (C) sing
    (D) sweep

You need to know the word **voz** to be clued in on this question. Only choice (C) has anything to do with one's voice.

19. You can't find your ring? I think I _____ it in the kitchen near the sink.

   (A) saw
   (B) went
   (C) gave
   (D) heard

This question is playing tricks with verb forms that all sound the same, which may lead to confusion. Only (A) is logical.

20. If I have a package, buy stamps, and then send it (the package) to someone, I am probably in the _____ office.

   (A) post
   (B) plates
   (C) education
   (D) presents

Again, vocabulary is essential in this question. The words **paquete**, **estampillas**, and **envío** make it obvious that you are in the post office.

21. When a movie confuses us, _____ it afterwards to understand it better.

   (A) you discuss
   (B) he/she discusses
   (C) **we discuss**
   (D) you (pl.)/they discuss

There has been no change in the subject that is apparent in the sentence. The indirect object pronoun **nos** gives us a "backdoor entry" into finding out the subject, **nosotros**.

22. The boss follows me as if he _____ for me to do something bad.

   (A) waited
   (B) **were waiting (imp. subj.)**
   (C) waits
   (D) waits (pres. subj.)

Remember that the expression **como si** always requires the imperfect subjunctive, regardless of the tense of the sentence.

23. When the professor finished the lesson, he erased _____ and left the classroom.

   (A) **the blackboard**
   (B) the garbage
   (C) the desk
   (D) the student (fem.)

Borró is the key word here, and the entire problem hinges upon knowledge of this word. Only (A) makes sense.

24. You need tomatoes and lettuce in the salad? I will
bring _____ to you immediately.

    (A) it (masc., sing.)
    (B) it (fem., sing.)
    (C) them (masc., pl.)
    (D) them (fem., pl.)

How many things am I bringing? *Two*, so I need a plural word, which eliminates (A) and (B). Remember that when a masculine and feminine noun are grouped together, the group retains the *masculine* article, so (C) is the proper answer.

25. Did it _____ strange to you that they weren't
wearing shoes in the snow?

    (A) saw
    (B) looked
    (C) looked for
    (D) seem

This question is playing with the English translation of this idea: "Did it *look* strange to you..." While this is a proper translation, it is not correct in Spanish. Only (D) is correct.

26. _____ whom were you preparing a big turkey and
mashed potatoes?

    (A) From
    (B) Where
    (C) To
    (D) For

Think about meaning here. Only (C) and (D) are possibilities, but (D) is more appropriate.

27. These two roses smell exactly similar, so this rose is
_____ that one.

    (A) little aromatic to
    (B) less aromatic than
    (C) more aromatic than
    (D) as aromatic as

If the roses are **exactamente similares**, then (B) and (C) make no sense. (A) is just awkward, and means nothing, so (D) is correct.

28. No one _____ the drums like Tito Puente.

    (A) played
    (B) played
    (C) played
    (D) played

All of these verbs can mean "to play" in the appropriate context. Only (C) is used with musical instruments, however.

29. When the company _____ who won the prize, I am sure it will be I.

    (A) announces
    (B) announces (pres. subj.)
    (C) announced
    (D) announced (imp. subj.)

The future tense at the end of the sentence tells us what tense we're in, which eliminates answers (C) and (D). Since the event is not *currently* happening, however, we cannot use the present tense—only the present subjunctive lets us know that the event is not happening right now—it is merely anticipated at this point.

PART B

En cada segundo vivimos un momento nuevo y único del universo, un momento que no existió <u>nunca</u> y no existirá otra vez. ¿Y qué <u>les</u> enseñamos a los niños en las escuelas? Enseñamos que dos más dos son cuatro y que París es la capital de Francia. ¿Cuándo enseñamos <u>lo que</u> ellos son? Deberíamos decirle a cada niño: ¿Sabes lo que eres? Eres una maravilla. Único. No <u>hay</u> en todo el mundo otro niño exactamente como <u>tú</u>. Todos debemos trabajar para hacer que este mundo <u>sea</u> digno de sus niños. <u>Nuestra</u> familia es una sola, cada uno de nosotros tiene un deber <u>para</u> sus hermanos. Todos somos hojas de un solo árbol y <u>ese</u> árbol es la humanidad.

In every second we live a new and unique moment of the universe, a moment that *never* existed and will not exist again. And what do we teach the children in schools? We teach that two plus two is four and that Paris is the capital of France. When do we teach *what* they are? We ought to tell each child: Do you know what you are? You are a wonder. Unique. *There is* not another child exactly like *you* in the world. We all should work to make this world worthy of its children. *Our* family is one alone, each one of us has a duty *to* his brothers. We are all leaves of a single tree and *that* tree is humanity.

30. (A) nothing
    (B) never
    (C) always
    (D) sometime

We're talking about a **momento**, which is a measure of time, so we can get rid of (A). The expression **no existió** is very important because it begins a negative clause, which means that all other words that follow must also be negative. (A) is the only negative word left.

31. (A) them (masc., pl.)
    (B) it (masc., sing.)
    (C) to him/her
    (D) to them

What are we teaching? We should be teaching **lo que ellos son**, which would function as the direct object of the sentence (yes, the direct object can be more than one word). Who is receiving this teaching? **Los niños**, who are the indirect object, which is what we're looking for, so we eliminate (A) and (B). Since we have the clarification of the identity of the indirect object already, we know that it is plural, so (D) is the correct answer.

32. (A) that
    (B) when
    (C) what
    (D) where

Let's look at each choice: (A) can't be right because it would leave a sentence fragment. (B) makes no sense. (D) cannot be right because it would require the use of the verb **estar**. Answer (C) is the idomatically correct way to say "what" in Spanish in this context.

33. **(A) there is**
    (B) is
    (C) is (subj.)
    (D) is

The key to this sentence is the expression **otro niño**, which is an *indefinite* expression. The verb **estar** is generally used with *definite* expressions, and thus (B) and (C) are not correct. **Ser** can be used with indefinite expressions, but not to express general existence, as this sentence does. The verb **haber** is used in such contexts, and so (A) is the correct answer.

34. (A) you
    (B) you
    (C) yours
    (D) his/hers

When making a comparison, the sentence is understood in the following way: "There is no other child exactly like you (*are*)," therefore, we are looking for a subject word to correspond with the verb, which is understood. Choice (B) is the only subject word among the choices.

35. (A) is
    (B) is (subj.)
    (C) was
    (D) was (imp. subj.)

The key expression in this sentence is **hacer que**, which means "to make," as in "to ensure that," which is a way of exerting one's desire or wish over the actions of someone or something else. Such an expression requires the use of the subjunctive, so choices (A) and (C) are wrong. Since the sentence is in the present tense, the present subjunctive is appropriate, and (B) is the answer.

36. (A) We
    (B) Us/To us
    (C) Our
    (D) No

In this sentence, we are looking for an adjective to modify the word **familia**. Since (A) and (B) are not adjectives, they are wrong. (D) is incorrect because it is masculine, and we are looking for a feminine adjective, which is choice (C).

37. (A) for
    (B) for
    (C) since
    (D) without

Choices (C) and (D) really don't make a tremendous amount of sense. The *destination* of our duty is our brothers, and **para** is used in contexts of destination, but, idiomatically, the preposition used with **deber** is always **con**. Choice (B) is the correct answer.

38. **(A) that (masc., sing.)**
    (B) that (fem., sing.)
    (C) that (neut., sing.)
    (D) this (neut., sing.)

Neutral demonstrative adjectives are used when there is no noun that follows. Since the word **árbol** follows the demonstrative, (C) and (D) cannot be right. Since **árbol** is masculine and singular, (A) is correct.

Una mañana se levantó y fue a buscar al amigo, al otro

lado de la valla. Pero el amigo no _(39)_ , y, cuando volvió, le

dijo la madre:

—El amigo se murió. Niño, no pienses más _(40)_ él y

busca otros para jugar.

El niño se sentó en el quicio de la puerta, con la cara _(41)_

las manos y los codos en las rodillas.

"Él _(42)_ ", pensó. Porque no podía ser que allí _(43)_ las

canicas, el camión y la pistola de hojalata, y el reloj que ya no

andaba, y el amigo no viniera a buscarlos. Vino la noche, con

_(44)_ muy grande, y el niño no quería entrar a comer.

—Entra niño, que _(45)_ el frío—dijo la madre. Pero,

_(46)_ entrar, el niño se levantó del quicio y se fue en busca del

amigo. Pasó buscándole toda la noche. Cuando llegó el sol,

el niño pensó: "Qué tontos y pequeños son _(47)_ juguetes.

Y ese reloj que no anda, _(48)_ sirve para nada." _(49)_ tiró al

pozo, y volvió a la casa, con mucha hambre.

One morning he got up and went to look for the friend, on the other side of the fence. But the friend *wasn't* there, and when he returned, the mother said to him: "The friend died. Child, don't think more *about* him and look for others to play." The child sat on the door frame with his face *in* his hands and his elbows on his knees.

"He *will return*," he thought. Because it couldn't be that the marbles, the truck, the tin pistol, and the watch that now didn't work were there and the friend didn't come to look for them. Night came, with a very big *star*, and the child didn't want to go inside to eat. "Come in child, it's *getting* cold," said the mother. But *instead of* entering, the child got up from the door frame and went to look for the friend. He spent all night looking for him. When the sun came up, the child thought: "How stupid and small *these* toys are. And that watch that doesn't work, it's *no* good for anything." He threw *it* into the well and returned home, very hungry.

39. (A) there were
    (B) was
    (C) went
    (D) was (there)

The sentence is trying to say that the friend could not be located, which would require the use of the verb **estar**, which is choice (D).

40. (A) of
    (B) about
    (C) that
    (D) above

Choice (C) cannot be right because the word **que** introduces clauses, and there is not one in the second part of the sentence. The expression **pensar de** is generally used only in questions, while (D) makes no sense. The expression **pensar en** means "to think about," and (B) is correct.

41. **(A) in**
    (B) above
    (C) below
    (D) without

Imagine the boy's posture: He has his elbows on his knees. What might be the relation between his face and his hands? (D) is silly, and (C) is only right if he is sitting upside down. While (B) makes sense, it seems more likely that the boy's head would be *in* his hands, since his mother just told him that his friend died. (A) is the best answer.

42. (A) returned
    (B) returns (subj.)
    (C) returned (imp. subj.)
    (D) will return

The boy doesn't know where his friend is, and his friend doesn't appear in the rest of the passage, so neither the past nor the present would be logical in this sentence, so (A), (B), and (C) are all eliminated. The boy is hopeful that his friend will return in *the future*, so (D) is correct.

43. (A) were
    (B) were
    (C) were (subj.)
    (D) are

No podía ser que is an expression of *doubt*, which, you'll remember, requires the use of the subjunctive. Only choice (C) is in the subjunctive mood.

44. **(A) a star**
    (B) a sun
    (C) a flower
    (D) an ocean

The night came *with* something—what is something that comes with the night? Even if you've never seen the word **estrella**, the other three answers don't make any sense.

45. (A) it's carrying
    (B) it's getting
    (C) it's raining
    (D) it's crying

Does the cold rain or cry? No. Does it carry anything? Possibly, but the sentence doesn't tell us what it could be carrying. The only choice that is logical is (B).

46. (A) in addition to
    (B) upon
    (C) in spite of
    (D) instead of

Does the boy actually enter his house when his mother calls him? No, he goes to look for his friend. (A), (B), and (C), which all suggest that he *has* entered the house, are wrong.

47. (A) those (fem., pl.)
    (B) those (neut., pl.)
    (C) that (fem., sing.)
    (D) that (masc., sing.)

We are looking for the correct demonstrative here. Since the word being modified is **juguetes**, which is masculine and plural, (B) is the correct answer.

48. **(A) doesn't**
    (B) no one
    (C) nothing
    (D) none

You have to follow the logic of the sentence here: The boy is complaining about the watch, saying it doesn't work. Since he's limiting his commentary to just a watch, (C) is wrong since it implies that he's dissatisfied with *everything* in his life. Answer (D) implies that there is more than one watch that doesn't work, which isn't true. Choice (B) is silly, so (A) is correct.

49. (A) It (fem., sing.)
   (B) It (masc., sing.)
   (C) To him/her
   (D) To them

What did the boy throw? The *watch*, which is the direct object, so answers (C) and (D) are incorrect. Since **reloj** is masculine, (B) is right.

> Hoy día, con la facilidad de la fotografía, tendemos
>
> a olvidarnos <u>de</u> la importancia que tenía la pintura en
>
> el pasado como modo de conservar <u>los recuerdos</u> de
>
> momentos históricos. El enorme <u>cuadro</u> *La rendición de*
>
> *Breda* fue pintado para conmemorar la victoria militar
>
> española de 1625 contra los holandeses. Velázquez <u>lo</u>
>
> pintó diez años después del incidente y <u>tuvo</u> que usar
>
> todo su ingenio para representar a personajes y un paisaje
>
> que nunca <u>había visto</u>. Pero, ¡qué sorpresa! No es típico
>
> de las pinturas militares, porque <u>evita</u> la violencia, la
>
> guerra y el orgullo nacional para evocar, en cambio, <u>un</u>
>
> <u>sentido</u> de tranquilidad y compasión humana.

Today, with the ease of photography, we tend to forget *about* the importance that painting had in the past as a means of preserving *memories* of historic moments. The enormous *painting The Surrender of Breda* was painted to commemorate the Spanish military victory of 1625 against the Dutch. Velázquez painted *it* ten years after the incident and *had* to use all his genius to represent people and a landscape that he *had* never *seen*. But, what a surprise! It is not typical of military paintings because *it avoids* violence, war, and national pride to evoke instead *a sense* of tranquility and human compassion.

50. (A) with
   (B) at
   (C) about
   (D) in

"To forget about" is an idiomatic expression that requires the use of **de**. Remember, idiomatic expressions don't necessarily have a rule: You either know them or you don't.

51. (A) the garbage
   (B) the memories
   (C) the music
   (D) the deaths

What exactly is the garbage of an historic moment? How does a painting preserve music? Do we actually preserve the deaths of historic moments, or the moments themselves? Interesting questions all, but (A), (C), and (D) are all wrong because they are not answered in this passage. An historic painting is a representation of a memory, so (B) is correct.

52. **(A) painting**
    (B) hug
    (C) Spaniard
    (D) event

Notice that *La rendición de Breda* is italicized. Generally, names of books, movies, ships, and, yes, paintings are italicized. Hugs, Spaniards, and events are not accorded this same special treatment, so (A) is the answer.

53. (A) to him/her
    (B) it (fem., sing.)
    (C) it (masc., sing.)
    (D) himself

What did he paint? The *painting*, which is the direct object, thus eliminating (A). (He did not paint himself, although that would have been interesting.) **Cuadro** is masculine, so (C) is the answer.

54. **(A) had**
    (B) had (imp. subj.)
    (C) would have
    (D) would have had

Choice (D) suggests that Velázquez *didn't* use all his genius (he *would* have, but...), but the sentence says just the opposite, so it is wrong. (B) is incorrect because there are no expressions that cue the use of the subjunctive. While (C) might sound correct in English, it is only right as an obscure, dramatic narrative technique in the past. (A) is the clearest way to get the point across.

55. (A) sees
    (B) will see
    (C) will have seen
    (D) had seen

The painting was dated 1625, long ago, so (A), (B), and (C) are simply not logical. (D) is the answer.

56. (A) shows
    (B) delineates
    (C) avoids
    (D) adopts

We're looking for something that *wouldn't* be typical of a military painting. Violence and war are the typical themes, and so showing, delineating, or adopting these themes would not be what we are looking for. (C) is more likely.

57. (A) some facts
    (B) an exit
    (C) a month
    (D) a sense

Choice (B) doesn't make sense in context, while choice (A) changes the intended purpose of the painting. Instead of being about a moment of military history, it has become a sort of spiritual self-help painting. It is also highly doubtful that Velázquez only wanted his painting to result in one month of tranquility, and so (D) is correct.

PART C

Se marchó y Luísa quedó sola. Absolutamente sola.
Se sentó desfallecida. Las manos dejaron caer el cuchillo
contra el suelo. Tenía frío, mucho frío. Por el ventanuco
entraban gritos de los vencejos, el rumor del río entre
las piedras. "Marcos, tú tienes la culpa...tú, porque
Amadeo..." De pronto, tuvo miedo. Un miedo extraño,
que hacía temblar sus manos. "Amadeo me quería. Sí: él
me quería." ¿Cómo iba a dudarlo? Amadeo era brusco,
desprovisto de ternura, callado, taciturno. Amadeo—a
medias palabras ella lo entendió—tuvo una infancia
dura, una juventud amarga. Amadeo era pobre y ganaba
su vida—la de él, la de ella y la de los hijos que hubieran
podido tener—en un trabajo ingrato que destruía su
salud. Y ella: ¿tuvo ternura para él? ¿Comprensión?
¿Cariño? De pronto, vio algo. Vio su silla, su ropa allí,
sucia, a punto de lavar. Sus botas, en el rincón, aún llenas
de barro. Algo le subió, como un grito. "Sí, me quería...
acaso ¿será capaz de matarse?"

He left and Luisa remained, alone. Absolutely alone. She sat down, weakened. Her hands dropped the knife on the floor. She was cold, very cold. Through the window the calls of the birds, the murmur of the river between the rocks entered. "Marcos, you are to blame...you, because Amadeo..." Suddenly, she was afraid. A strange fear that made her hands shake. "Amadeo loved me. Yes: He loved me." How was she going to doubt it? Amadeo was abrupt, lacking tenderness, quiet, sullen. Amadeo—at mid-sentence she understood it—had a tough childhood, a bitter adolescence. Amadeo was poor and earned his living—his, hers, and that of the children that they could have had—at an ungrateful job that was destroying his health. And she: Did she have tenderness for him? Understanding? Affection? Suddenly, she saw something. She saw his chair, his clothes there, ready for washing. His boots, in the corner, still full of mud. Something rose in her, like a shout. "Yes, he loved me...by any chance will he be capable of killing himself?"

58. What has the narrator always doubted?

(A) **that Amadeo had feelings for her**
(B) that Marcos was to blame for her problems
(C) that Amadeo and she could have children
(D) that Amadeo and she were going to be rich

The narrator spends the majority of the passage convincing herself that Amadeo loved her—**Sí, me quería**—so she must not have believed it in the past.

59. What type of person is Amadeo?

    (A) he is very friendly and extroverted
    (B) he is profoundly cruel and violent
    (C) he is passionate and sensitive
    (D) he is pretty quiet and is not very well refined

Amadeo is described as **brusco** and **callado**, descriptions that are paraphrased nicely in choice (D).

60. According to the passage, why is Amadeo's personality like it is?

    (A) the narrator didn't love him
    (B) he always fought with Marcos
    (C) he had a difficult life
    (D) his health is bad

The narrator speaks of **una infancia dura** and **una juventud amarga**, which are hardly qualities of a happy life.

61. Where does the narrator think that Amadeo went?

    (A) to the river to fish
    (B) to work to earn money
    (C) outside the house to kill himself
    (D) to his children's room

The phrase **será capaz de matarse** at the end of the passage is a good clue of what's on the narrator's mind.

62. What is the central point of this passage?

    (A) the narrator hasn't known that Amadeo loves her until this moment
    (B) Marcos is the cause of the problems between Amadeo and the narrator
    (C) Amadeo's and the narrator's life is incredibly prosperous
    (D) Amadeo and Marcos hate each other

We can look at the reasoning for question 58 to explain choice (A).

Muchos científicos advierten con alarma que la Tierra está calentándose. Explican que esto podría significar un gran peligro debido al efecto invernadero. Un invernadero es un edificio donde se cultivan plantas usando el techo de vidrio (cristal) que permite la entrada de los rayos del sol, pero no deja que salga todo el calor reflejado. Según esta comparación, la atmósfera de nuestro planeta funciona como el techo de vidrio.

En realidad, el efecto invernadero, en proporciones moderadas, es positivo y aun necesario. Si no tuviera esta función nuestra atmósfera, la Tierra sufriría los radicales cambios de temperatura que ocurren en la luna, con un frío espantoso de noche y un calor insoportable de día. Mirándolo así, debemos darle gracias al efecto invernadero. Sin embargo, algunos expertos temen que la acumulación del bióxido de carbono, del metano y de otros gases producidos por las actividades humanas, aumente la eficiencia de nuestro "techo de vidrio" a tal punto que atrape demasiado calor.

Muchos factores, como los terremotos y las erupciones de volcanes, influyen momentáneamente en el clima, pero el gradual calentamiento de la Tierra parece casi inevitable. De acuerdo con sus cálculos, los científicos afirman que desde el año 1850 el aumento de la temperatura global ha sido de uno a cinco grados centígrados y que, hacia el año 2030, podría llegar a aumentar entre 1,5 a 4,5 grados más. Junto con esta subida, se pronostican consecuencias drásticas en las economías de muchas regiones debido a fluctuaciones en la producción agrícola, pérdida o ganancia en el negocio del turismo, y otros cambios.

Many scientists warn with alarm that the Earth is warming. They explain that this could signify a great danger because of the greenhouse effect. A greenhouse is a building where one grows plants using a glass roof that permits the entry of the sun's rays but doesn't allow all the reflected warmth to leave. According to this comparison, the atmosphere of our planet functions as a "glass roof."

In reality, the greenhouse effect, in moderate proportions, is positive and even necessary. If our atmosphere didn't have this function, the Earth would suffer the radical temperature changes that occur on the moon, with a frightful cold at night and an insufferable heat during the day. Looking at it in this way, we should give thanks to the greenhouse effect. However, some experts fear that the accumulation of carbon dioxide, methane, and other gases produced by human activities, will increase the efficiency of our "glass roof" to the point that it will trap too much heat.

Many factors, such as earthquakes and volcanic eruptions, momentarily influence the climate, but the gradual warming of the Earth seems almost inevitable. In accordance with their calculations, scientists affirm that since the year 1850, the increase of the global temperature has been from one to five degrees centigrade and that, near the year 2030, it could increase between 1.5 and 4.5 degrees more. Along with this increase, they predict drastic consequences in the economies of many regions because of fluctuations in agricultural production, loss or gain in tourism, and other changes.

63. What is the function of a greenhouse effect?

(A) to increase the temperature of the Earth
(B) to have positive effects in the planet's atmosphere
(C) to allow the sun to enter but the heat doesn't leave
(D) to produce gases for the benefit of the atmosphere

The answer can be found in the second sentence of the passage.

64. What is a positive result of the greenhouse effect?

(A) the temperature of the Earth doesn't vary much
(B) the cold is frightful and the heat insufferable
(C) it traps the heat of the sun to heat the planet
(D) agricultural production fluctuates

The passage states that we should really **darle gracias** to the greenhouse effect because we don't have the drastic temperature shifts of the moon.

65. Why do some experts think that the atmosphere is a "glass roof?"

(A) it allows us to see the stars
(B) it effectively encloses the planet
(C) the temperature fluctuates a lot
(D) it causes economic problems

This question requires a little careful thinking. Choice (A) is silly, while (D) is not the reason for this expression being coined—rather, that it is a result of the phenomenon. Choice (C) looks good only if you misunderstand it—the temperature would only fluctuate if we *didn't* have this "glass roof." (B) is therefore the correct answer.

66. What is the great fear of some scientists?

   (A) that the situation will get worse
   (B) that the gases produced by human activity will
         disappear
   (C) that one will not be able to see the universe
         outside of the "glass roof"
   (D) that the temperature will drop drastically before the year 2030

The entire last paragraph is dedicated to telling of the "doom and gloom" that the greenhouse effect promises for us in the next twenty-five years or so.

67. What could be the total increase in the Earth's
    temperature near the year 2030?

   (A) between 1 and 5 degrees centigrade
   (B) between 1.5 and 4.5 degrees centigrade
   (C) between 2.5 and 9.5 degrees centigrade
   (D) between 5 and 15 degrees centigrade

The passage states that the temperature has increased from 1 to 5 degrees centigrade since 1850, then states that it could increase an *additional* 1.5 to 4.5 degrees before 2030. The potential totals are given in choice (C).

68. Why would the economy suffer if the greenhouse
    effect continued in the future?

   (A) earthquakes and volcanoes would destroy
         much of the planet
   **(B) the quantity of food grown on Earth could
         drop a lot**
   (C) scientists would need more money to
         investigate this phenomenon more
   (D) we would need more industries that didn't depend so
         much on the weather

The last sentence of the passage speaks of the **consecuencias drásticas** of a continued warming of the planet, and a potential shortage of crops is mentioned.

El gobierno de los incas sera muy centralizado y
autoritario. Estaba situado en la capital, Cuzco, que en
su idioma, el quechua, quería decir *ombligo del mundo*.
Todo se administraba desde allí. La propiedad no era
privada. Cada parcela de tierra era cultivada por un
ayllu, un grupo de familias que compartían el trabajo y
los animales domésticos (llamas, alpacas y vicuñas). Al
final del año, un tercio de los cultivos le correspondía al
ayllu, un tercio a los sacerdotes y un tercio al Estado. El
Estado usaba su parte para ayudar a las personas viejas
o enfermas y para mantener a los artesanos y soldados.
También guardaba una parte para dársela al pueblo en
tiempos de escasez o emergencia. Por eso había una
gran seguridad. Todo el mundo tenía dónde vivir y casi
no había hambre. Pero, por supuesto, la gente tenía que
pagar un impuesto, aunque no en moneda, ya que el

dinero no existía en aquella sociedad, sino en trabajo. Cada hombre tomaba su turno en la *mita*, el servicio del estado, luchando como soldado en las guerras o trabajando en las minas, o en la construcción de obras públicas. Se ha calculado que el gobierno de los incas disponía anualmente de más de mil millones de horas de mano de obra.

The government of the Incas was very centralized and authoritarian. It was situated in the capital, Cuzco, which in their language, *Quechua*, means "umbilicus (navel) of the world." Everything was administered from there. Property was not private. Each parcel of land was cultivated by an *ayllu*, a group of families that shared the work and the domestic animals (*llamas, alpacas, vicuñas*). At the end of the year, a third of the crop belonged to the *ayllu*, a third to the priests, and a third to the State. The State used its part to help old or sick people and to maintain artisans and soldiers. They also kept a part to give to the town in times of shortage or emergency. For this reason there was a great security. The whole world had a place to live and there was almost no hunger. But, of course, the people had to pay a tax, although not in money, since money didn't exist in that society, rather in work. Each man took his turn in the *mita*, service to the state, fighting as a soldier in wars or working in the mines or in the construction of public works. It has been calculated that the government of the Incas annually had more than a billion hours of manpower at its command.

69. What was the "umbilicus of the world"?

(A) *Quechua*
(B) the capital
(C) property
(D) the Incas

The relative pronoun **que**, which always introduces a descriptive clause modifying the word immediately preceding it, is right after the word **Cuzco**, which was the capital of the Incan civilization.

70. To whom did property and its products belong in the Incan society?

(A) the Church
(B) the State
(C) individuals
(D) a combination of these three groups

The passage states that the **cultivos** were divided into **tercios**: one for the Church, one for the State, and one for the family groups. Each group is thus part-owner of the land and its crops.

71. What was an *ayllu*?

    (A) it was the name of a third of the crops
    (B) it was the name of each parcel of land
    **(C) it was the name of a group of families united
         by their work**
    (D) it was a pet of the Incas

The comma after the word *ayllu* tells us that a further description of an *ayllu* is coming: **un grupo de familias** is sufficient description to see that the answer is (C).

72. What happened in times of emergency?

    (A) the priests helped the people
    **(B) the State gave part of the crops to the people
         to help them**
    (C) the soldiers fought for the security of the town
    (D) the crops were distributed among the townspeople

This question requires some careful reading. Crops were distributed at the end of the year, so (D) is incorrect. Choice (C) sounds good, but it assumes that the only types of emergencies the Incas had were wars, which is not necessarily true. Choice (A) also sounds good, but the priests didn't help everyone—only the old and the sick. (B) is the best answer.

73. What type of society was Incan society?

    **(A) a society that gave much protection and
         benefits to its people**
    (B) a very advanced society in terms of
        its technology
    (C) a society in which every person cultivated
        his/her own parcel of land
    (D) a warlike society that was always involved in a war

There is no discussion of technology here, so (B) is out. The passage states that **La propiedad** *no* **era privada**, which cancels (C). Choice (D) is also not really discussed, so (A) is the answer.

74. What was a *mita*?

    (A) the name of an Incan soldier
    (B) the name of the public mines where the Incas
        worked
    **(C) the name of the service that each Inca did for
         his society**
    (D) the name of the money of the Incas

Once again, we see a comma after the word *mita*, followed by a nice description of what it was: **el servicio al Estado**. (C) is the answer.

Producto de enorme importancia cultural y comercial en el mundo, el café tiene una historia pintoresca y de origen incierto. Según una conocida leyenda, fue en Etiopía, por el año 850, que un pastor observó que su rebaño se agitaba tras ingerir los frutos de un arbusto misterioso, el cafeto. Él mismo probó los frutos, y le gustó tanto la sensación, que compartió los frutos con otros en su poblado.

Varios siglos más adelante, el café llegó a Venecia por medio de los turcos. Desde esta ciudad italiana, el café pasó al resto de Europa, llegando primero a París, y pocos años después, a Londres. En el año 1723 Gabriel de Clieu llevó un cafeto al Caribe, y así llegó esta deliciosa bebida a las Américas. Hoy en día, el café es la bebida más popular del mundo.

Los expertos dicen que hay cuatro factores clave en la producción del café: el clima, es decir, la proporción de sol y lluvia; la altura (cuanto mayor sea, mejor es la calidad); el terreno (el suelo volcánico es el más rico en nutrientes); y el cuidado durante la cosecha. Cada árbol tarda entre tres y cuatro años antes de dar fruto, pero una vez maduro, el árbol permanece activo y productivo durante muchas décadas.

Así, lo que conocemos como el café tuvo que pasar por una interesante historia antes de llegar a la taza que nos tomamos.

A product of enormous cultural and commercial importance throughout the world, coffee has a history that is both picturesque and uncertain. According to popular legend, it was in Ethiopia in the year 850 that a shepherd observed that his herd of goats became excited and energetic after ingesting the berries of a mysterious shrub, the coffee tree. The shepherd tried the berries for himself and he liked the sensation so much that he shared them with others in his village.

Several centuries later, the Turks brought coffee to Venice. From this Italian city coffee traveled to the rest of Europe, arriving first in Paris and a few years later in London. In 1723, Gabriel de Clieu took a coffee plant to the Caribbean and that's how this delicious beverage arrived in the Americas. Now, coffee is the most popular beverage in the world.

The experts say there are four key factors in the production of coffee: the climate, that is to say, the proportion of sun and rain; the altitude—the higher the altitude the better the quality; the land—volcanic land is richest in nutrients; and the care during the harvest. Each tree takes between three and four years to produce the first berries, but once it's mature, the tree remains active and fruitful for many decades.

So, that which we know as coffee had to go through an interesting history before arriving in our cup.

75. Where did coffee supposedly originate?

    (A) The Caribbean
    (B) Ethiopia
    (C) Turkey
    (D) Venice

The passage mentions that a shepherd discovered coffee in Ethiopia in the year 850. The passage does indeed also mention Turkey, Venice, and the Caribbean in the second paragraph, but it does so only to show how coffee traveled throughout the world. The correct answer is (B).

76. Who discovered coffee?

    (A) some savage animals in the desert
    (B) Muslim farmers
    (C) a shepherd who observed his goats in an animated state
    (D) some uncertain painters

The first paragraph indicates that **un pastor** observed his herd acting strange after ingesting the fruit of the mysterious coffee tree. The passage makes no mention of wild animals, Muslim farmers, or uncertain painters. So (C) is the best answer.

77. The popularity of coffee is due to

    (A) how easy it is to cultivate
    (B) the stimulation that it produces
    (C) its flavor of chocolate
    (D) its low price

It would be relatively easy to answer this question without even reading the passage. Why do most people drink coffee? Usually it's to experience the jolt of the caffeine. Again the answer to this question comes from the first paragraph where the author states that the shepherd enjoyed the sensation of the coffee so much that he shared it with others in the village. One could easily be tricked by answer choice (A) because the passage mentions how to best cultivate coffee. Since the passage makes no mention of chocolate or the price of coffee. (B) is the correct answer here.

78. One can infer that the best place to cultivate coffee would be

    (A) the beach
    (B) the desert
    (C) a big city
    (D) the mountains

In the third paragraph, experts outline the four keys to the successful production of coffee. One of these is the altitude of the coffee plants. Since mountains have the greatest altitude of the four answer choices, (D) is the best answer.

79. A coffee tree

    (A) has a short lifespan
    (B) produces a pound of seeds beginning in the
         first year
    (C) can flourish for more than ten years
    (D) takes several decades to produce its first berries

According to the end of the third paragraph, the coffee tree takes three or four years to produce its first fruit. This helps us eliminate answer choices (B) and (D). The author then tells us that the coffee tree can continue to produce fruit for many decades. Now we can eliminate answer choice (A) and select answer choice (C).

Nos gustaba la casa porque, aparte de espaciosa y antigua, guardaba los recuerdos de nuestros bisabuelos, el abuelo paterno, nuestros padres y toda la infancia.

Nos habituamos Irene y yo a vivir solos en ella, lo que era una locura, pues en esa casa podían vivir ocho personas sin estorbarse. Hacíamos la limpieza por la mañana, levantándonos a las siete, y a eso de las once yo le dejaba a Irene las últimas habitaciones por repasar y me iba a la cocina. Almorzábamos a mediodía, siempre puntuales; ya no quedaba nada por hacer fuera de unos pocos platos sucios. Nos resultaba grato almorzar pensando en la casa profunda y silenciosa. A veces llegamos a creer que era ella la que no nos dejó casarnos. Irene rechazó dos pretendientes sin mayor motivo, a mí se me murió María Esther antes que llegáramos a comprometernos. Entramos en los cuarenta años con la inexpresada idea de que el nuestro, simple y silencioso matrimonio de hermanos, era necesaria clausura de la genealogía asentada por los bisabuelos en nuestra casa.

Pero es de la casa que me interesa hablar, de la casa y de Irene, porque yo no tengo importancia. Me pregunto qué hubiera hecho Irene sin el tejido. No necesitábamos ganarnos la vida, todos los meses llegaba la plata de los campos y el dinero aumentaba. Pero a Irene solamente le entretenía el tejido, mostraba una destreza maravillosa y a mí se me iban las horas viéndole las manos. Era hermoso.

We liked the house because, aside from being spacious and old, it guarded the memories of our great-grandparents, paternal grandfather, our parents, and all of childhood.

Irene and I became accustomed to live alone in it, which was a crazy thing since in that house eight people could live without getting in each other's way. We did the cleaning in the morning, getting up at seven, and at about eleven I left the last rooms to Irene to finish and went to the kitchen. We ate lunch at noon, always punctual; there now remained nothing to do aside from a few dirty dishes. We found it pleasing to eat lunch thinking about the deep and silent house. At times we believed that it was she (the house) that didn't allow us to marry. Irene rejected two suitors for almost no reason at all, María Esther died before we could get engaged. We entered our forties with the unexpressed ideal that our simple and silent marriage of brother and sister was a necessary closure of the genealogy laid down by our great grandparents in our house.

But it is the house about which I am interested in speaking, the house and Irene, because I am not important. I ask myself what Irene would have done without weaving. We didn't need to earn a living, every month the money arrived from the fields and the money grew. But only weaving entertained Irene, she showed marvelous skill and, watching her hands, the hours flew by for me. It was beautiful.

80. How is the life of the narrator and Irene?

   (A) it is exciting and full of adventure
   (B) it is repetitive and pretty passive
   (C) it is sad and very depressing
   (D) it isn't very prosperous

The narrator and his sister do *the same thing every day*, which pretty much amounts to nothing. The use of the imperfect tense tells us that all of the actions the narrator describes are habitual. (B) is a nice summary of this description.

81. How is the house of the narrator and Irene?

   (A) it's small and basically comfortable
   (B) it's badly constructed
   (C) it's very dirty
   (D) it's enormous and is pretty empty

The narrator says **en esa casa podían vivir ocho personas**. Sounds pretty big, huh? (D) is the perfect answer.

82. Why did Irene reject her two boyfriends?

   (A) there is no apparent reason
   (B) the narrator didn't like them
   (C) they didn't want to live in the house
   (D) Irene's parents rejected them also

The narrator doesn't tell us what he thought of Irene's boyfriends, so (B) is incorrect. He also doesn't say much about the boyfriends themselves, so (C) is wrong. Irene's parents are apparently not living, so their opinion is not relevant in her decision, therefore (A) is the best answer.

83. Who is María Esther?

   (A) another sister of the narrator
   (B) the narrator's mother
   (C) the narrator's dead girlfriend
   (D) the narrator's wife

The narrator says that María Esther died before they could **comprometerse**, which means "to get engaged." This is a pretty serious (and strange) step for brother and sister to take ((A) is wrong), or mother and son (so is (B)). If she died before they got engaged, they couldn't have been married, so (C) is the answer.

84. What is the financial state of the narrator and Irene?

    (A) they are very poor because they don't work
    (B) they have a difficult life, but they have few financial problems
    (C) one can't determine their financial state in the passage
    (D) they are very rich with the money from their property

The narrator says **No necesitábamos ganarnos la vida** but that **el dinero aumentaba** anyway. Doesn't sound like too much of a struggle. (D) is correct.

85. How does the narrator spend his time?

    (A) he goes out with María Esther
    (B) he researches the genealogy of his family
    (C) he weaves
    (D) he watches Irene do her own work

The narrator says in the next to the last line **a mí se me iban las horas viéndole las manos**. Loads of fun, huh? (D) is the answer.

ABOUT THE AUTHORS

George Roberto Pace was born in Miami in 1966. The native Spanish speaker moved to New York City at the age of two months, where he grew up and attended Hunter College High School. He received his BA from Oberlin College in 1988, and he currently resides in Chicago, where he is Director of The Princeton Review of the Great Plains.

David Stewart grew up in Manhattan Beach, California, and studied Spanish for several years before completing high school in San Pedro Sula, Honduras, as part of an AFS foreign exchange program. He later studied Spanish literature in Madrid and majored in Spanish at Occidental College, where he received his BA in 1992. He now lives with his wife Lisa in Sunrise, Florida, and is the National Consultant for The Princeton Review.

Practice Test Form

Completely darken bubbles with a No. 2 pencil. If you make a mistake, be sure to erase mark completely. Erase all stray marks.

The Princeton Review

1.
YOUR NAME: _____
(Print)   Last   First   M.I.

SIGNATURE: _____ DATE: ___/___/___

HOME ADDRESS: _____
(Print)   Number and Street

_____
City   State   Zip Code
(Print)

SAT Spanish Section 1

1. (A) (B) (C) (D) (E)	26. (A) (B) (C) (D) (E)	51. (A) (B) (C) (D) (E)	76. (A) (B) (C) (D) (E)
2. (A) (B) (C) (D) (E)	27. (A) (B) (C) (D) (E)	52. (A) (B) (C) (D) (E)	77. (A) (B) (C) (D) (E)
3. (A) (B) (C) (D) (E)	28. (A) (B) (C) (D) (E)	53. (A) (B) (C) (D) (E)	78. (A) (B) (C) (D) (E)
4. (A) (B) (C) (D) (E)	29. (A) (B) (C) (D) (E)	54. (A) (B) (C) (D) (E)	79. (A) (B) (C) (D) (E)
5. (A) (B) (C) (D) (E)	30. (A) (B) (C) (D) (E)	55. (A) (B) (C) (D) (E)	80. (A) (B) (C) (D) (E)
6. (A) (B) (C) (D) (E)	31. (A) (B) (C) (D) (E)	56. (A) (B) (C) (D) (E)	81. (A) (B) (C) (D) (E)
7. (A) (B) (C) (D) (E)	32. (A) (B) (C) (D) (E)	57. (A) (B) (C) (D) (E)	82. (A) (B) (C) (D) (E)
8. (A) (B) (C) (D) (E)	33. (A) (B) (C) (D) (E)	58. (A) (B) (C) (D) (E)	83. (A) (B) (C) (D) (E)
9. (A) (B) (C) (D) (E)	34. (A) (B) (C) (D) (E)	59. (A) (B) (C) (D) (E)	84. (A) (B) (C) (D) (E)
10. (A) (B) (C) (D) (E)	35. (A) (B) (C) (D) (E)	60. (A) (B) (C) (D) (E)	85. (A) (B) (C) (D) (E)
11. (A) (B) (C) (D) (E)	36. (A) (B) (C) (D) (E)	61. (A) (B) (C) (D) (E)	
12. (A) (B) (C) (D) (E)	37. (A) (B) (C) (D) (E)	62. (A) (B) (C) (D) (E)	
13. (A) (B) (C) (D) (E)	38. (A) (B) (C) (D) (E)	63. (A) (B) (C) (D) (E)	
14. (A) (B) (C) (D) (E)	39. (A) (B) (C) (D) (E)	64. (A) (B) (C) (D) (E)	
15. (A) (B) (C) (D) (E)	40. (A) (B) (C) (D) (E)	65. (A) (B) (C) (D) (E)	
16. (A) (B) (C) (D) (E)	41. (A) (B) (C) (D) (E)	66. (A) (B) (C) (D) (E)	
17. (A) (B) (C) (D) (E)	42. (A) (B) (C) (D) (E)	67. (A) (B) (C) (D) (E)	
18. (A) (B) (C) (D) (E)	43. (A) (B) (C) (D) (E)	68. (A) (B) (C) (D) (E)	
19. (A) (B) (C) (D) (E)	44. (A) (B) (C) (D) (E)	69. (A) (B) (C) (D) (E)	
20. (A) (B) (C) (D) (E)	45. (A) (B) (C) (D) (E)	70. (A) (B) (C) (D) (E)	
21. (A) (B) (C) (D) (E)	46. (A) (B) (C) (D) (E)	71. (A) (B) (C) (D) (E)	
22. (A) (B) (C) (D) (E)	47. (A) (B) (C) (D) (E)	72. (A) (B) (C) (D) (E)	
23. (A) (B) (C) (D) (E)	48. (A) (B) (C) (D) (E)	73. (A) (B) (C) (D) (E)	
24. (A) (B) (C) (D) (E)	49. (A) (B) (C) (D) (E)	74. (A) (B) (C) (D) (E)	
25. (A) (B) (C) (D) (E)	50. (A) (B) (C) (D) (E)	75. (A) (B) (C) (D) (E)	

Practice Test Form

Completely darken bubbles with a No. 2 pencil. If you make a mistake, be sure to erase mark completely. Erase all stray marks.

1.

YOUR NAME: _____
(Print)
                     Last   First   M.I.

SIGNATURE: _____   DATE: _____ / _____ / _____

HOME ADDRESS: _____
(Print)
                                        Number and Street

_____
                     City   State   Zip Code

(Print)

SAT Spanish Section 2

1. Ⓐ Ⓑ Ⓒ Ⓓ Ⓔ
2. Ⓐ Ⓑ Ⓒ Ⓓ Ⓔ
3. Ⓐ Ⓑ Ⓒ Ⓓ Ⓔ
4. Ⓐ Ⓑ Ⓒ Ⓓ Ⓔ
5. Ⓐ Ⓑ Ⓒ Ⓓ Ⓔ
6. Ⓐ Ⓑ Ⓒ Ⓓ Ⓔ
7. Ⓐ Ⓑ Ⓒ Ⓓ Ⓔ
8. Ⓐ Ⓑ Ⓒ Ⓓ Ⓔ
9. Ⓐ Ⓑ Ⓒ Ⓓ Ⓔ
10. Ⓐ Ⓑ Ⓒ Ⓓ Ⓔ
11. Ⓐ Ⓑ Ⓒ Ⓓ Ⓔ
12. Ⓐ Ⓑ Ⓒ Ⓓ Ⓔ
13. Ⓐ Ⓑ Ⓒ Ⓓ Ⓔ
14. Ⓐ Ⓑ Ⓒ Ⓓ Ⓔ
15. Ⓐ Ⓑ Ⓒ Ⓓ Ⓔ
16. Ⓐ Ⓑ Ⓒ Ⓓ Ⓔ
17. Ⓐ Ⓑ Ⓒ Ⓓ Ⓔ
18. Ⓐ Ⓑ Ⓒ Ⓓ Ⓔ
19. Ⓐ Ⓑ Ⓒ Ⓓ Ⓔ
20. Ⓐ Ⓑ Ⓒ Ⓓ Ⓔ
21. Ⓐ Ⓑ Ⓒ Ⓓ Ⓔ
22. Ⓐ Ⓑ Ⓒ Ⓓ Ⓔ
23. Ⓐ Ⓑ Ⓒ Ⓓ Ⓔ
24. Ⓐ Ⓑ Ⓒ Ⓓ Ⓔ
25. Ⓐ Ⓑ Ⓒ Ⓓ Ⓔ

26. Ⓐ Ⓑ Ⓒ Ⓓ Ⓔ
27. Ⓐ Ⓑ Ⓒ Ⓓ Ⓔ
28. Ⓐ Ⓑ Ⓒ Ⓓ Ⓔ
29. Ⓐ Ⓑ Ⓒ Ⓓ Ⓔ
30. Ⓐ Ⓑ Ⓒ Ⓓ Ⓔ
31. Ⓐ Ⓑ Ⓒ Ⓓ Ⓔ
32. Ⓐ Ⓑ Ⓒ Ⓓ Ⓔ
33. Ⓐ Ⓑ Ⓒ Ⓓ Ⓔ
34. Ⓐ Ⓑ Ⓒ Ⓓ Ⓔ
35. Ⓐ Ⓑ Ⓒ Ⓓ Ⓔ
36. Ⓐ Ⓑ Ⓒ Ⓓ Ⓔ
37. Ⓐ Ⓑ Ⓒ Ⓓ Ⓔ
38. Ⓐ Ⓑ Ⓒ Ⓓ Ⓔ
39. Ⓐ Ⓑ Ⓒ Ⓓ Ⓔ
40. Ⓐ Ⓑ Ⓒ Ⓓ Ⓔ
41. Ⓐ Ⓑ Ⓒ Ⓓ Ⓔ
42. Ⓐ Ⓑ Ⓒ Ⓓ Ⓔ
43. Ⓐ Ⓑ Ⓒ Ⓓ Ⓔ
44. Ⓐ Ⓑ Ⓒ Ⓓ Ⓔ
45. Ⓐ Ⓑ Ⓒ Ⓓ Ⓔ
46. Ⓐ Ⓑ Ⓒ Ⓓ Ⓔ
47. Ⓐ Ⓑ Ⓒ Ⓓ Ⓔ
48. Ⓐ Ⓑ Ⓒ Ⓓ Ⓔ
49. Ⓐ Ⓑ Ⓒ Ⓓ Ⓔ
50. Ⓐ Ⓑ Ⓒ Ⓓ Ⓔ

51. Ⓐ Ⓑ Ⓒ Ⓓ Ⓔ
52. Ⓐ Ⓑ Ⓒ Ⓓ Ⓔ
53. Ⓐ Ⓑ Ⓒ Ⓓ Ⓔ
54. Ⓐ Ⓑ Ⓒ Ⓓ Ⓔ
55. Ⓐ Ⓑ Ⓒ Ⓓ Ⓔ
56. Ⓐ Ⓑ Ⓒ Ⓓ Ⓔ
57. Ⓐ Ⓑ Ⓒ Ⓓ Ⓔ
58. Ⓐ Ⓑ Ⓒ Ⓓ Ⓔ
59. Ⓐ Ⓑ Ⓒ Ⓓ Ⓔ
60. Ⓐ Ⓑ Ⓒ Ⓓ Ⓔ
61. Ⓐ Ⓑ Ⓒ Ⓓ Ⓔ
62. Ⓐ Ⓑ Ⓒ Ⓓ Ⓔ
63. Ⓐ Ⓑ Ⓒ Ⓓ Ⓔ
64. Ⓐ Ⓑ Ⓒ Ⓓ Ⓔ
65. Ⓐ Ⓑ Ⓒ Ⓓ Ⓔ
66. Ⓐ Ⓑ Ⓒ Ⓓ Ⓔ
67. Ⓐ Ⓑ Ⓒ Ⓓ Ⓔ
68. Ⓐ Ⓑ Ⓒ Ⓓ Ⓔ
69. Ⓐ Ⓑ Ⓒ Ⓓ Ⓔ
70. Ⓐ Ⓑ Ⓒ Ⓓ Ⓔ
71. Ⓐ Ⓑ Ⓒ Ⓓ Ⓔ
72. Ⓐ Ⓑ Ⓒ Ⓓ Ⓔ
73. Ⓐ Ⓑ Ⓒ Ⓓ Ⓔ
74. Ⓐ Ⓑ Ⓒ Ⓓ Ⓔ
75. Ⓐ Ⓑ Ⓒ Ⓓ Ⓔ

76. Ⓐ Ⓑ Ⓒ Ⓓ Ⓔ
77. Ⓐ Ⓑ Ⓒ Ⓓ Ⓔ
78. Ⓐ Ⓑ Ⓒ Ⓓ Ⓔ
79. Ⓐ Ⓑ Ⓒ Ⓓ Ⓔ
80. Ⓐ Ⓑ Ⓒ Ⓓ Ⓔ
81. Ⓐ Ⓑ Ⓒ Ⓓ Ⓔ
82. Ⓐ Ⓑ Ⓒ Ⓓ Ⓔ
83. Ⓐ Ⓑ Ⓒ Ⓓ Ⓔ
84. Ⓐ Ⓑ Ⓒ Ⓓ Ⓔ
85. Ⓐ Ⓑ Ⓒ Ⓓ Ⓔ

Practice Test Form

Completely darken bubbles with a No. 2 pencil. If you make a mistake, be sure to erase mark completely. Erase all stray marks.

1.

YOUR NAME: _____
(Print)   Last   First   M.I.

SIGNATURE: _____   DATE: ___ / ___ / ___

HOME ADDRESS: _____
(Print)   Number and Street

_____
City   State   Zip Code

(Print)

SAT Spanish Section 3

1. Ⓐ Ⓑ Ⓒ Ⓓ Ⓔ	26. Ⓐ Ⓑ Ⓒ Ⓓ Ⓔ	51. Ⓐ Ⓑ Ⓒ Ⓓ Ⓔ	76. Ⓐ Ⓑ Ⓒ Ⓓ Ⓔ
2. Ⓐ Ⓑ Ⓒ Ⓓ Ⓔ	27. Ⓐ Ⓑ Ⓒ Ⓓ Ⓔ	52. Ⓐ Ⓑ Ⓒ Ⓓ Ⓔ	77. Ⓐ Ⓑ Ⓒ Ⓓ Ⓔ
3. Ⓐ Ⓑ Ⓒ Ⓓ Ⓔ	28. Ⓐ Ⓑ Ⓒ Ⓓ Ⓔ	53. Ⓐ Ⓑ Ⓒ Ⓓ Ⓔ	78. Ⓐ Ⓑ Ⓒ Ⓓ Ⓔ
4. Ⓐ Ⓑ Ⓒ Ⓓ Ⓔ	29. Ⓐ Ⓑ Ⓒ Ⓓ Ⓔ	54. Ⓐ Ⓑ Ⓒ Ⓓ Ⓔ	79. Ⓐ Ⓑ Ⓒ Ⓓ Ⓔ
5. Ⓐ Ⓑ Ⓒ Ⓓ Ⓔ	30. Ⓐ Ⓑ Ⓒ Ⓓ Ⓔ	55. Ⓐ Ⓑ Ⓒ Ⓓ Ⓔ	80. Ⓐ Ⓑ Ⓒ Ⓓ Ⓔ
6. Ⓐ Ⓑ Ⓒ Ⓓ Ⓔ	31. Ⓐ Ⓑ Ⓒ Ⓓ Ⓔ	56. Ⓐ Ⓑ Ⓒ Ⓓ Ⓔ	81. Ⓐ Ⓑ Ⓒ Ⓓ Ⓔ
7. Ⓐ Ⓑ Ⓒ Ⓓ Ⓔ	32. Ⓐ Ⓑ Ⓒ Ⓓ Ⓔ	57. Ⓐ Ⓑ Ⓒ Ⓓ Ⓔ	82. Ⓐ Ⓑ Ⓒ Ⓓ Ⓔ
8. Ⓐ Ⓑ Ⓒ Ⓓ Ⓔ	33. Ⓐ Ⓑ Ⓒ Ⓓ Ⓔ	58. Ⓐ Ⓑ Ⓒ Ⓓ Ⓔ	83. Ⓐ Ⓑ Ⓒ Ⓓ Ⓔ
9. Ⓐ Ⓑ Ⓒ Ⓓ Ⓔ	34. Ⓐ Ⓑ Ⓒ Ⓓ Ⓔ	59. Ⓐ Ⓑ Ⓒ Ⓓ Ⓔ	84. Ⓐ Ⓑ Ⓒ Ⓓ Ⓔ
10. Ⓐ Ⓑ Ⓒ Ⓓ Ⓔ	35. Ⓐ Ⓑ Ⓒ Ⓓ Ⓔ	60. Ⓐ Ⓑ Ⓒ Ⓓ Ⓔ	85. Ⓐ Ⓑ Ⓒ Ⓓ Ⓔ
11. Ⓐ Ⓑ Ⓒ Ⓓ Ⓔ	36. Ⓐ Ⓑ Ⓒ Ⓓ Ⓔ	61. Ⓐ Ⓑ Ⓒ Ⓓ Ⓔ	
12. Ⓐ Ⓑ Ⓒ Ⓓ Ⓔ	37. Ⓐ Ⓑ Ⓒ Ⓓ Ⓔ	62. Ⓐ Ⓑ Ⓒ Ⓓ Ⓔ	
13. Ⓐ Ⓑ Ⓒ Ⓓ Ⓔ	38. Ⓐ Ⓑ Ⓒ Ⓓ Ⓔ	63. Ⓐ Ⓑ Ⓒ Ⓓ Ⓔ	
14. Ⓐ Ⓑ Ⓒ Ⓓ Ⓔ	39. Ⓐ Ⓑ Ⓒ Ⓓ Ⓔ	64. Ⓐ Ⓑ Ⓒ Ⓓ Ⓔ	
15. Ⓐ Ⓑ Ⓒ Ⓓ Ⓔ	40. Ⓐ Ⓑ Ⓒ Ⓓ Ⓔ	65. Ⓐ Ⓑ Ⓒ Ⓓ Ⓔ	
16. Ⓐ Ⓑ Ⓒ Ⓓ Ⓔ	41. Ⓐ Ⓑ Ⓒ Ⓓ Ⓔ	66. Ⓐ Ⓑ Ⓒ Ⓓ Ⓔ	
17. Ⓐ Ⓑ Ⓒ Ⓓ Ⓔ	42. Ⓐ Ⓑ Ⓒ Ⓓ Ⓔ	67. Ⓐ Ⓑ Ⓒ Ⓓ Ⓔ	
18. Ⓐ Ⓑ Ⓒ Ⓓ Ⓔ	43. Ⓐ Ⓑ Ⓒ Ⓓ Ⓔ	68. Ⓐ Ⓑ Ⓒ Ⓓ Ⓔ	
19. Ⓐ Ⓑ Ⓒ Ⓓ Ⓔ	44. Ⓐ Ⓑ Ⓒ Ⓓ Ⓔ	69. Ⓐ Ⓑ Ⓒ Ⓓ Ⓔ	
20. Ⓐ Ⓑ Ⓒ Ⓓ Ⓔ	45. Ⓐ Ⓑ Ⓒ Ⓓ Ⓔ	70. Ⓐ Ⓑ Ⓒ Ⓓ Ⓔ	
21. Ⓐ Ⓑ Ⓒ Ⓓ Ⓔ	46. Ⓐ Ⓑ Ⓒ Ⓓ Ⓔ	71. Ⓐ Ⓑ Ⓒ Ⓓ Ⓔ	
22. Ⓐ Ⓑ Ⓒ Ⓓ Ⓔ	47. Ⓐ Ⓑ Ⓒ Ⓓ Ⓔ	72. Ⓐ Ⓑ Ⓒ Ⓓ Ⓔ	
23. Ⓐ Ⓑ Ⓒ Ⓓ Ⓔ	48. Ⓐ Ⓑ Ⓒ Ⓓ Ⓔ	73. Ⓐ Ⓑ Ⓒ Ⓓ Ⓔ	
24. Ⓐ Ⓑ Ⓒ Ⓓ Ⓔ	49. Ⓐ Ⓑ Ⓒ Ⓓ Ⓔ	74. Ⓐ Ⓑ Ⓒ Ⓓ Ⓔ	
25. Ⓐ Ⓑ Ⓒ Ⓓ Ⓔ	50. Ⓐ Ⓑ Ⓒ Ⓓ Ⓔ	75. Ⓐ Ⓑ Ⓒ Ⓓ Ⓔ	

NOTES

NOTES

NOTES

NOTES

NOTES

NOTES

AP Exams

Cracking the AP Biology Exam,
2004–2005 Edition
0-375-76393-7 • $18.00/C$27.00

Cracking the AP Calculus AB & BC Exam,
2004–2005 Edition
0-375-76381-3 • $19.00/C$28.50

Cracking the AP Chemistry Exam,
2004–2005 Edition
0-375-76382-1• $18.00/C$27.00

**Cracking the AP Computer Science
A & AB Exam ,** 2004-2005 Edition
0-375-76383-X • $19.00/C$28.50

**Cracking the AP Economics (Macro &
Micro) Exam,** 2004-2005 Edition
0-375-76384-8 • $18.00/C$27.00

Cracking the AP English Literature Exam,
2004–2005 Edition
0-375-76385-6 • $18.00/C$27.00

Cracking the AP European History Exam,
2004–2005 Edition
0-375-76386-4 • $18.00/C$27.00

Cracking the AP Physics B & C Exam,
2004–2005 Edition
0-375-76387-2 • $19.00/C$28.50

Cracking the AP Psychology Exam,
2004–2005 Edition
0-375-76388-0 • $18.00/C$27.00

Cracking the AP Spanish Exam,
2004–2005 Edition
0-375-76389-9 • $18.00/C$27.00

Cracking the AP Statistics Exam,
2004–2005 Edition
0-375-76390-2 • $19.00/C$28.50

**Cracking the AP U.S. Government
and Politics Exam,** 2004–2005 Edition
0-375-76391-0 • $18.00/C$27.00

Cracking the AP U.S. History Exam,
2004–2005 Edition
0-375-76392-9 • $18.00/C$27.00

Cracking the AP World History Exam,
2004–2005 Edition
0-375-76380-5 • $18.00/C$27.00

SAT Subject Tests

Cracking the SAT Biology E/M Subject Test,
2005-2006 Edition
0-375-76447-X • $19.00/C$27.00

Cracking the SAT Chemistry Subject Test,
2005-2006 Edition
0-375-76448-8 • $18.00/C$26.00

Cracking the SAT French Subject Test,
2005-2006 Edition
0-375-76449-6 • $18.00/C$26.00

Cracking the SAT Literature Subject Test,
2005-2006 Edition
0-375-76446-1 • $18.00/C$26.00

**Cracking the SAT Math 1 and 2
Subject Tests,** 2005-2006 Edition
0-375-76451-8 • $19.00/C$27.00

Cracking the SAT Physics Subject Test,
2005-2006 Edition
0-375-76452-6 • $19.00/C$27.00

Cracking the SAT Spanish Subject Test,
2005-2006 Edition
0-375-76453-4 • $18.00/C$26.00

**Cracking the SAT U.S. & World History
Subject Tests,** 2005-2006 Edition
0-375-76450-X • $19.00/C$27.00

Available at Bookstores Everywhere
PrincetonReview.com

Necesitas más?

If you want to learn more about how to excel on the SAT Subject Test in Spanish, you're in the right place. Our expertise extends far beyond just this test. But this isn't about us, it's about getting you into the college of your choice.

One way to increase the number of fat envelopes you receive is to have strong test scores. So, if you're still nervous—relax. Consider all of your options.

We consistently improve students' scores through our books, classroom courses, private tutoring and online courses. Call 800-2Review or visit *PrincetonReview.com*.

If you like our *Cracking the SAT Spanish Subject Test*, check out:
- *The Best 357 Colleges*
- *Cracking the New SAT*
- *11 Practice Tests for the New SAT and PSAT*
- *Cracking the AP Spanish Exam*